Making Feminist Sense of the Global Justice Movement

Catherine Eschle and Bice Maiguashca

ROWMAN & LITTLEFIELD PUBLISHERS, INC.
Lanham • Boulder • New York • Toronto • Plymouth, UK

Published by Rowman & Littlefield Publishers, Inc.
A wholly owned subsidiary of The Rowman & Littlefield Publishing Group, Inc.
4501 Forbes Boulevard, Suite 200, Lanham, Maryland 20706
http://www.rowmanlittlefield.com

Estover Road, Plymouth PL6 7PY, United Kingdom

British Library Cataloguing in Publication Information Available

**The hardback edition of this book was previously cataloged by the Library of
Congress as follows:**

Eschle, Catherine.
  Making feminist sense of the global justice movement / Catherine Eschle and
Bice Maiguashca.
    p. cm.
  Includes bibliographical references and index.
  1. Feminism. 2. Globalization—Social aspects. 3. Globalization—Moral and
ethical aspects. I. Maiguashca, Bice, 1965– II. Title.
HQ1155.E83 2010
305.4209—dc22

2009043130

ISBN 978-0-7425-5592-1 (cloth : alk. paper)
ISBN 978-0-7425-5593-8 (pbk. : alk. paper)
ISBN 978-0-7425-6781-8 (electronic)

Making Feminist Sense of the Global Justice Movement

Contents

Figures and Textboxes

FIGURES

TEXTBOXES

Acknowledgments

This book would not have been possible without the help of many friends, colleagues, and family members.

Our first and biggest debt, one we will never repay, is to the interviewees whose words we use in this book. They were unfailingly generous and open with us, and the book would not have been possible without them. We hope that we have managed to do justice to their politics and contributed in a small way to their continued struggle for full inclusion in the World Social Forum and the global justice movement. And we hope they will forgive any infelicities in our interpretations of their words.

We are also grateful to the grant bodies who gave financial support for the preparation of this project and for the fieldwork—the Nuffield Foundation, the British Academy, and, most importantly, the Economic and Social Research Council. The last of these funded our trip to Brazil and also some time away from teaching to enable us to write up our work on our return. Moreover, our interviews in Brazil would not have been possible without the amazing translation work of Magaly Pazello, Tatiana Wells, Adriana Veloso, and Caroline Commandulli, and the help of Rekha Pande in India. All of these individuals really looked after us and made our trips to India and Brazil much more enjoyable experiences, and we cannot thank them enough.

Data construction was aided by hours of photocopying by Alix Kelso, and the drafting process by feedback at various academic conferences, and by e-mail, from Ellen Reese, Janet Conway, Nicholas Onuf, Barry Gills, and Karena Shaw. We would like to express thanks to Jessica Gribble at Rowman & Littlefield for her enthusiasm for the project and for taking us on, and to Susan McEachern for her kindness and patience while waiting for us to deliver. Mary Hawkesworth, who reviewed the manuscript for Rowman & Littlefield, was also very supportive. In the final writing-up stages, Jocelyn Vaughan and Keith Smith offered invaluable assistance in formatting, reference chasing, and the like. We are grateful to David Armstrong and the EU Network of Excellence Garnet fund for paying for Jocelyn's assistance, and to Kirsty Alexander and Manuela Maiguashca for last minute read-throughs. Catherine would also like to thank her parents, Sheila and John Eschle, for their support and hospitality over the years, as she has stayed with them on many an occasion while working on the book with Bice.

Finally, thank you from the bottom of our hearts to Juan Maiguashca and Denis Donoghue. Juan translated interview consent forms between three languages, read innumerable drafts, and was an indefatigable and constructive source of advice and copyediting despite being a continent away. Denis was almost squeezed out of his own home by this project, but remained a most supportive partner to Catherine and a genial host to Bice. Patient with us to a fault, he also supplied diagrams and copyedited chapters far above and beyond the call of duty. That this is not a better book is no fault of theirs. We dedicate it to the pair of them, with love.

Abbreviations and Acronyms

ABONG   Associação Brasiliera de Organizaçãoes não Governmentais (Brazilian Association of Non-Governmental Organisations)

AFM   Articulación Feminista Marcosur (Marcosur Feminist Network)

AIDWA   All India Democratic Women's Association

ALRA   Abortion Law Reform Association

AMB   Articulação de Mulheres Brasilieras (Network of Brazilian Women)

AMNB   Articulação de Mulheres Negras Brasilieras (Network of Black Brazilian Women's NGOs)

APCMS   Andhra Pradesh Chaitanya Mahila Samakhya ("Mahila" means woman)

APMSS   Andhra Pradesh Mahila Samatha Society

ATTAC   Association pour la Taxation des Transactions pour l'Aide aux Citoyens/ Association for the Taxation of Financial Transactions for the Aid of Citizens

AWID   Association for Women's Rights in Development

CADAC   Coordination Nationale d'Associations pour le Droit à l'Avertement et la Contraception (Network for the Right to Abortion and Contraception)

CAVOW   Campaign against Violence on Women

CBJP   Brazilian Justice and Peace Commission

CDD   Católicas por les Derechos de Decider (Catholics for the Right to Decide)

CEDAW	Convention on the Elimination of All Forms of Discrimination against Women
CEMINA	Communicação, Educação e Informação em Gênero (Communication, Education and Information on Gender)
CEPIA	Cidadania, Estudo, Pesquisa, Informação, Ação (Citizenship, Study, Research, Information, Action)
CFEMEA	Centro Feminista de Estudos e Assessoria (Feminist Centre for Study and Analysis)
CIVES	Brazilian Business Association for Citizenship
CMI	Centro de Midia Independente (Indymedia Centre)
CMP	Centro de la Mujer Peruana (Center for Peruvian Women)
CNDF	Collectif National pour les Droits des Femmes (National Collective for the Rights of Women)
CPI	Communist Party of India
CPI-M	Communist Party of India–Marxist
CRIOLA	(Not an acronym but usually capitalized: a play on words indicating a black woman)
CUT	Central Trade Union Federation
CWGL	Centre for Women's Global Leadership
DAWN	Development Alternatives with Women for a New Era
DIY	Do-it-yourself
DRC	Democratic Republic of the Congo
ESF	European Social Forum
FEMNET	(Not an acronym as such, indicates the African Women's Development and Communication Network)
GLBT	Gay, lesbian, bisexual, and transexual
IBASE	Brazilian Institute of Social and Economic Analysis
ICT	Information and communication technology
IFI	International financial institution
IGTN	International Gender and Trade Network
ILGA	International Lesbian and Gay Association
ILPS	International League of People's Struggles
IR	International Relations (the academic discipline)
ISIS	Information and Communication Service
LGBT	Lesbian, gay, bisexual, and transexual
MST	Movimento Sim Terra (Movement of the Landless)
NAAR	National Association Against Racism
NAC	National Abortion Campaign
NATFHE	National Association of Teachers in Further and Higher Education
NFIW	National Federation of Indian Women
NGO	Nongovernmental organization
NNAWG	National Network of Autonomous Women's Groups

OPEC	Organization for Petroleum Exporting Countries
PS	Parti Socialiste (Socialist Party)
PT	Partido dos Trabalhadores (Worker's Party)
PUC	Pontificia Universidade Católica (Catholic University)
Quango	Quasi-autonomous nongovernmental organization
REDEH	Rede de Desenvolvimento Humano (Network for Human Development)
REMTE	Red Latinoamericana Mujeres Transformando la Economía (Latin American Network of Women Transforming the Economy)
REPEM	Red de Educacíon Popular entre Mujeres (Network of Women in Popular Education)
RSHR	Reproductive and Sexual Health and Rights
SAP	Structural adjustment policy
SMO	Social movement organization
SOF	Sempreviva Organização Feminista (Living Feminism Organization)
TAN	Transnational advocacy network
TINA	There is no alternative
TSMO	Transnational social movement organization
WEDO	Women's Environment and Development Organization
WEN	Women's Environmental Network
WGNRR	Women's Global Network for Reproductive Rights
WHRNet	Women's Human Rights Network
WICEJ	Women's International Coalition for Economic Justice
WID	Women in Development
WIDE	Women in Development Europe
WILPF	Women's International League for Peace and Freedom
WLUML	Women Living Under Muslim Laws
WSF	World Social Forum
WTO	World Trade Organization

1

Introduction

Making Feminist Sense of the Global Justice Movement

In this book we seek to shine a light on feminist activism within the global justice movement. The seeds of this undertaking lie in another book, one we coedited a few years ago, in which we sought to apply diverse critical-theoretical perspectives to the global justice movement and to bring them into dialogue with each other (Eschle and Maiguashca 2005). It was while working on that project that we realized the theory and practice of feminism were largely absent from the emergent literature on the new movement. Pursuing our intuition that feminist activists are nonetheless involved and that feminist theory has relevant things to say, we undertook fieldwork at the World Social Forum between 2003 and 2005 and read a range of related feminist scholarship. In the resulting book we offer an empirical and conceptual study of what we call "feminist antiglobalization activism." In so doing, we hope not only to bring into relief a distinctive sector of the global justice movement, but also to draw out the significance of feminism for rethinking this movement more generally.

WHY A BOOK ON THIS TOPIC?

For more than a decade, struggles against the violences and exclusions of neoliberal globalization have been grabbing headlines and reshaping political imaginations worldwide. Such struggles range from the Zapatista uprising in the Chiapas region of Mexico to the high-profile protest against the World Trade Organization in Seattle, and from Bolivian campaigns against water privatization to the enormous gatherings of the World Social Forum at Porto Alegre in Brazil. Taken together, these mobilizations, according to

many writers and commentators, constitute one of the most significant social movements to emerge on the world stage in recent years. Thus Michael
Hardt and Antonio Negri (2003: xvi) write about "a great movement of the
multitude" in their foreword to a collection of essays on the World Social
Forum while Benjamin Shepard and Ronald Hayduk, in the introduction
to a reader on community struggles in the United States, speak of "a new
global activism" (2002: 1–2). Or take Brazilian sociologist Boaventura de
Sousa Santos who sees these "movements of resistance" as "an alternative,
counter-hegemonic globalization" characterized by "huge political and
cultural diversity" (2006: ix).

Given this diversity, it is not surprising that commentators disagree on
what the movement should be called. The "antiglobalization" label became
widespread after the Seattle demonstration, apparently "a coinage of the US
media" (Graeber 2002: 63). The term has always been strongly contested by
activists as overly negative and falsely implying an isolationist, parochial,
and protectionist orientation (e.g., Thomas and Klein 2002). As we discuss
at more length in chapter 8, many activists prefer to describe the movement
in which they participate as "antineoliberal," "anticapitalist," or "anti–
economic globalization," although the term "antiglobalization" is still a
useful shorthand or code word for some (including ourselves) to indicate
opposition to contemporary global economic processes. It is in this sense
that we use it to identify a distinct feminist orientation. There have been
efforts to formulate a more accurate and more aspirational appellation,
however, including the "global democracy movement," "globalization
from below," and the "global justice movement," with the last becoming
particularly widespread in Anglophone academic circles in recent years.[1] It
is for this reason that we prefer to use "the global justice movement" in this
book when describing the movement as a whole.[2]

Whatever it is called, writings on the movement have proliferated since
the late 1990s. Simon Tormey points out that this literature is varied, serving different purposes and speaking to multiple audiences (2004b: 2–4).
We find it helpful to distinguish two broad categories of texts. First, there
is an enormous activist-oriented body of work that writes about and on
behalf of the movement, in a partisan, politically committed way and from
an insider standpoint. Examples range from analyses of the operations of
globalization (e.g., Klein 2000; Burbach, Núñez, and Kagarlitsky 1996)
to overviews of the global movement (e.g., Notes from Nowhere 2003;
Kingsnorth 2003; Polet 2004b) and from advocacy of political visions and
strategies (e.g., Callinicos 2003; Broad 2002) to dispatches from the front
line of protest (e.g., Cockburn, St. Clair, and Sekula 2000; *On Fire* 2001).
Second, although academics have been rather late to the game, there is now
a growing body of literature striving to analyze the movement in a more
scholarly, objective fashion and from a more outsider perspective. For ex-

ample, academics in the discipline of International Relations and its associated field of International Political Economy have generated some interesting reflections on global justice activism.[3] The most sustained theoretical and empirical engagement, however, has been undertaken by sociologists drawing on social movement theory.[4] Of course, as Tormey stresses, the boundary between activist and academic commentary is unstable and we acknowledge the conscious efforts of many authors to bridge this divide (e.g., Reitan 2007; Harvie et al. 2005; Shepard and Hayduk 2002).

For us, as we noted above, what is most striking about all types of commentary on the global justice movement is the near-invisibility of feminism as an active force and influence within it. This neglect became evident to us early on when, while still working on our edited book, we undertook a review of English-language texts that sought to represent this emergent global justice movement as a new form of political activism. Our search uncovered only a smattering of references to feminism as an organized presence or distinctive perspective. So, for example, despite proclaiming "the new movement" as "less sexist" than previous mobilizations, the authors of a book on protests at Seattle and beyond introduce the key protagonists without mentioning feminists (Cockburn, St. Clair, and Sekula 2000: 2–3). Feminism is equally absent from Amory Starr's otherwise thorough-going early survey of the main ideological strands of the movement (2000). Our examination of more recent literature reveals a similar pattern. The U.S. anthology *Confronting Capitalism* (Yuen, Burton-Rose, and Katsiaficas 2004), for instance, declares the movement to have a "deep engagement with patriarchy" (Yuen 2004: xvi) and has two pieces on women's organizing around environmental issues, but there is no discussion of how patriarchy is being tackled or by whom. Again, in a global survey titled *The State of Resistance* (Polet 2007) there is not one chapter that focuses on feminist organizing.

There are, of course, some exceptions to this tendency. Women mobilizing to contest gendered inequalities, among other forms of power, merit their own chapter in a compendium titled *Anti-capitalism* (Bircham and Charlton 2001; Egan and Robidoux 2001). Starhawk's collection of essays on the movement (2002b) is suffused with references to her feminist politics and to her women's group, and an edited collection on the World Social Forum contains several chapters on feminists, and feminist ideas, by feminist authors.[5] Yet, despite these important efforts, the overall impression left by prevailing representations of the global justice movement is that feminism is not part of the story.

This book begins from the premise that the neglect of feminism leads to an inaccurate depiction of the global justice movement in empirical and theoretical terms and that it is also politically problematic. Starting with the empirical rationale, we demonstrate in what follows that feminism is actually a vibrant presence within the movement. Indeed, we suggest that it can be seen as a distinctive form of collective action we call "feminist antiglobalization activism." Although the individuals we include under this heading have diverse political views, we see them all as participating in a shared effort to transform gender hierarchies as well as the global economy.[6] Moreover, while this definition does not imply that feminist antiglobalization activists are always, necessarily women, our research suggests that, in fact, most are. This is perhaps not surprising given that it tends to be women who see gender relations as oppressive and who are left with the task of challenging this form of power. Last but not least, although most of the activists we studied do self-label as feminist and/or as antiglobalization, it is important to note that some do not, given that the meaning of such terminology varies widely according to country and strategic context. In sum, we conceptualize feminist antiglobalization activism as a movement sector that lies at the intersection of the feminist movement and the global justice movement, fusing the concerns of both in a single political project (see figure 1.1).

In our view, the emergence of feminist antiglobalization activism must be seen as an exciting new development in feminist politics, one that merits empirical investigation in its own right. Moreover, a richer, more inclusive picture of the contours and trajectories of the global justice movement will only be possible when feminist antiglobalization activism is taken into account.

Yet another reason for studying feminist antiglobalization activism is theoretical. In our view, analysis of this movement sector can open up potentially

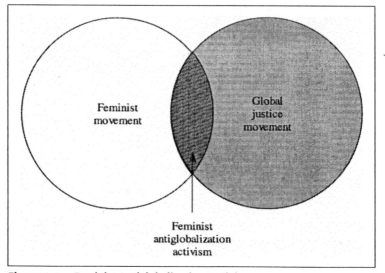

Figure 1.1. Feminist Antiglobalization Activism

interesting and important conceptual lines of inquiry that are currently not explored in the global justice movement literature. In other words, what feminist activists are doing and saying in this movement may offer theoretical insights, both in their own terms and as a lucrative starting point for a more academic theoretical endeavor. In this regard, we note that feminist scholars have yet to focus on the global justice movement per se and by extension, on the feminists within it. Thus, despite generating a rich body of work analyzing women's organizing in the context of globalization in general and globalized feminist networks in particular,[7] feminist scholars have not conceptualized the particular movement sector that we identify above or sought to systematize the conceptualizations of activists within it.[8] Recognizing the importance of deepening and expanding feminist research in this area, Mohanty says, "at this time I believe the theory, critique and activism around antiglobalization has to be a key focus for feminists" (2003. 230). Our book is a response to this call.

The third and last rationale for this book is unashamedly political. By this we do not mean that it can be read as an activist text. After all, we are not insiders to the groups we analyze; we do not try to evaluate their strategies and we are nonpartisan in the sense that we avoid taking sides in intergroup debates. But if not an activist text, this book remains a political intervention. As feminist scholars, we suspect that the marginalization of feminists in representations of the global justice movement reflects and reproduces deeper power relationships within the movement itself. Indeed, as we demonstrate in chapter 2, gender hierarchies scar the World Social Forum and, by extension, the wider movement of which the Forum is a part.[9] By exposing these power relations and by seeking to speak to and from the feminist struggles that have emerged to confront them, this book is written in solidarity with feminist antiglobalization activists.

WHAT IS THIS BOOK ABOUT?

In what follows, we seek to answer three questions. What are the trajectories and characteristic features of feminist antiglobalization activism? What conceptual tools do we need to make sense of them? And how does our analysis of feminist antiglobalization activism encourage new ways of thinking about the global justice movement?

Turning to our first question, we argue that feminist antiglobalization activism emerged from the reconfigurations of feminism and the Left during the 1980s and was driven by the responses of individuals to injustices experienced in their own lives and in the lives of others. These injustices, understood to be the consequence of economic and political power relations that have become globalized, are seen as requiring urgent transformation. To this end, feminist antiglobalization activists offer evocative and imaginative visions of a more just world, pursue a wide range of political activities, and seek to forge solidarity with others in ways that foster diversity as well as integration into a broader political struggle. Part II of the book maps these features of feminist antiglobalization activism in some detail.

Moving on to the second question, for the conceptual underpinnings of our analysis we bring feminist activist arguments into conversation with feminist scholarly resources from a range of fields. In order to illuminate movement origins, we turn to feminist claims about the importance of recovering women's agency at the collective and individual levels (e.g., Gardiner 1995; Roseneil 2000; Hercus 2005). Our approach to activist beliefs has been shaped by our reading of the work of Amy Allen (1998) and Iris Marion Young (1990) on oppression, and that of Seyla Benhabib (1992) and Greg Johnson (2002) on the utopian dimension of feminist aspirations for change. We draw on feminist social movement scholars to underpin our expansive conceptualization of activist practices (e.g., Sudbury 1998; Katzenstein 1990, 2003; Banaszack, Beckwith, and Rucht 2003), and, finally, from feminists working on philosophy and epistemology we glean tools to help us understand the dynamics of activist identity (Alcoff 2000, 2006; Weir 2008; Moya 1997, 2001).

So how does our feminist framing of feminist antiglobalization activism compel us to rethink the global justice movement, our third question above? We will show by the end of the book that taking feminist antiglobalization activism seriously requires a more expansive empirical view of the global justice movement than is typically found in the literature. We also contend that the conceptual scaffolding of this literature needs revisiting. In other words, we seek to do more than simply add and stir feminist activism into current accounts of the global justice movement. Instead, we aim to persuade readers that "making feminist sense" of that movement requires a reassessment of how best to think about where it comes from, what its activists believe, what they do, and what binds them together as a collective actor.

HOW HAVE WE GONE ABOUT OUR RESEARCH AND PUTTING THE BOOK TOGETHER?

The research for this book is rooted in fieldwork conducted at the World Social Forum. The decision to pursue fieldwork was influenced by two important methodological considerations. The first concerns how we understand the nature of social movements. Following sociologist Alberto Melucci, we reject the idea that movements act as "unified empirical data" or "personages"—each with a coherent identity, preformed interest, and single will—seeing them rather as heterogeneous, negotiated constructions (Melucci 1989: 28; see also Eschle 2004b). Although academic accounts of activism often mask internal complexity or seek to fix shifting boundaries, our conviction has long been that it is only from a vantage point in the middle of the action that we are able to uncover the detail of and debates within feminist antiglobalization activism as an unfolding process.

A second important methodological consideration stems from our commitment to building our analysis around feminist voices and agency. In our view, feminist scholarship should take care not to reduce women and men to mere effects of power, but instead strive, as Brooke Ackerly and Jacqui True state, to "reveal the *agency* of the seemingly excluded" (2006: 249, emphasis in original). In our fieldwork, we thus sought to move beyond the lamentation and explanation of feminist marginalization, exploring instead the efforts of women to resist the hierarchies that shape their lives and create an alternative social order. In this context, it was particularly important to pay attention to women's "ideas, thoughts and memories in their own words, rather than in the words of the researcher" (Reinharz 1992: 19), and to treat what women said as a crucial source of knowledge, rather than simply an object of inquiry (Oakley 1981).

Not being empiricists, however, we recognize the impossibility of innocent factual accounts unshaped by interpretative framing. Our fieldwork was thus complemented from the start with an attempt to construct a feminist conceptual framework for our narrative. This dual-track effort has required us to shift back and forth between our theoretical lens and our fieldwork in order to create a comfortable fit between the two, with the resulting analysis in this book fusing empirical and conceptual labor. As a consequence, while we have tried to document and learn from the self-understandings, practices, and written statements of feminist antiglobalization activists, we have not sought to represent them directly. Instead, what we offer here is a highly mediated story that, though inspired by the words and deeds of others, is articulated in our own terms and develops arguments about what we take to be its significance for understandings of the global justice movement.

Our choice of the World Social Forum as our specific fieldwork site was influenced by several factors. To begin with, the Forum is arguably the most accessible and high-profile gathering of the global justice movement in recent years, attracting activists from a range of causes, including feminism, from all over the world. The first-ever Forum was held in Porto Alegre, Brazil, in the last week of January 2001. Only 2,000 participants were originally expected (Klein 2001), but 20,000 showed up, representing 1,000 activist groups from 117 countries (World Social Forum 2006). By the time of the fifth edition of the World Social Forum, which met again in Porto Alegre, there were 200,000 in the opening demonstration and over

155,000 registered participants (World Social Forum 2005a). Clearly, these annual events, during the period of our research, steadily expanded in size and popularity. At the same time, the World Social Forum since 2002 has become a global process, rolling out around the world in a series of local, national, and regional meetings including, for example, annual European Social Forums.[10] Such geographical expansion has meant that the Forum provides yet more opportunities for activist involvement.

Another reason for choosing the World Social Forum and European Social Forum for our fieldwork is because these events seek to foster the articulation of critiques of the current world order and, importantly, visions of other possible worlds (e.g., Fisher and Ponniah 2003). In addition, they serve as a staging ground for extensive networking and strategizing between groups and across movements. Thus, it was our hope that by attending we would catch a glimpse of not only the varied activities of feminist antiglobalization activists on site, but also their efforts to reach out to others and to build campaigns that go beyond the confines of the Forum. In this way, the Forum provided us with a portal through which we could see and begin to map the much wider terrain of feminist antiglobalization activism.

Despite these strengths of the World Social Forum as a starting point for our research, we recognize that it is not a fully representative space. Many individuals and groups choose not to or are unable to participate in the Forum in its various manifestations. As we discuss in more detail in chapter 3, it is, after all, a contested process and space, shaped by power relations that allow some activist orientations and practices to be privileged over others. This is true, however, of all other political gatherings from which the global justice movement can be mapped, from Seattle to Chiapas, and, in our view, does not militate against using the Forum as a starting point for research and analysis.

We carried out our fieldwork at four events: the second European Social Forum, held in Paris in November 2003; the World Social Forum in Mumbai in January 2004; the London edition of the European Social Forum held in the autumn of 2004; and, finally, the fifth meeting of the World Social Forum, back at its Porto Alegre birthplace in January 2005. In addition, we conducted research before or after each gathering in all the host countries except France.[11] We used three main methods to gather information, namely participant observation, interviewing, and document collection. Taken together, these afforded us "multiple lines of sight" (Berg 2004: 5) into our subject and, thereby, breadth of vision. Thus, while not seeking to offer a comprehensive, representative snapshot of feminist activism at the World Social Forum—an impossibility for two researchers in a series of such huge, open, fluid meetings—we did want to find ways of widening our lens and of offering as panoramic a view of it as we could. And although it is our view that none of these methods is intrinsically feminist, they provide us with different ways of recording the self-understandings and practices of feminist activists and, thereby, a means to make them audible and visible within the global justice movement (see Reinharz 1992: 48).

More concretely, in terms of participant observation, our first method of gathering information, we attended a wide range of sessions at the forums, including the major opening and closing plenaries that sought to galvanize the crowds and to reflect on and speak to the movement as a whole. In addition, we involved ourselves in a great number of workshops we identified as feminist,[12] ranging from the Feminist Dialogues prior to the 2005 World Social Forum in Porto Alegre to much smaller sessions in all the sites, in which we had the opportunity to talk directly with an activist audience about a range of topics including our own research. Finally, we kept extensive field notes of both our observations and our more analytical reflections, mostly written up immediately in the wake of each day on site (Reinharz 1992: 65–71).

Our second method consisted of interviewing activists both in and outside the World Social Forum. Several techniques were used to identify potential interviewees including "purposive" approaches to activists whom we perceived to be "key informants," that is, the main organizers of feminist groups involved in each forum or speakers on forum panels who voiced what seemed to us to be feminist concerns. We identified more people to talk to through "snowballing," that is, asking our interviewees to recommend others and according to "convenience," that is, through chance encounters on site (for a discussion of all three, see Berg 2004: 34–37). In total, we conducted 78 semistructured interviews with 85 activists, drawing on an evolving interview guide (Arksey and Knight 1999: ch. 7; Lofland and Lofland 1995: 78–84).

Our third method was the gathering of group documentation from every event we attended and from stalls on-site showcasing advocacy material from feminist groups. We also collected documentation from group offices when interviewing off-site. These documents served the important function of filling in factual gaps left by our interviews while also providing a glimpse of the collective ideological orientations of each group, something that was harder to ascertain through conversations with individuals.

However fruitful, these methods do raise feminist dilemmas for those applying them, as we discovered in the course of our research. To begin with, much of our analysis in this book is built around interview transcripts that inescapably reflect certain power hierarchies involved in their production. Two power differentials in our favor both derive from our positioning as academics. The first was specific to the Indian context, and relates to the fact that were only able to obtain interviews in Hyderabad before the World Social Forum because of the efforts of an academic colleague and friend of ours, Rekha Pande, a professor of women's studies at Hyderabad

University. Our academic networks here gave us an overall advantage, but also a very particular entry point into interviewing. Since Rekha had taught a number of our interviewees when they were university students, there is no doubt that a hierarchy was established by her presence, one that served to grant us associated authority. The second power differential simply had to do with our structural positioning as white, middle-class, western academics traveling to India and Brazil on grant money in order to write a book about activists there. No matter how junior we may have appeared to our interviewees (some even commented on it), in the end we were still seen as having particular advantages in the political economy of knowledge production. In this context we were not only outsiders but ones with the perceived capacity to publish knowledge claims about these activists in formal academic contexts. This undoubtedly shaped the interview process and outcomes, resulting in a very different kind of conversation than one between, say, two friends within the same organization. As one interviewee reminded us, activists can have real and meaningful anxieties around the use made of their words in academic contexts.

As Ann Phoenix points out, however, power in the interview process rarely travels entirely one way (2001: 204). At the start of the interview, we asked each of our interviewees to sign a consent form. This required us to explain our project, its goals, and main themes and to ask permission to use their name and the contents of the interview. While most agreed to sign the form immediately, some asked to wait until the end of the interview, leaving us in suspense about its potential use. Moreover, in the name of accountability, we committed to sending all our interviewees, if they wished, a complete transcript that they were invited to edit as they saw fit. This process proved extremely challenging to administer to the extent that it often involved lengthy negotiations with interviewees (see Taylor 1998: 370). As such, this could be seen as involving a shift in power to the interviewee in terms of the process of data construction, albeit not in terms of the final interpretation of that data.

Regardless of the direction of power, interviews are always a mediated product to the extent that they do not offer access to authentic experience but rather reflect strategies of "self-presentation" (Jacoby 2006: 162). In this regard, three dynamics are worth addressing in our own interviews. The first is that introducing ourselves as feminists and as sympathetic to the overall aims of the global justice movement most likely influenced the strategies of self-presentation pursued by our interviewees. As we argue in subsequent chapters, activists are highly strategic in the ways in which they mobilize political identifiers and we provided a context in which a feminist identity was safe to articulate; other identities may have been less so. A second dynamic that shaped the interviews pertained to the fact that these were formal, recorded interactions and the resulting words were going to be used in published material, in the public domain. In this context, it is likely that our interviewees were very selective and careful in how they presented themselves. In fact, several took the opportunity to brief us on their own political priorities, regardless of the questions we asked. A third dynamic had to do with the translation of interviews, particularly in Brazil. In such cases, the mediation process was even more complex in that we had, in effect, a three-way negotiation between our interviewee, our translators, and ourselves over meaning. Thus, these transcripts incorporate greater ambiguities than usual as to whether they capture what an interviewee truly intended to say.

Like interviewing, participant observation also presents challenges for the feminist researcher, most hinging on the character of the relationships established with those who are being observed. Reinharz, for example, indicates potential difficulties in forging relations of trust and in deciding whether or not to maintain "respectful distance" or to strive for the erasure of such distance (1992: 65–71). In the context of our fieldwork, trust was not assumed but neither was it difficult to establish: we were not sharing people's lives, after all, but rather participating in a large public event in which all present were seeking an audience for their views and hoping to make new connections. The spectrum of closeness and distance took a little more navigating, however. Given our efforts to achieve a panoramic view of activists at the forum, we did not want to assume an insider status by associating ourselves with a particular faction within it (Blee and Taylor 2002: 98). Nonetheless, our outsider academic role had a tendency to fade from view as we met activists repeatedly over time and developed friendly relationships with some of them. Out of respect for these relationships, we have been careful in this book to avoid any reference to things told to us informally in the interstices of meetings and when socializing, and to draw solely on those views put forward for public consumption. We feel that we have been less successful responding to the expectations of some of our interviewees that we contribute to feminist antiglobalization activism more directly. So, for instance, while we were able to meet some requests to lead workshops, we were surprised by and unable to fulfill activist's hopes of getting their texts published (see discussion in Maiguashca 2006b). Thankfully, our inability to reciprocate in this way did not adversely affect our relationships on-site.

After completing our fieldwork, we undertook the task of translating our research materials into data, a process that involved four stages. The first revolved around the transcription of all our interviews and, when requested, facilitating the review and editing of the resulting transcripts by interviewees. The second stage involved the identification of feminist groups to which our interviewees belonged. In this regard it is important to note that we had approached some of our interviewees because they articulated a feminist discourse rather than because of their membership in feminist organizations and, consequently, a proportion of our sample are members of mixed-gender networks of a range of political orientations. Moreover, the majority of our interviewees belong to more than one group, feminist or otherwise. Given this, we initially identified all the groups to which our interviewees belonged and then selected only those that prioritize overturning gender oppression as our core groups (see textbox 1.1).

Having thus determined our core groups, we moved on to systematize all the documentation that we had collected on them. This took us to the third stage of the process, namely, that of supplementing field-site information with online searches for published documentation. This allowed us to compile more complete profiles of our chosen groups as well as to develop a broader perspective on what had been happening over the years at the World Social Forum. The fourth and final stage saw us code both the transcripts and the relevant group documentation along with our field notes using computer software that enabled us to fillet and rearrange an enormous amount of data under gradually more specific category headings. From the resulting empirical material, in tandem with a continual review of feminist theory, we developed the lines of argumentation that constitute the backbone of this book.

We want to end this introduction with a few reflections on the status of the knowledge claims that we are making in the chapters that follow. More specifically, we suggest that our work should be seen as a form of "situated knowledge" (Haraway 1988). Feminists have long argued that conventional understandings of academic knowledge production that privilege the "view from nowhere" are fundamentally flawed. This is so because the standards of detachment and objectivity on which they rely serve to disguise their masculinist, elitist underpinnings and to validate as knowers only those who can assert authority from the "unmarked positions of 'White' and 'Man'" (Haraway 1988: 581). In response, feminists insist on an understanding of knowledge production that situates it within particular geopolitical and social locations and that sees it as reflecting specific configurations of power and interests (Collins 2000: ch. 11; Ramazanoğlu and Holland 2002; Harding 1991). Knowledge claims, then, are by their very nature a "view from somewhere" to the extent that they are bound to their point of origin, partial in character and limited in scope (Collins 2000: 269–70). In agreement with this view, our effort to construct a narrative of feminist antiglobalization activism must be seen as reflecting a situated, located perspective and as therefore tentative and incomplete.

In this epistemological scheme, feminists identify two key principles for the production of knowledge, namely reflexivity and dialogue. The first means placing oneself as researcher "within in the same critical plane" as the research one produces (Harding 1987: 9) and paying explicit attention

Textbox 1.1.   Core Groups

1. Abortion Rights
2. AfricaWoman
3. Akshara
4. All African Women's Group
5. All India Democratic Women's Association (AIDWA)
6. Andhra Pradesh Chaitanya Mahila Samakhya (APCMS)
7. Andhra Pradesh Mahila Samatha Society (APMSS)
8. Articulação de Mulheres Brasilieras (AMB)
9. Articulação de Mulheres Negras Brasilieras (AMNB)
10. Articulación Feminista Marcosur (AFM)
11. Asmita
12. Association for Women's Rights in Development (AWID)
13. ATTAC (Feminist groups)
14. Capetinas
15. Católicas por los Derechos de Decidir
16. CEMINA—Communicação, Educação e Informação em Gênero
17. Center for Women's Global Leadership (CWGL)
18. Centro Feminista de Estudos e Assessoria (CFEMEA)
19. Cidadania, Estudo, Pesquisa, Informação, Ação (CEPIA)
20. Codepink
21. Coletivo Feminino Plural
22. Collectif National pour les Droits des Femmes (CNDF)
23. CRIOLA
24. Dalit Feminist Group
25. Dalit Women's Federation
26. Development Alternatives with Women for a New Era (DAWN)
27. Fala Preta!
28. Feminist Centre
29. Femmes Solidaires
30. FEMNET—The African Women's Development and Communication Network
31. Flora Tristán: Centro de la Mujer Peruana
32. Forum against the Oppression of Women
33. Furcaza Feminista
34. Global Women's Strike
35. Grail
36. Indymedia Women
37. Instituto Eqüit
38. International Feminists for a Gift Economy
39. International Free Women's Foundation
40. International Gender and Trade Network (IGTN)
41. Mahila Jagruthi
42. Maria Mulher
43. National Federation of Indian Women (NFIW)
44. National Network of Autonomous Women's Groups (NNAWG)
45. NextGENDERation
46. Phoenix: Organisation for Woman and Child
47. Rede de Desenvolvimento Humano (REDEH)
48. Rede Mulher de Educação
49. Sempreviva Organização Feminista (SOF)
50. Themis—Assessoria Jurídica e Estudos de Gênero
51. Umas e Outras
52. Women in Black
53. Women Living Under Muslim Laws (WLUML)
54. Women Speak Out
55. Women's Environment and Development Organization (WEDO)
56. Women's Environmental Network (WEN)
57. Women's Global Network of Reproductive Rights (WGNRR)
58. Women's International Coalition for Economic Justice (WICEJ)
59. Women's International League for Peace and Freedom (WILPF)
60. World March of Women

to how the politics of one's location (Rich 1986: 210–31) shapes what is chosen for study and to the way it is studied. Or, to put it more simply, the feminist emphasis on reflexivity pushes us to write ourselves into our research as honestly and openly as we can as a counterweight to the false pretence of objectivity (Stanley and Wise 1993: 169). We have started this process here and continue it in chapter 3 by telling a personal story about our journey through the World Social Forum sites. In so doing, we seek to bring to the fore the ways our encounter with the Forum as a physical and political space, as well as our own individual positioning as academics with funding and linguistic privileges, serve to situate and render partial the knowledge claims of this book.

With regard to the second principle, feminists emphasize the importance of forging knowledge through a process of open-ended dialogue with others from different social and epistemic locations. It is only by means of this collective process, they argue, that a fuller, more inclusive understanding of reality can be constructed (Ackerly and True 2006: 258; Collins 2000: 269–70). Reaching for this "larger perspective" (Alice Walker quoted in Collins 2000: 270) is essential for feminists because it is only from here that one can begin to lay the foundations of a broader movement for transformative change. Our efforts to apply this dialogical principle in our own work begin with the conversations we have had with each other. In our commitment to collaborative scholarship, we have sought to adhere to respectful negotiation at every stage of the research and writing process, continually renegotiating and refining the arguments we lay out in this book. Casting the net more widely, we would include as part of this dialogical process the discussions we have had with our interviewees over their transcribed interviews and in workshops about the book, and our interactions with other academics in conferences at which we have presented our work and sought advice on refining it. In the final chapter of the book, we bring our knowledge claims into dialogue with the literature on the global justice movement, seeking to reflect on how our story might alter the perspectives presented there as well as on what further research still needs to be done. In this way, we hope to contribute to a constructive and exciting conversation about the politics of the global justice movement, one that is still ongoing.

What follows is divided into two main parts. Part I, "Constructing Feminist Antiglobalization Activism," consists of two chapters on the World Social Forum, our fieldwork site. In chapter 2, through a discussion of the collective efforts of feminists to challenge gendered hierarchies at the World Social Forum, we attempt to demonstrate that feminist antiglobalization activism has emerged as a coherent and significant form of collective action worthy of our attention. Chapter 3 shifts into a different register, telling a story about our journey through the Paris, Mumbai, London, and Porto Alegre forums between 2003 and 2005 in order to emphasize not only the heterogeneity of feminist antiglobalization activism on the ground, but also the situated nature of our encounter with it and thus our very particular view of the subject matter of this book.

Part II, "Mapping Feminist Antiglobalization Activism," unfurls a picture of the wider terrain of feminist antiglobalization activism, insofar as we glimpsed it from our vantage point at the World Social Forum. We begin in chapter 4 with an exploration of the origins of that activism. Our interviewees' critiques of the contemporary world order is the subject of our analysis in chapter 5 and their aspirations to build a better world are unpacked in chapter 6. In chapter 7, we explore the political activities undertaken in pursuit of this normative vision, while the final mapping chapter turns to how activists create and sustain a sense of solidarity. We conclude in chapter 9 by pulling together our arguments about feminist antiglobalization activism from across the book, and by drawing out their empirical and conceptual implications for thinking about the global justice movement.

NOTES

1. See, e.g., Graeber 2002: 63; Klein 2002: 77–78; Danaher and Burbach 2000: introduction; Waterman 2003; Brecher, Costello, and Smith 2002; della Porta et al. 2006.

2. See, e.g., Starhawk 2002b: 11; della Porta and Diani 2006: especially 2–5; della Porta 2007a; Graeber 2007; Hadden and Tarrow 2007; Wennerhag 2008.

3. See, e.g., Rupert 2000; Amoore 2005; Drainville 2004; Munck 2007.

4. See, e.g., Smith and Johnston 2002; Bandy and Smith 2005; della Porta and Tarrow 2005b; della Porta and Diani 2006.

5. These include chapters by Alvarez, Faria, and Nobre 2004; Brenner 2004; Vargas 2004; World March of Women 2004d. For one more example of an edited book that does include several chapters by feminists offering an analysis of gender as a site of political practice, see Amoore 2005: 215–56.

6. Gender is "a complex and contested concept" (Squires 1999: 54). Certainly many of our activists do not use the term. Nonetheless, we find it useful as "a category that was developed to explore what counts as 'woman' and as 'man'" (Squires 1999: 54). For us, as for many feminists, there is an assumption that gender categories are relational, gaining their meaning from an implied opposition to each other; that they are hierarchically arranged, with man/masculine privileged over female/feminine; and that gender intersects in complex, context-specific ways with other forms of power and oppression. In other words, feminist analysis begins with gender but does not end there.

7. Examples include Antrobus 2004; Waller and Marcos 2005; Moghadam 2005; Hawkesworth 2006; Marchand and Runyan 2000b; Naples and Desai 2002; Rowbotham and Linkogle 2001; Wichterich 2000.

8. See hints in this direction in Mohanty 2003: 230. A more developed empirical study has been offered recently by Valentine Moghadam (2009), although in

contrast to our book, Moghadam still treats feminism and the global justice move-ment as essentially separate political forces and thus is not able to draw out the the-oretical implications of feminist antiglobalization activism as we strive to do here.

9. References to the Forum, capitalized, are intended to indicate the World So-cial Forum as an ongoing, holistic process occurring at many levels.

10. For a fuller list see Leite 2005: chronology

11. We also talked to activists we recognized from the Forum whom we ran into again while at a Women's Studies conference in Dublin, and we conducted a couple of interviews while in Amsterdam for personal reasons.

12. We picked these sessions on the basis of a careful examination of the pro-gram at each forum for those events whose titles indicated that they addressed issues around feminism, women, or gender. We also prioritized those sessions organized by groups identified in the program as having *feminist* or *women* in their names or self-descriptions.

I

CONSTRUCTING FEMINIST ANTIGLOBALIZATION ACTIVISM

2

Skeleton Woman at the World Social Forum

Feminist Struggles for Visibility, Voice, and Influence, 2001–2005

> Skeleton woman—the uninvited guest—also showed up. . . . And the illusion of wealth, the imaginings of unfettered growth and expansion, became small and barren in the eyes of the world. Dancing, drumming, ululating, marching in black with a symbolic coffin for the world, Skeleton woman wove through the sulphurous rainy streets of the night. She couldn't be killed or destroyed. (Hawken 2000: 33)

In a powerful piece on the 1999 protests in Seattle against the World Trade Organization, Paul Hawken uses the image of a "Skeleton woman" to describe the tenacious way in which resistance haunts the neoliberal world order. Although Hawken does not focus on the role of women or feminists in this resistance, we find his metaphor evocative of the shadowy presence of feminism within the global justice movement.[1] In what follows, we reveal Skeleton woman at the World Social Forum in the shape of feminist struggles for visibility, voice, and influence. As will become clear, a wide range of feminist groups have been involved, over several years in several different countries, in a shared effort to ensure that the Forum includes feminist visions of equality and justice in the struggle for a better world. It is our view that, in so doing, they have constituted themselves as a coherent and significant form of collective action.

As we pointed out in chapter 1, the World Social Forum was first held in January 2001, in Porto Alegre, Brazil. There were two more annual gatherings in the same place until, in 2004, the decision was made to shift the location of the fourth World Social Forum to Mumbai, India, where we conducted fieldwork. We were also present in January 2005, when the global gathering returned to Porto Alegre for its fifth edition. At the same time as these global forums were being organized, an increasing number of associated events were being held around the world. At the regional level, for example, the first European Social Forum was held in Florence in the autumn of 2002, the second in Paris in November 2003, and the third in London in October 2004. We conducted fieldwork at the latter two.[2] While there have been forums in many other parts of the world (for a fuller account, see Leite 2005: chronology), and also several European Social Forums since 2004, we do not look at these here. To be clear, in what follows we focus on feminism at the World Social Forums and European Social Forums held from 2001 to 2005 (see figure 2.1).

This chapter is divided into two parts. In the first, we begin by tracing the gendered hierarchies that were in operation in the preparatory processes of the Forum and its annual events during this period, and the ways in which they served to marginalize feminist actors and discourses. In the second, we identify the main strategies deployed by feminists in order to avert what the southern network Development Alternatives with Women for a New Era (DAWN) called "the materialisation of Porto Alegre Men" (2002).[3] Feminist struggles to gain visibility, voice, and influence, we conclude, have resulted in the emergence of feminist antiglobalization activism as a significant political force deserving of our attention.

GENDERED MARGINALIZATIONS/
THE MARGINALIZATION OF GENDER

According to its Charter of Principles, the World Social Forum is intended as:

> an open meeting place for reflective thinking, democratic debate of ideas, formulation of proposals, free exchange of experiences and interlinking for effective action, by groups and movements of civil society that are opposed to neoliberalism and to domination of the world by capital and any form of imperialism. (WSF 2002)

The charter makes it clear that the Forum founders did not intend to establish a political actor nor to take on a determining vanguard role. In contrast, wherever they are organized, forums are meant to be open spaces in which alternatives to power relations can be developed, rather than a "locus of power" (WSF 2002). Nonetheless, they are not as open as the originators hoped they would be. Since the outset, critics have pointed out that the Forum has reflected and reified hierarchies in the wider social, economic, and political context.[4] One set of criticisms in this regard has focused on the overweening influence of specific political groups—such as the French group Association pour la Taxation des Transactions pour l'Aide aux Citoyens (ATTAC) and the Porto Alegre branch of the Brazilian Partido dos Trab-

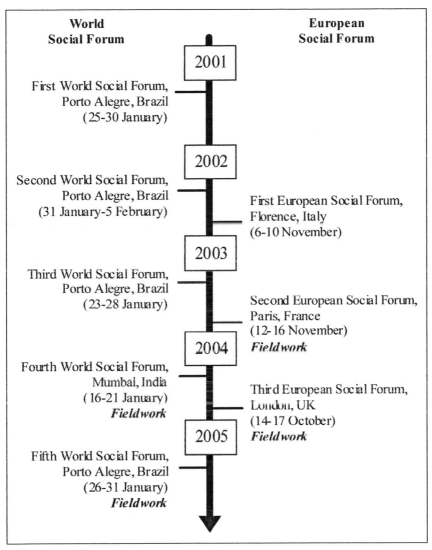

Figure 2.1. World Social Forum Time Line, 2001–2005

alhadores (PT or Worker's Party)—of certain strands of the Left, and of large nongovernmental organizations (NGOs) (e.g., Hardt 2002; Research Unit on Political Economy 2003). Another set of criticisms has focused on the exclusionary impact of certain methodological decisions, such as the frequency of the gatherings, the high travel costs, the distances to be covered between events at the different sites, the emphasis on large-scale, officially organized plenaries over smaller, autonomously organized workshops, and the privileging of academic discourses. Taken together, critics argue, these have functioned to ensure the inclusion of only small numbers of black Africans, for example, and the underrepresentation of young people on the official program (e.g., Klein 2001; Marin 2002).

In this part of the chapter we focus on the claim of many feminist participants that the World Social Forum and European Social Forum have also been shaped by gender hierarchies.[5] At this point, it must be acknowledged that women have attended the annual World Social Forum in huge numbers. Indeed, it has been estimated that they constituted just over half of the total attendees in Porto Alegre in 2001 and 2003 and, although the proportion was slightly lower in 2005, more than half of the young people taking part in that year were female (Francisco 2001; Grzybowski 2002; IBASE 2005: 19–20). Given the remarks above, it can be assumed that these women are, in general, relatively privileged in terms of their access to resources, educational background, and/or racial and geopolitical positioning (see, e.g., Latoures 2007: 167). What is striking, nonetheless, is the extent to which women have not been as visible as men in the main events of the Forum—and certainly not feminist women speaking about gendered hierarchies. Relatedly, feminist concerns have not been widely aired or heard within Forum processes.

It is our view that there are four main ways in which gendered hierarchies have shaped the Forum. The first can be seen in the *dominance of elite men and masculine modes of interaction in the leadership and organization of the Forum process*, particularly in its early stages (cf. Wilson 2007: 20–21). Feminists had little concrete involvement in the activities leading up to the first edition in Porto Alegre, 2001. According to an account by Brazilian activist Chico Whitaker (n.d.), his acquaintance Oded Grajew had the original idea and by early 2000, Bernard Cassen, president of ATTAC in France, was also involved. It seems Cândido Grzybowski of the Brazilian Institute of Social and Economic Analysis (IBASE) followed shortly thereafter. Eight Brazilian organizations then became responsible for organizing the event.[6] Although the initiative gained more diverse support at its international launch (at a gathering of social movements and NGOs parallel to a UN conference in Geneva, June 2000), not one of the eight founding groups was explicitly feminist in orientation, and the key players were "four white men and also more than fifties, older" (Magaly Pazello, interview, Porto Alegre, January 23, 2005). Indeed, these men are frequently referred to as "founding fathers" (Patomäki and Teivainen 2005), and Sonia Corrêa of DAWN describes discussion of their roles as a "paternity debate" (interview, Rio de Janeiro, January 10, 2005).

Consequently, the opening press conference of the first World Social Forum, according to Nicola Bullard of Focus on the Global South, "looked like the Last Supper: twelve men with an average age of 52" (cited in Klein 2001). Things had not improved much by the second forum, given that the press conference was led by one woman flanked by nine men. "As one woman journalist wisely said: 'This is so boring! It happens everywhere. She's the only woman but she is the one doing all the work!'" (Grzybowski 2002: 19). This led "founding father" Grzybowski to reflect that the organization of the World Social Forum was not immune from a "structural bias that hinders women from exercising leadership roles," for which he blamed a "Jurassic macho culture . . . in civil society" (2002: 19).

Things were perhaps even worse for the few feminists involved in the organization of the first European Social Forum in Florence later that year. Sarah Bracke, a participant in a network of feminist scholars and students called NextGENDERation, attended the final European preparatory assembly and commented:

> there was one black guy . . . he was the only one consistently raising issues of racism and migrant issues. And then there was Nadia [De Mond of the transnational network of feminist groups, the World March of Women], and she was the only one consistently raising feminist issues. . . . Why does it fall on the shoulders of this one person, this person who in a sense embodies the issue somehow, while the others seemingly can take disembodied positions of speaking about the struggle "in general"? (interview, Dublin, July 10, 2004)

Preparation for the European Social Forum in London a couple of years later posed further challenges. It seems that the organizing process was particularly conflictual, in that it "polarized the 'alternative' political scene" in the UK (Triggs 2004; see Eurotopia n.d.; Hennig 2004). The two opposed sides became known as the "verticals" and "horizontals." The former was associated with a preference for vertically organized chains of command and responsibility, electorally based models of representation and instrumental strategizing; the latter with more participatory, decentralized modes of organizing, through which individuals and groups speak only for themselves and aim to "prefigure" the world they would like to achieve (De Angelis 2004).[7] Our point here is not that one or the other was more feminist-friendly. In fact, British feminists were found on both sides of the divide. But the division itself, and the rather aggressive disagreements it generated and symbolized, arguably worked to the disadvantage of the full involvement of women, among others, in the organizational process. One interviewee told us that meetings were "violent, really violent . . . people were actually shouted down, and it became really personal" (Isabelle Fremeaux, interview, November 9, 2004). She abandoned the organizing process after being physically sick. Another admitted that "it took me months, *months*, to get up [to speak]; I was absolutely petrified" (Emma Dowling, interview, Dublin, July 9, 2009). The interviewee concluded that those women who succeeded in getting their voices heard in such a fraught context "are like men! Masculine in style. They are older women as well, they have been activists for a number of years and they have had to be strategic and acquire a number of behavioral patterns in order to be heard" (Emma Dowling, interview, Dublin, July 9, 2004).

This brings us to our second gendered dynamic, *the dominance of elite men and masculine modes of interaction in the annual Forum space or event.* While this may be an unsurprising consequence of the male domination of the prior organizing process, we point to the privileging of the large-scale "conference" or "plenary" format for the most high-profile official events as another relevant factor. Reinforcing the celebrity status of prominent activists, usually male, plenaries are also showcases for the kind of visceral confrontations mentioned above or for long-winded speeches from on high to passive, distant throngs. Neither of these modes of communication are particularly feminist-friendly. Thus, it is not surprising that the most important plenaries during the first World Social Forum at Porto Alegre were:

> almost entirely male, with only one or two females. And when you listened to that female she was an honorary male, she was patriarchal, she was not saying the feminist issues you would expect. . . . And when you did find on the main panels a feminist angle, it was something that had been organized by a feminist organization, like the Women's March [the World March of Women]. And . . . they were all female panelists. (Sara Longwe, interview, Porto Alegre, January 25, 2005)

In other words, feminists were not widely seen or heard outside of the sessions they organized themselves.

Cynthia Peters (2002) argues that things were much the same on this score at the second World Social Forum a year later. The size of the event had increased enormously, almost doubling in size to incorporate 50,000 attendees (WSF 2006), but women, including feminist women, were still underrepresented as speakers at panels and workshops. At the 2003 World Social Forum, which saw over 100,000 participants, things improved somewhat (WSF 2006). Feminist speakers were significantly more in evidence on those panels held under the auspices of the "thematic axes" organized by two feminist groups, the World March of Women and the Latin American network Articulación Feminista Marcosur (AFM). Our reading of the documentation on these panels is that fully half of the total of eighty-seven listed speakers were women and of those at least twenty-one were self-declared feminists or from feminist and pro-women groups (WSF 2003; AFM 2003a, 2003b). Of the remaining official panels, however, we calculate that just over a quarter of the speakers were women (thirty three out of a total of 119), of whom only seven were feminists or from women's groups (see WSF 2003). Furthermore, the introduction of larger, more TV-friendly conferences along with the showcasing of big names at the Gigantinho football stadium (Karadenizli et al. 2003; AFM 2003b) served to reinforce the phenomenon of what Naomi Klein (2003) described as "big men and swooning crowds" (see also Huijg 2003b). This was to reoccur in 2005 when high-profile stadium sessions were again held by male celebrities of the Left, Lula and Chavez.

At the European level, the first event in 2002 saw between 40,000 and 60,000 people descend on Florence to attend workshops, with nearly one million participating in the closing march (Hodkinson 2002). Yet feminist sessions were few and far between. As Sarah Bracke from NextGENDERation informed us:

> I counted because it's basic but it's necessary. In the official programme—more or less fifty panels—one dealing with feminism, women's issues; more or less 250 seminars—[only] three . . . the two by World Women's March and one by Punto di Partenza, our workshop. . . . There was also Les Pénélopes who were doing feminist media. . . . So that was more or less our sense of the forces. (interview, Dublin, July 10, 2004)

While some feminists had a productive experience in Florence at the non-feminist sessions, undertaken in what they considered to be "an atmosphere of solidarity and friendliness" (Collins 2002), others argued that "at times . . . the formal sessions seemed pre-feminist in their platforms and style" (Wainwright 2002). By the time of the second European Social Forum in Paris, in which similar numbers of activists were involved (see Zehetbauer 2003; Hubbard 2003; Dybeck 2003), feminist representation on panels had improved somewhat. Our count of those sessions in the program that had *women* (or a category of women), *gender*, or *feminism* in the title indicates four plenaries, ten seminars, and twelve workshops, significantly more than in Florence but still only 3.6 percent of the total. Feminist and women's groups also fielded speakers in other plenaries and were involved in the preparation of mixed or broad sessions, of which it is impossible to do a definitive count. Nonetheless, many interviewees lamented that the visibility and influence of feminists remained limited in Paris. And our search of the online program for sessions specifically on feminist and women's themes in London the subsequent year indicates that these composed 6 percent of sessions. Although this was a much smaller event (Callinicos 2004), the important point is that feminists had almost doubled their proportion of speakers since Paris. Yet they still remained invisible on the podiums in 94 percent of the occasion.

A third gendered dynamic shaping Forum politics concerns the *prevalence of gender-blind characterizations of "the enemy" and visions of social change*. We have argued elsewhere that Left critiques of globalization are frequently economically determinist, rendering gender either invisible or superstructural, and making it difficult to see how feminism might contribute to the struggle for other possible worlds (Eschle 2004a). This charge was echoed in the testimony of several feminists at the 2001 and 2002 World Social

Forum gatherings, who commented on the "lack of a robust gender perspective in the analyses of globalization" (DAWN 2002) and the "clearly sexist language" used (Vargas 2001) "outside of explicitly feminist groups" (Rebick 2002). Or as activists associated with NextGENDERation described it in Florence, "the power relations involved in gender and ethnicity (let alone sexuality) were not considered a common, transversal, concern but were seen as 'particular' issues, particular to certain groups or certain subjects" (Andrijasevic, Bracke, and Gamberi 2002). Even in 2003, with levels of feminist visibility improving, there were continued, repeated complaints about the lack of integration of feminist concerns into the dominant discourses at the Porto Alegre event. The final declaration issued by the World March of Women (2003a) lamented that "[t]he struggle against capitalism is still considered to be the primary struggle in the minds of many," while a report from Women in Development Europe (WIDE) declared that "gender issues were as usual very marginalized as not being a 'priority' given these troubled times and the more 'serious' issues to tackle" (Karadenizli et al. 2003). In this regard, one interviewee pointed out that none of the male participants at a World March–sponsored session on the economy considered gender issues in their talks and that when directly asked about it "they did not answer" (Nalu Faria, interview, São Paolo, January 17, 2005).

Finally, gendered power relations at the Forum sites have manifested in *sexist actions that have served to directly intimidate, demean, and silence women,* feminist or otherwise. The Youth Camp, a space where mostly young people stay during the World Social Forum, seems to have had particular problems in this regard. Intended to be a self-organized, self-conscious attempt at "horizontal" forms of collective living, free from hierarchies (Juris 2005), in 2002 the camp generated several complaints of sexual harassment and two allegations of rape (Huijg 2003a). In 2005—by which time it had expanded to over 35,000 people (Juris 2005; WSF 2005b)—the camp saw a shocking total of ninety reported complaints of sexual harassment and the last day of the World Social Forum was again blighted by claims that one or more rapes had taken place there (Obando 2005; WHRNet 2005; Koopman 2007). Beyond the confines of the camp, a rape allegation was also made against a speaker at the official sessions in Mumbai in 2004 (Sargent and Albert 2004: 6–7). We acknowledge that these incidents seem to have been localized and were unlikely to have affected the majority of women on site. As such, they are undoubtedly less directly causal of the marginalization of the feminist presence at the Forum than the more diffuse structural processes highlighted above, however terrible they must have been for those women directly affected. Having said this, we interpret the repeated surfacing of sexual harassment and violence as an indicator, in the bluntest possible form, of the limited acceptance or integration of feminist arguments and ethics among sections of Forum participants.

FEMINIST STRUGGLES FOR
VISIBILITY, VOICE, AND INFLUENCE

Although it has been argued that feminists were rather "late and light" in their involvement in the Forum (Peter Waterman, interview, October 13, 2004; see also Karadenizli et al. 2003: 2), it was not long after the initial process was launched that feminists began sustained, coordinated efforts to challenge the gendered hierarchies described above. We begin this part of the chapter by examining those strategies intended to *contest elite male dominance of the organization process*. It was in 2000, at a crucial meeting at the headquarters of IBASE, that feminists first intervened in this process. Activists from DAWN and AFM sought to persuade the organizers that "there is a problem with the panels because there are no women and there are no feminists. The voices there are so male mainstream" (Magaly Pazello, interview, Porto Alegre, January 23, 2005; see also DAWN 2000). During the first World Social Forum gathering, feminists circulated a statement titled "Practicing Gender Justice Now," which urged "the organizers to practice the democratic principle of gender and regional balance in the constitution of the advisory and organizing committee" (cited in DAWN 2002) Activists from the World March of Women who attended that first event immediately took the decision to become more involved:

> we went there and we found . . . the same analysis of the World Bank and of neoliberalism and so on. . . . But they lack a gender analysis . . . so that's what we have to bring in because no one else is going to. . . . [At that point we decided] we want to be much more in the preparation process and in the conferences . . . and the World March of Women was one of the international networks that immediately entered the International Council. (Nadia De Mond, interview, Paris, November 14, 2003)

The International Council was established a few months after the first World Social Forum in 2001, in recognition of the need to globalize the organizing process given "the global character of the fight against capitalist globalization" (Leite 2005: 98). We know that DAWN and AFM joined the World March in the International Council shortly after its formation and that by 2003 another six feminist groups had become members.[8] Although these groups constituted less than 10 percent of the International Council at this stage (Waterman 2003), they do seem to have gained some influence. Crucially, as we have seen, the World March and AFM were granted control of two of the thematic axes around which panels were organized in the 2003 World Social Forum.

Turning to the organization of the European Social Forums, the build-up to the Paris event in 2003 saw a small number of key feminist activists integrate into the preparatory process. These women were associated not only with the World March but also with ATTAC, the trade unions, and the Left parties that dominated organizing committees (see Reyes and Hodgkinson 2004). They were thus very well connected and could wear several hats, their activities ensuring both some attention to "patriarchy" as a theme in the official program (Zehetbauer 2003; Hodgkinson 2002) and "more plenaries and seminars integrating women's questions than had previously been the case in Florence" (Leclerc 2003). The momentum increased as the World Social Forum moved to India for the 2004 meeting, with the establishment of a Women's Movement Caucus on the Indian Organizing Committee (see WSF 2004a, 2004b). This caucus was very effective in pushing patriarchy as a theme of the forum,[9] and in its lobbying for more women in the official plenaries and conferences, including in a dedicated "women's conference."

This takes us to the second set of feminist strategies we want to discuss, those aimed at *ensuring enhanced visibility at the World Social Forum event.* Most obviously, feminists have attempted to infiltrate the high-profile plenaries and conferences of the official program. For example, during the first World Social Forum, the "Practicing Gender Justice Now" statement discussed above was read out by Sara Longwe of the African Women's Development and Communication Network (FEMNET), among others, in a highly public "coup d'état [during] the last plenaries":

> We just went to the token women on the panels and said "can you please give me five minutes of your time?" We did this without announcing to the chairs of the panels to avoid being stopped . . . and I read this statement, which in part said "if we are having a new world or an order alternative to neoliberalism, we must get women on board and women's issues on board, and this must start with the representation on the panels and the issues." (Sara Longwe, interview, Porto Alegre, January 23, 2005)

In the wake of the first World Social Forum and European Social Forum, feminists on the International Council and on the European preparatory assemblies have fought for systematic mechanisms for the higher representation of women on panels. They have insisted on actual parity of representation, or "50 percent women speakers [and chairs] as an aim" in the official sessions "and alternate women and men speakers in the assemblies and all those things" (Nadia De Mond, interview, Paris, November 14, 2003), albeit with varying degrees of success. We pointed out above that it was not until the 2003 Porto Alegre meeting that women in general and feminist women in particular became more visible on plenaries, albeit on those sessions organized under the thematic axes controlled by AFM and the World March, on which parity was achieved. It was at the Indian meeting of 2004, however, that feminists—or perhaps more accurately in the Indian context, activists from the Indian women's movement—really established a strong presence. The opening event, for example, included several women speakers whose contributions framed the concerns of the World Social Forum through a gender lens, as we discuss below. Subsequently, approximately 30,000 people gathered at the women's conference a few days later, officially titled "Wars against Women, Women against Wars," to listen to speakers such as Arundhati Roy, Nawal El Saadawi, and Gayatri, a young victim of rape by the police (see, e.g., Salazar 2004: 8). In addition, there were a further 144 events organized by feminists and women's groups, both official and self-organized—at our calculation, 11.6 percent of the total held at the Mumbai forum.[10] While still a relatively small proportion overall, this is by far the highest total of the first few years, and it should be remembered that it does not include the many mixed panels into which speakers from the Indian women's movement were integrated.

Feminist efforts to gain visibility at the forum have not been limited to official panels or self-organized workshops, but have also included organizing at street level. For some, the "best feminist moment" at the first World Social Forum was the "diverse and colourful protest" against U.S. abortion policy (DAWN 2001). At the second World Social Forum there was a similar demonstration, this time a "noisy, carnival-like rally for the decriminalisation of abortion in Latin America and the Caribbean" (Rosenberg 2002; see also Vargas 2003: 916). This was linked to the launch of the Campaign against Fundamentalism, organized at this stage chiefly by AFM, "an impressive (and expensive) media or cultural campaign, including posters on Porto Alegre hoardings, a hot air balloon, tee shirts, masks, public testimonies and professional-looking brochures" (Waterman 2002). At the 2003 World Social Forum, the campaign took a float to the opening demonstration and distributed 15,000 face masks (AFM 2003b; see also AFM n.d.). Gaining similar grassroots visibility at this time was the World March. Thus in 2002, one participant remarked that the "World March flags and women wearing March T-shirts are omnipresent on the site. . . . 10,000 flyers have been distributed" (Burrows 2002). In 2003 the World March "headed the protest march with its 10-metre tall coloured dolls" (Estima 2003) and organized two well-attended workshops and a protest march in the Youth Camp.

Nonetheless, it was at the Mumbai event in 2004 that feminist and women's groups were most evident throughout the space. With estimates of attendees reaching 150,000 (WSF 2004c; Duddy 2004b), the unprecedented street life of this World Social Forum has been widely noted. "Most remarkable was the visible presence of women from grassroots mass movements of Dalits and Adivasi [tribal people]" (Salazar 2004: 6; see also Di Giovanni 2004). In combination with the stronger presence of women on official panels integrating an awareness of gender inequality and women's rights into their speeches, these street protests created a significantly more feminist-friendly environment than previous World Social Forums. As Dianne Matte of the World March put it, "I saw the presence of feminism [in Mumbai] more than I ever saw in Brazil" (cited in Conway 2007a: 57).

Yet another strategy that feminists have pursued in order to permeate the Forum is to create their own autonomous feminist spaces. As well as carving out room for feminist networking and offering a retreat for feminists, this strategy can also be linked to the overall project of enhancing visibility in the Forum because it enables coordination of feminist integration into other sessions and into broader alliances, and showcases feminist speakers and methods. This is the reasoning behind, for example, the proposal that emerged from a NextGENDERation workshop in Florence to hold a larger feminist meeting before the subsequent European Social Forum in Paris. As Sarah Bracke put it, "let's meet up before the next ESF and . . . we will spread like a virus, you know a feminist virus . . . a feminist fire!" (interview, Dublin, July 10, 2004). What was ultimately to become the "European Assembly for Women's Rights" was judged to be a great success by its organizers because far more women than anticipated, from more countries, eventually turned up:

> we thought, optimistically, about 2,000 perhaps would come. . . . 3,300 turned up and in the afternoon we were turning people away because we could not exceed 2,500 in the tent. . . . We also invited women from Eastern Europe and gave them a place in the workshop, and it was very important to make this relationship. . . . Forty-two countries were represented. (Anne Leclerc, interview, Paris, November 16, 2003)

Interestingly, in the organizational process for the European Social Forum in London the subsequent year, the model of what became known as the Paris "Women's Day" did not receive widespread support among feminist groups. Indeed, such an event was pushed for by only one British-based group, the Global Women's Strike (2004a, 2004b, 2004c).[11] In the end, the Global Women's Strike held its own Women's Day prior to the London gathering.

At the global level, in contrast, there seems to be more consensus around the utility of autonomous spaces for raising the profile of feminists. The second edition of the World Social Forum in 2002 saw the organization of the Planeta Fêmea women's tent by the Brazilian groups Rede de Desenvolvimento Humano (REDEH) and Coletivo Feminino Plural.[12] Intended as "a space where groups could meet informally, discuss strategies and mount various activities" (Women's Environment and Development Organization 2002), the tent also provided an alternative feminist aesthetic: "[It] was very beautifully decorated. It made a difference, you know. It was a place people wanted to go" (Thais Corral, interview, Rio de Janeiro, January 17, 2005). In 2003, unfortunately, the Planeta Fêmea was moved to a less central position, was less well used, and has not been organized since.[13] Other autonomous spaces emerged subsequently, however, including the Feminist Dialogues initiated by AFM, which have their roots in feminist strategy meetings held before and after the 2003 World Social Forum and which have subsequently become more formalized and more inclusive in scope, allowing participants to strengthen links between each other before going on to attend World Social Forum events.[14] In addition, in 2005, the same cluster of groups associated with the Feminist Dialogues organized a Barco de Diversidad, or Diversity Boat. This sought not only to flag the need for greater acknowledgment of identity differences at the Forum, but also to offer women and other marginalized groups a safe space in which to strategize on site (Wilson 2007: 15). Simultaneously, the World March of Women set up a "feminist laboratory" in the Youth Camp, a "kind of an action center, an autonomous space for activities   Our criteria was only to accept activities proposed by women," which were then taken out into the Youth Camp as a whole (Julia Di Giovanni, interview, Porto Alegre, January 27, 2005).

These wide-ranging and diverse efforts to gain visibility are closely related to a third set of strategies aimed at *integrating feminist concepts into the analyses of oppression and the visions of change developed at the Forum*. Indeed, this has been a central objective of feminist spaces, plenaries, workshops, round tables, and campaigns on site and of feminist participation in many mixed sessions with other nonfeminist groups. For example, Virginia Vargas (2002) draws attention to the Diversity Roundtable organized by AFM at the second World Social Forum, which brought feminists together with Dalits and "sexual minorities" and which "place[d] at centre stage issues of intolerance," seeking to unpack the "deceptive" and "exclusive" character of claims to "universality." In parallel, World March participants raised issues around gender at plenary conferences on labor, on the solidarity economy, and on globalization and militarism, besides organizing their own events (Burrows 2002). The World March also managed to ensure that the high-profile "Call of Social Movements" at the end of the second World Social Forum contained a critique of "the central role of . . . patriarchy in neoliberal globalization" (Burrows 2002). Outside of the official panels and large assemblies, the specific issues of reproductive rights and abortion were dramatically highlighted by the demonstrations mentioned above, as well as in workshops (see Rosenberg 2002), and by a widely circulated DAWN supplement issued just before the third event in Porto Alegre that challenged the Forum's neglect of the "critical geo-political issue" of abortion (Corrêa 2003: 4). Yet another innovative example is provided by the sustained efforts of the Campaign against Fundamentalism to extend the concept of fundamentalism to incorporate neoliberalism, thus targeting all "those religious, economic, scientific or cultural expressions that attempt to negate humanity in its diversity" (cited in Vargas 2003:

915). In so doing, the campaign seeks to challenge economistic discourses that sideline culture and sexuality.

In India, there was also a widespread preoccupation among women activists with gender inequality, violence against women, and women's economic rights. Thus, on top of the large-scale conference, Wars against Women, Women against Wars mentioned above and the sessions organized by international feminist networks (World March of Women 2003b; Di Giovanni 2004; Santiago 2005), there was a whole range of seminars on related topics arranged by local Indian groups (see, e.g., Salazar 2004; Kumar 2004). Moreover, as already mentioned, the Women's Caucus succeeded in integrating an explicit concern with patriarchy into the main themes of the whole event. As Janet Conway concludes of Mumbai, "this more explicit recognition of the multiplicity of oppressions and the expansion of political discourses beyond capitalism and imperialism was, in terms of feminism, probably the most significant development" (2007a: 57).

A final way in which feminists have challenged gendered dynamics at the Forum is by *taking direct action against sexist treatment of women on site*. Take, for example, the demonstration organized by the World March of Women in the Youth Camp in 2003, which developed out of a workshop on sexist advertising and graffiti and took the form of a loud and lively march through the camp with about forty women and men banging drums and chanting slogans against sexual harassment and violence (Beaulieu and Giovanni 2003; Huijg 2003a). In 2005, in the wake of a proliferation of sexual harassment complaints, another demonstration took place in the camp, with over 200 participating this time and the Brigada Lilás, a group of women wearing lilac armbands, serving as safety chaperones to other women (see Koopman 2007: 151; also Centro de Midia Independente Brasil 2005). As Sara Koopman reports (2007: 151), however, the 2005 demonstration was met with hostility from some in the camp, which ultimately crystallized into a competing march of nearly 100 men, some naked, demanding what they proclaimed to be "sexual liberation." Koopman elaborates that "[t]here generally seems to be a 'will to forget' these events that seem so contradictory to the image, the discourse and the ideals of the Forum. The rumours of rapes, and the protest march against them, were largely invisibilized" (2007: 151).

So what was the balance sheet for feminists by 2005? Overall, the story told here is one of fluctuating feminist fortunes rather than inevitable progress. Clearly, the feminist strategies enumerated above have ensured some significant gains in visibility, voice, and influence since the first edition. A small core of feminist groups did manage to integrate into the International Council, and later years witnessed the continued incorporation of feminist voices into mainstream panels and the development of autonomous transnational networks and spaces in the European and international events.

In tandem with the integration of local women's groups into the Indian Organizing Committee in the form of the Women's Movement Caucus, this degree of feminist mobilization and coordination resulted in the 2004 Mumbai World Social Forum becoming one of the "historical high points" (Conway 2007a: 50) in terms of the visibility of women in official plenaries and throughout the meeting and the widespread adoption of the concept of patriarchy and a women's rights discourse. It should not, however, be concluded that Mumbai was a feminist paradise, given the rape accusation that marred it.

Moreover, progress seemed to stall in Porto Alegre in 2005. Most significantly, this fifth World Social Forum saw the abolition of the distinction between, on the one hand, the officially organized program of conferences and plenaries and, on the other, self-organized workshops. As Hilary Wainwright explains, the International Council experimented with a new organizing methodology, "inia[ting] a 'consulta' with all the past participants in the Forum, asking them to propose the main themes" around which all sessions would be organized:

> The results formed the basis of 11 clusters or "terrains" around particular themes: militarism, trade and debt, common goods, social movements and democracy and more. Organizations then proposed and registered their activities within these terrains which were also the physical focal points of the WSF. The theory was that groups would put their plans on the WSF website . . . and there would be a process of merging and connecting. . . . In practice, the new methodology was only half implemented . . . but most people I've talked to found the break from the centrally planned programme a real liberation. (Wainwright 2005; see also WSF 2004d)

Most Brazilian feminists we interviewed welcomed this methodological shift as being in line with feminist democratic principles. The two-tier system did not disappear entirely, however, as stadium sessions with male stars of the Left, Lula and Chavez, were held again. Even more worryingly, it is in the context of the democratization process that the feminist presence seems to have dipped. As a crude yardstick, our count of events in the 2005 program that were primarily for or about women, gender, or feminist agendas yields a total of 116, or 4.6 percent of the total number of 2,500 sessions (see also Haralanova 2005). This is back to the levels of Paris and London and significantly lower than in Mumbai. Furthermore, 2005 saw not only an increased incidence of claims of harassment and violence against women in the World Social Forum space, but also continued complaints about the discursive marginalization of concerns about gender equality outside of feminist-organized events. Koopman indicates, for example, that there should have been—but wasn't—discussion of the rape complaints in the daily forum newspaper (2007: 157), while Barbara

Klugman (2007: 89) claims that sexual and reproductive rights were disconnected from the supposedly "transversal" themes of the World Social Forum and discussed mainly in parallel events. In sum, in 2005 the articulation of feminist concerns at the World Social Forum remained dependent on the physical presence of self-declared feminists, and this presence was not as integrated or extensive as that of women's movement activists in India in the previous year. As one interviewee concluded:

> It is not that it [the World Social Forum] is open to feminism. It was opened to feminism. If we compare the first or second World Social Forum to this one now you can see that we have developed a lot . . . but I still don't believe that the World Social Forum is a space that managed to make a break from patriarchal logic. We are still questioning this culture but we haven't ruptured it. (Telia Negrão interview, Porto Alegre, January 22, 2005)

Commentary on subsequent meetings confirms that feminist fortunes at the World Social Forum have continued to fluctuate.[15]

CONCLUSION

This chapter has explored feminist efforts to gain visibility, voice, and influence at the Forum, in response to the dominance of elite men and masculine styles in the organizing process and Forum events, the prevalence of gender-blind characterizations of "the enemy" and of social change, and incidents of sexual harassment. Feminists have integrated into the International Council and local organizing committees; they have fought for feminist speakers on high-profile plenaries, conducted campaigns on the ground, and organized feminist spaces and networks on site; they have circulated gendered and intersectional analyses of power relations; and they have demonstrated against sexist actions and sexual violence on site. Although we concluded above that these activities have had only partial and fluctuating success, it is clear that ongoing feminist pressure has helped to ensure that the hegemony of "Porto Alegre Men" remains incomplete.

Most importantly for our purposes, the chapter has demonstrated the existence of Skeleton woman at the World Social Forum—sometimes obscured and glimpsed through shadows, but steadfastly refusing to die away. To put this another way, notwithstanding the range of groups involved in the different forums, their shared struggle to combat gender hierarchies and to integrate feminist visions of justice constitutes them as a coherent and significant form of collective action, one we have labeled "feminist antiglobalization activism." This is not to deny the highly heterogeneous and even conflictual character of the feminist presence at the Forum, however, especially when viewed from the ground. The differences and contestations between the myriad groups involved in feminist antiglobalization activism are the subject of the next chapter, along with our own particular encounters with these groups while undertaking our fieldwork.

NOTES

A shorter version of this chapter, focusing purely on the World Social Forum rather than the European Social Forum, will be published in Jai Sen (ed.), *Facing History: The World Social Forum and Beyond* (forthcoming).

1. See Eschle 2005 for the first exploration of this metaphor.
2. Bice also attended Florence; see Maiguashca 2006b.
3. This is a deliberate reference by DAWN to the looming shadow of "Davos Man," or the elite men and their masculinist assumptions found at the World Economic Forum in Davos, to which the World Social Forum is intended as a counterpoint.
4. The openness of the Forum has explicit as well as implicit limits, given that political parties and armed organizations have been officially excluded (Sen 2004).
5. Similar criticisms have been made about forum events elsewhere. For example, on the African Social Forum held in Mali early in 2002, Elvire Beleoken writes that only one theme, titled "gender and equity," was devoted to women's issues. Two workshops were held on this and the second was retitled "women's talents and creativity . . . which resulted in a drop of attendance of 50 per cent. . . . Major African women's organizations were neither present nor represented. . . . [R]eproductive and sexual rights and health were not on the agenda" (Beleoken 2002).
6. These were the Brazilian Association of Non-Governmental Organizations (ABONG), ATTAC, the Brazilian Justice and Peace Commission (CBJP), the Brazilian Business Association for Citizenship (CIVES), the Central Trade Union Federation (CUT), the Brazilian Institute for Social and Economic Studies (IBASE), the Centre for Global Justice, and the Landless Rural Workers Movement (MST) (Whitaker n.d; Sen 2004: 72).
7. Simon Tormey (2004a) claims that a similar divide characterized European Social Forum organization in Paris the previous year, so it was not unique to London, although it may have played out in a particularly vitriolic way there. It certainly featured widely in our London interviews and not at all in our Paris ones. We would also acknowledge that there are some problems with the labels. One interviewee points out that they came originally from those self-identified as horizontal: "it is completely their own choice of language. . . . I don't like it at all" (Milena Buyum, interview, London, November 5, 2004).
8. The other feminist groups on the International Council by 2003 were the International Gender and Trade Network, REMTE (Latin American Network of Women Transforming the Economy), Rede Latinamericana y Caribena de Mujeres Negras (Latin American and Caribbean Network of Black Women), Red Mujer y Habitat (Network of Women and the Environment), the Women's Global Network for Reproductive Rights, and REPEM (Network of Women in Popular Education) (AFM 2003a).

9. Technically, patriarchy was included as a transversal or cross-cutting theme at the Mumbai forum (WSF 2004a), rather than a "thematic axis" around which panels were organized. However, it is our impression that there was a much greater emphasis on patriarchy, communalism, and casteism than this official categorization perhaps reveals and certainly much greater than in Paris, where patriarchy was also a theme.

10. This is according to a handout of feminist and women's sessions circulated at the Feminist Dialogues prior to the World Social Forum in 2005.

11. In the end, after continued pressure from the Global Strike and also from European feminists associated with the World March, an official plenary on women and oppression was supplemented at the last minute by a three-hour Women's Assembly, held on the first morning of the first full day of the European Social Forum and apparently necessitating the sacrifice of several other feminist sessions (Cruells 2004).

12. The Planeta Fêmea was held first at the UN Conference on Environment and Development in 1992.

13. Telia Negrão of Coletivo Feminino Plural, key local organizers of the Planeta Fêmea, told us they "didn't feel motivated enough to cope with all the difficulties," particularly of coalition building, in the face of criticisms in previous years (interview, Porto Alegre, January 22, 2005).

14. For more on the Feminist Dialogues, and for debates about their function, see Feminist Dialogues 2009; Women's International Coalition for Economic Justice 2003; AFM 2003b; Duddy 2004a, 2004b; Santiago 2005; Wilson 2007; Gouws 2007; Conway 2007b.

15. For example, Aurelie Latoures claims that self-organized activities on "gender sensitive issues" at Bamako in 2006 totaled 13 percent of all activities, a higher proportion than our similar calculation of Mumbai—but these were concentrated mainly in one thematic area, Women's World, not "mainstreamed" (2007: 172–73). According to Latoures, the proportion was significantly lower in the other venues for the polycentric 2006 World Social Forum (2007: 177). See Oloo 2006 and Oloo's interview in Willis 2007 for one man's assessment of the ongoing struggle for "parity" before and during the World Social Forum held in Nairobi in 2007.

3

Feminist Encounters at the World Social Forum, 2003–2005

Uncovering Diversity and Situating Knowledge

> I am speaking my own small piece of truth as best as I can. . . . [W]e each have only a piece of the truth. So here it is: I'm putting it down for you to see if our fragments match anywhere, if our pieces, together, make another larger piece of the truth that can be part of the map we are making together to show us the way to get to the longed-for world. (Minnie Bruce Pratt, cited in Moya 2001: 7)

If the previous chapter offered a panoramic view of the feminist presence at the World Social Forum, in this one we want to tell a more personal story of our own voyage through the Forum and of the manifold kinds of feminist organizing we encountered there. There are two reasons for this shift in perspective. The first is our wish to draw attention to the diverse, heterogeneous, and fluid character of feminist antiglobalization activism. We presented this movement sector earlier as a distinct form of collective action, one with a degree of coherence in terms of shared mobilization against gender hierarchies at the World Social Forum. Here we want to remind the reader that feminist antiglobalization activism, like all social movement activism, is not unified and stable but a site of struggle and contestation.

The second reason pertains to the feminist imperative of reflexivity, which requires us to situate ourselves as researchers and to show the ways in which our specific experiences during our fieldwork shaped the story we tell in the book. In this chapter, we strive to show how our social positioning, our academic status, the methods we deployed, and our choices made on site interacted with structural and contingent features of the Forum to produce a partial, nonreplicable image of feminist antiglobalization activism. In what follows, then, we draw selectively on our field notes to relate

our encounters with feminist antiglobalization activism in and around the
four events we visited.

PARIS, NOVEMBER 2003

We begin our research in the summer of 2003. Driven by a conviction that
feminist antiglobalization activists are vital to the global justice movement
but invisible in most representations of it, we put an initial grant proposal
together in the hopes of obtaining financial support for our search for them.
While waiting to hear back from academic funding bodies, we attend a
conference in Graz, Austria, on the feminist contribution to opposition to
neoliberalism, organized by activists there and in Vienna who are members
of a feminist caucus in the Association for the Taxation of Financial Transactions for the Aid of Citizens (ATTAC). At the conference we have a chance to
talk informally to activists from ATTAC in several European countries, such
as Kaarina Kailo from Finland, and to participants from other groups, like
Nadia De Mond from Italy. Nadia tells us she is involved in the European-
level coordination of the World March of Women, a network of feminist
anticapitalist organizations from around the world. We are directed toward
relevant e-mail lists and, on our homecoming, start to follow online arrangements for a day-long "Women's Assembly" preceding the upcoming
European Social Forum in Paris. We find preparations are already at an
advanced stage, centered on the Paris-based branch of the World March of
Women. The e-mails flying backward and forward reveal that one of the
participating networks, NextGENDERation, is withdrawing from the organizational process. Member Sarah Bracke, from Belgium, later explains to
us that this was because of incompatible expectations about the character of
that process—"we probably have a more . . . autonomous spirit"—as well as
disagreement over the interpretation of particular themes:

> for me it's important to keep that in mind, because often it is forgotten, that
> . . . [o]n so many issues and ways of working . . . [feminists] can really clash
> politically. . . . [I]t makes a difference if you are a feminist Trotskyist or a
> feminist anarchist. . . . Not that I'm so attached to such labels, but sometimes
> they help to situate some of the differences. Especially in the light of tempt-
> ing outcries like "but why can't we just work together as women?" (Interview,
> Dublin, July 10, 2004)

As November rolls around, we head off to Paris to pilot our project. We
want to see if feminists are there to any great extent, to check whether or
not it will be possible to talk to them, to gather initial documentation on
groups, and to get a sense of the Forum as a fieldwork site and how best
to navigate it. Thus, the day before the official event starts, on a wintry

Wednesday morning, we join the long queues waiting patiently outside a cluster of enormous white marquees in the suburb of Bobigny. This is the Women's Assembly—the "European Assembly for Women's Rights" to give it its full title—and we are amazed and impressed at the size and scale of it all, and at the sheer numbers of women. The queue is processed surprisingly quickly and, after an initial introduction, the workshops begin. These are not the small-scale, participatory gatherings we expected, however, but rather more plenary-style events with enormous audiences. At the "Women and War" workshop Catherine attends, there is a row of podium speakers elevated above the crowd. Dressed in black, most are obviously from the peace network Women in Black and, as it turns out, not just from Paris but also Belgrade, Italy, and Jerusalem. A white-scarved Chechen refugee weeps as she gives her testimony. Interventions from the floor are finally permitted, but only a few can speak, for a short time. One woman berates the audience passionately for not focusing sufficiently on Palestine.

At lunch, we gather documentation from all the stalls around the main tent before returning in the afternoon to a closing plenary. They are now turning women away from the huge main tent for safety reasons and there are more people here than we can count. Certainly, on the podium there are no fewer than fourteen speakers. The chair, who introduces herself as Anne Leclerc from the World March in Paris, asks everyone to quiet down for the reading of the preprepared manifesto, hastily amended to accommodate some of the day's workshop proposals. "We protest against this macho, sexist, patriarchal and discriminatory Europe," it asserts; "the struggles and demands of women are not 'specific,' on the contrary they are at the heart of the struggles against neoliberal globalization." Then the floor opens for debate and a long and noisy queue for the microphone immediately forms. A British woman from Globalize Resistance argues that Muslim women have a right to wear *hijab* or the headscarf, and a French speaker responds that we should protest for the right not to wear "the veil." A group of young women in pink from NextGENDERation then crowd around the microphone to criticize the placement of the topic of prostitution in the workshop on violence, rather than with work or migration, and diverse interventions on a range of issues continue into the evening.

Flagging at the end of this marathon session, our spirits are soon revived by the vibrant and enthusiastic demonstration that takes us through the cold and darkening streets of Bobigny. It includes many mixed male and female groups from trade unions and Palestinian rights organizations. Elderly white women line up behind a long banner from the Women's International League for Peace and Freedom; NextGENDERation women and men rush by us waving pink parasols; and large cardboard silhouettes of dancing women bob in the air. This demonstration marks the end of the Women's Assembly and the official start of the European Social Forum.

The forum is spread out over four different parts of Paris and on November 13, the opening day, we head to La Villette. This is an enormous building of steel and glass, filled with stalls and artwork and set in huge grounds in which several tents are also erected. We explore the building, collecting group documentation from stalls, but our main reason to be here is a session titled "The Contribution of Feminism to the Social Movement Strategies," chaired by Kaarina Kailo, whom we know from Graz. There seems to us to be a clear effort here to pull the energy and agenda from the Women's Assembly into the main European Social Forum. The session is notable for the mix of women and men in the audience and on the podium, and for an ongoing debate over whether we should focus our attention on gender or class. An intervention from the floor is made in defense of "intersectional" understandings of oppression by an Indian woman who turns out to be Nandita Shah from the Indian Organizing Committee for the next World Social Forum event, in Mumbai.

As the session winds down, Catherine departs for a prearranged interview with Daniela Pamminger, who had been involved in setting up the ATTAC conference in Graz. Bice wades through the crowds in search of Kaarina and Nandita, in the hope of obtaining agreement to an interview. This is our first effort to tackle the daunting task of getting extremely busy people to spontaneously consent to speak to us on the record, and we are relieved that Kaarina and Nandita (like most others subsequently) so readily do. In fact, the more difficult challenge turns out to be finding appropriately quiet spaces for conducting interviews. More often than not this proves impossible: Catherine, for instance, talks to Daniela in the busy gardens of La Villette, amid high levels of background noise, and Bice ends up interviewing Kaarina over lunch in a crowded restaurant between other appointments. Sticking to our interview guide and producing audible tapes proves more difficult than we anticipated.

The next day, November 14, we head to yet another of the four forum sites. This time it is a long metro journey to the suburb of Saint Denis, where sessions are dispersed in various buildings and tents. We eventually track down a venue where a local feminist gathering is supposed to be taking place, only to find this has been canceled. After exploring the area, we find a feminist café, staffed by local women, where we are able to talk to Simone Bernier, coordinator of the French organization Femmes Solidaires. The interview is conducted entirely in French—we have no translator—but Simone makes every effort to help us understand, gives us some helpful documentation on her organization, and introduces us to the other women staffing the café. In the afternoon, we trek back to Bobigny to a meeting of the European coordinators of the World March, who are publicizing the progress of their Charter for Humanity through the continent. At this meeting, we renew our acquaintance with Nadia De Mond, and in our subsequent interview with her we learn a lot about the role of the World March globally, including in the early stages of the Forum in Porto Alegre.

On November 15, the final day of the forum, we attend another workshop on feminism and the "social movement," this time in a beautifully carved wooden tent in the grounds of La Villette. This session is dominated by reflections on the experiences of the last few days, and many of those present express frustration with what they see as the marginalization of feminist voices at the forum. After a hectic lunchtime spent interviewing in a crowded café, we join the enormous closing demonstration. This weaves from the Place de la République through the streets of Paris. It is on an entirely different scale from the opening march, composed of thousands and thousands of people, interspersed with farmers' tractors and weird and wonderful floats and sculptures. We join up with the World March contingent, many dressed in purple, led by Spanish and Portuguese members who are dancing boisterously and chanting slogans.

Although the forum is now officially over, it is an early rise for us again on November 16 for the "Assembly of Social Movements," described in the program as "a conference open to all organizations taking part in the European Social Forum" but which, in contrast to the forum proper, is aimed at "conceiving propositions and strategies for actions common to participating organizations." It is another huge and crowded tent, with long queues of representatives from different strands of the forum, each waiting to get to the microphone for a few minutes to air their specific agenda. Anne Leclerc and a friend are first in line, speaking on behalf of the Women's Assembly. Interviewing Anne later over a coffee, we hear about her role in an education trade union, her affiliations with feminist networks like the Collectif National pour les Droits des Femmes (CNDF) and the World March, and her involvement in arrangements for the Paris forum. We are impressed by her generosity in granting an interview to us at the end of what must have been for her an exhausting few days.

HYDERABAD AND MUMBAI, JANUARY 2004

As the World Social Forum in India looms, we learn that we have been successful in obtaining two small grants from the Nuffield Foundation and the British Academy. These enable us to get our research properly underway by providing us with money for travel, for better recording equipment, and for help with transcribing the resulting interviews.

A week before the World Social Forum is due to be held in Mumbai, we head for Hyderabad. This is for two reasons. First, we have learned in Paris how difficult it is to interview in situ while a forum is taking place. Second, we know the Asian Social Forum was held in Hyderabad the previous year, so there are many participants locally and we have a friend who lives here, Rekha Pande, who has generously offered to put us in contact with them. As a women's studies scholar at the local university, Rekha is well connected with Hyderabadi feminists and particularly with the local women's rights and development NGO sector.

This sector strikes us as very tightly networked. Many of the people to whom Rekha introduces us, such as A. Padma of the women's educational quango,[1] Andhra Pradesh Mahila Samatha Society, are her ex-students; others, such as Kalpana Kannabiran of the women's rights campaign group Asmita, are academic colleagues. Certainly, most of the people we interview in Hyderabad seem to know each other. It is also through our interviews with Kalpana and with others such as Mahe Jabeen of the NGO Phoenix that we are alerted to the need to broaden our interviewing strategy to encompass a wider range of social forces and factions on the Left, and, to this end, to attend Mumbai Resistance, being organized in parallel to the World Social Forum by Maoist and Leninist groups.

A few days before the forum, we travel to Mumbai. We are not able to attend the "Feminist Dialogues" taking place at this time, having had our e-mail request several months earlier politely turned down on the grounds of limited space. Instead, we spend the time getting our bearings and trying to get hold of a program. In contrast to Paris, the forum is taking place all on one site, in a disused industrial park called Goregaon, which proves relatively easy to navigate despite its immense size. It is clear from the outset that this is a place of paradox. Communist Party of India banners drape the entrance, despite the ostensible ban on party involvement, and western delegates like us stay in hotels in town while many poorer Indian participants sleep on site under the trees and beggars cluster at the gates. Furthermore, the overwhelming scale of this event is immediately apparent. Demonstrations and parades continually push their way through the huge crowds, ranging from the Tamil Nadu Women's Collective to North Korean trade unionists and federations of Dalits fighting against their stigmatization as low caste. Local food vendors are dispersed throughout, many from local women's groups and charities. There is constant music, chanting, and dancing in the incredible heat, and an exhilarating, celebratory atmosphere. We are particularly struck by the numbers of women in the Dalit and *adivasi* (tribal) groups, and also more generally, filling the space.

Our efforts to obtain the program in the days before the forum prove fruitless as it is only made available on the opening day, January 16. In the evening, events start with a major plenary in the *maidan*, a great open field, in front of a crowd of tens of thousands, many of whom have danced and sung their way here. As the sky grows dark, the tiny figures on the faraway stage, predominantly women, are spotlit against the dramatic black and white backdrop. Speeches are mostly in English, so as visitors from the old imperial power we have an advantage over many of the local people in the crowds who may not have had access to English-language education. Still, there is an incredible effort by facilitators and participants to translate much of what is said into Hindi, Urdu, and other languages on the spot. The elderly Lakshmi Saghal, who led a women's regiment during the Indian fight for independence from the British Empire, begins by declaring "this time the enemy is an invisible one. . . . [G]lobalization is very much anti-women." She is joined by the novelist and campaigner Arundhati Roy, who focuses on the "new imperialism": "Debating imperialism is like debating the pros and cons of rape. Are we supposed to say that we really miss it?"

The next day, we seek out the Mumbai Resistance event we have been told about, and find it close by, albeit on the other side of a chaotic, eight-lane highway. The opening event here is much smaller scale, less international, with fewer resources. We gather documentation from the stalls and watch several hundred mostly Indian participants parade around the small ochre-colored grounds in the bright morning sun. A representative from one women's group, P. Pavana of the Andhra Pradesh Chaitanya Mahila Samakhya (APCMS), is called up on stage during the opening plenary to join in songs about overthrowing imperialism, but otherwise the event is overwhelmingly male dominated, with several older men giving long speeches in English developing Marxist critiques of globalization and of the World Social Forum.

Bice stays on at Mumbai Resistance to attend the workshop organized by women's groups there, titled "Imperialist Globalization and Its Impact on Women." This opens with young *adivasi* girls singing about women's liberation to a large crowd that includes many men. The men trickle out, however, as speeches begin on topics ranging from the commodification of women's bodies in the sex industry to gender discrimination in education. There are also repeated attacks against "bourgeois feminism," often conflated with feminism per se, and against the Forum. Across the road, meanwhile, Catherine is attending a parallel panel on "Women and Globalization," where discussants debate what seem to us to be very similar themes despite the different ideological setting, including the need to make links to trade unions and to contest fundamentalism, violence against women, and globalized economic insecurity. Songs, slogans, and theatrical performances enliven the sessions at both sites.

Bice manages to conduct some interviews at the women's workshop at Mumbai Resistance, including one with Sujatha Surepally of the Dalit Women's Federation. Sujatha's insistence on the "triple oppression" of gender, class, and caste is an important reminder for us of the distinctive experiences of Dalit women in India, experiences we are otherwise not able to tap into for our research. This is for two interconnected reasons. First, our focus is on key informants—those we have seen speaking on platforms and panels, where Dalit women are rarely to be found. Second, we are working without a translator and, therefore, are unable to talk to those who do not speak English. This includes the poorest and most marginalized members of Indian society, those without access to education, who are present in their thousands in the audiences and on the streets. Thus we know that there are important sectors of women's organizing in India that are under-represented in our data-gathering process.

On our third day at the forum, January 18, Catherine attends "Diverse Alternatives for Global Change," organized by a range of groups, from the World March to the radical, women-dominated, Latin American peasant network Via Campesina. The session opens with a striking ceremony: a figure swathed in a yellow cloth is gradually unwrapped of her bonds by singing women, who then distribute seeds to the audience. The Via Campesina representative speaks of the need for food security and urges more respect for indigenous peoples and women because of their role in maintaining food supplies. We spend the rest of the day weaving in and out of different sessions, here and at Mumbai Resistance, observing, collecting documents, and interviewing on both sites. We manage to talk, for example, to Virginia Vargas of Articulacíon Feminista Marcosur (AFM). Shouting over the noise of an entire brass band, Virginia tells us about the activities of her group in the preparatory processes of the World Social Forum. We also interview P. Pavana of APCMS, whom we had noticed previously at the opening ceremony of Mumbai Resistance. She draws our attention to the negotiations around the role of and facilities for women in Mumbai Resistance, as well as to the links between globalization and increased levels of violence against women.

That evening sees the so-called Women's Conference, officially titled "Wars against Women, Women against Wars," held in the *maidan*. We sit among the enormous crowd of women and men in the twilight listening to prominent speakers such as Egyptian writer Nawal El Saadawi, who criticizes U.S. policy in the Middle East and violence against women, and Arundhati Roy (again), who talks about the cooptation of feminist agendas by the United States in Afghanistan and communal violence in Gujarat. Roy gives up most of her speaking time, however, to Gayatri, a young woman who had been raped by the Indian police. Only the outline of Gayatri's increasingly passionate testimony is translated for English speakers, but her rage and sense of injustice is palpable. The panel finishes with chants of "From patriarchy! From all hierarchy!" and a song for peace, thousands of people clapping along.

The next day, Catherine attends "A Dialogue between Four Movements," organized by feminist groups including AFM and the National Network of Autonomous Women's Groups, an Indian organization. The audience is told that this is an effort to create a genuine exchange between representatives of women's, lesbian/gay/transsexual, Dalit/racial justice, and labor movements. And there seems to be a genuine dialogue here as each speaker (including Virginia Vargas, one of those representing the "women's movement") listens carefully and responds to others. Catherine then goes to a smaller, crowded session on violence and globalization run by the National Federation of Indian Women (NFIW), a mass organization we know to have links to the Communist Party of India. The audience there is almost entirely Indian, with lots of men present, tightly packed within an extremely hot tent. A series of testimonies focuses on shocking forms of violence, all then swiftly translated into English. A woman with a savagely burned face tells how she was thrown on the fire by her husband in front of their child, and several speak of their rescue from abusive marriages or from prostitution, sometimes in whispers. The president of NFIW, Amarjeet Kaur, then gives a speech in several languages that explains the reasons for violence in India as she sees them: globalization, in collusion with the Indian state and forces of fundamentalism, means the further perpetuation of patriarchy, the commodification of women, and the loss of human dignity. The day ends for us both at the Assembly of Social Movements. As in Paris, the purpose of this gathering is to allow activists from different campaigns to generate a common agenda. It is chaired by Nancy Burrows from the World March, ensuring a feminist voice is even more central at this event.

On the final day, Catherine attends another NFIW session, this time on work, while Bice goes to one on "honor killings," organized by a group affiliated to a rival communist party, the All India Democratic Women's Association (AIDWA). Bice manages to interview the president of AIDWA, Subhashini Ali, immediately after the session, albeit with several other interviewers jostling for Ali's attention and intervening with a range of questions. Later, we head to the final, large-scale conference in the *maidan,* "Religious Ethnic and Linguistic Exclusion and Oppression." Amarjeet Kaur of the NFIW is one of the speakers here as well and we manage to talk to her afterward—although it is now very late at night, she is called to a press conference in the middle of the interview, and loses her voice by the end. Kaur is keen to tell us about the agenda of the NFIW and yet again it is hard to keep to our interview guide. But we are extremely grateful for the time she gives us and impressed by her eloquence and energy, as we are with all our interviewees.

LONDON, OCTOBER 2004

The hosting of the European Social Forum in London means that we are on home turf. It is much easier for us to get to the city and to navigate the fieldwork sites within it. As in India, we have the advantage that the dominant language of the forum is our native tongue. In addition, the political terrain is more familiar to us. Our preexisting knowledge of some of the ideological differences and tensions at play is augmented by the fact that we join several organizational e-mail lists over the summer in which disagreements are aired and by Bice's attendance at a preparatory meeting in London in July. Finally, it is easier for us to identify a number of key informants and to hold interviews before and after the event. Thus, we head for London a couple of days in advance of the European Social Forum in order to talk to Anne Kane of Abortion Rights, who has played an important role in the preparatory process and is able to explain what happened at some of the meetings and committees. We also meet Anna, Sara, and Mary of the Global Women's Strike, a group that has been a prominent critic of the organizing process and that we know has set up its own autonomous "Women's Day." The three women tell us about the reasons why they felt the Strike and "grassroots" women were excluded from the forum and why they do not use the feminist label to describe their pro-women politics.

On the evening of October 13, we head for Middlesex University for the launch of the "Beyond the ESF" strand of workshops, organized separately from, and in opposition to, the official European Social Forum by so-called horizontal groups. Called the "Autonomous Assembly" and run under the auspices of the Wombles direct action network, this event attracts a friendly, mostly white crowd to listen to a series of speakers, including several young women, who tell the audience about the various initiatives happening under the Beyond the ESF umbrella. These range from a cultural carnival on a bus to a workshop reflecting on the possibilities of "Life Beyond Capitalism." Although there is no explicitly, self-labeled feminist discourse or documentation, there seems to us to be an implicit feminist discourse bubbling under the surface, particularly in the contributions of the young women, who mention the upcoming Women's Day organized by the Global Women's Strike, the provision of space for children, and a session with a Ugandan women's group.

The next morning, we join a long queue to register and get our program. As with the other forums we have attended, this has not been made available beforehand in paper form, although we have seen some sessions advertised online. Then it's off to the Women's Day organized at a church hall at King's Cross by the Global Women's Strike, based at the Crossroads women's center nearby. We enter to see a small group of women watching a film about the revolution in Venezuela. The crowd grows in size to around a hundred over the course of the morning: mostly, but not entirely, women, it is ethnically mixed and seems embedded in the local social context. A row of African women sit behind us dressed in printed fabrics, several with small children on their laps. Among the banners at the front, there is a mock-up of a broken wall declaring that 742 refugees have died trying to get into the UK. As the film ends, we collect documents from all the stalls in the room and then listen to a short speech from Sara, one of the organizers and our interviewee from a couple of days previously, about the "heavy racism and sexism" in the organizing spaces of the European Social Forum. Sara stresses that this "speakout" is a kind of intervention in the European Social Forum and the arguments made will be taken to the official event. Then a steady trickle of immigrant women from the audience go to the microphone and speak movingly of the terrible traumas and difficulties they have faced as refugees in this country, often with broken health and in complete isolation other than the lifeline thrown to them by the center.

Unfortunately, we have to leave early. We are committed to participating in another autonomously organized session, the "Radical Theory Forum," which is taking place in a squatted gallery in Leytonstone some distance away. Here we meet lots of people we know among the crushing throng. There are many academics and students, mostly white and often young. We run a workshop here ourselves, "Feminism and the European Social Forum." To our delight, the session is crowded, with about thirty people in a very small space, and the discussion is wide-ranging, intense, and passionate. Our plan for the session is to discuss the contemporary meaning of feminism, its relation to the European Social Forum, and what we should be researching for our project. The conversation never gets beyond the first, however, as there are so many voices wanting to talk about their relationship to feminism, raising themes such as internalized oppression, sexual practices, and eugenics.

The official European Social Forum program starts the next day, October 15, with events mostly based at the Alexandra Palace. This may be a beautiful space with its elegant plants and vast windows, but we are struck by its relative isolation from the streets of London and by its commercialism: the catering is branded, multinational and expensive, and the waiters and cleaners are markedly people of color serving a predominantly white crowd. Stalls and events may be easier to find here but sessions take place simultaneously within great halls, divided from one another by low, black-curtained partitions, and we struggle to hear in the crowds and noise.

The "Women's Assembly," which takes place on this first morning, is very different from both the Bobigny event in Paris and the meeting organized by the Global Strike. It is much smaller in scale than Paris, a seminar of around 200 people, mostly older white women, all of whom are crammed into a rather small and dark space. The convenor, Maureen O'Mara of the National Association of Teachers in Further and Higher Education, apologizes for the delayed start due to technical problems with the translation. Once we get going, there are a range of speakers, from a Swedish parliamentarian to several women from European branches of the World March and from the Bobigny organizing process. The last of these express their disappointment with the London event in comparison to Paris and argue for the need to continue to push for a feminist presence at the forum. At this point, the discussion changes direction to focus on the politics of race and religion, with Salma Yaqoob from the British organization Stop the War warning us of "Islamaphobia," which she associates with "a new phase of imperialism" and "a new phase of racism." She castigates the women's movement for its difficulty in dealing with women of faith and declares that the *hijab*, or headscarf, which she is wearing, has to be a personal choice. Partly in response, Sissy Vovou of the Greek World March declares that she does not accept that campaigns against fundamentalist Islam are racist. Jackie Lewis of the International Lesbian and Gay Association (ILGA) strikes yet another note, pointing to the marginalization of lesbian voices and insisting "not all women are the same: some of us are black, disabled, lesbian." Catherine speaks to Jackie after the session, setting up a future interview. Jackie also kindly directs Catherine to the new head of ILGA, Rosanna Flamer-Caldera, with whom she arranges yet another interview for the weeks ahead.

The next day we decide to separate. Bice visits Bloomsbury where additional European Social Forum events are being held and where she conducts several interviews and attends a vibrant, interactive Women's Environmental Network session on consumerism and gender. During the afternoon, Bice attends the workshop "Life Beyond Capitalism," which is being held at the London School of Economics under the rubric of the Beyond the ESF umbrella (and about which we had been informed at the Middlesex University orientation). The alternatives to capitalism articulated at this session, while interesting and imaginative, are notably lacking in feminist framing. No one speaks as a feminist other than Bice, and she is left wondering whether the low profile of feminism in more anarchist-influenced, horizontal or autonomous events is due to the fact that feminists are not present or that we are simply looking in the wrong places.

Catherine stays at Alexandra Palace where tensions over religion and racism are brought into high relief at a session titled "*Hijab*: A Woman's Right to Choose." Over 500 people are present at the start and more pour in throughout. Among the speakers are several wearing *hijab* who speak in its defense as a civil right and as a challenge to the objectification of women. The French law banning the headscarf from schools is the particular target of prominent feminist theorist Christine Delphy, who reminds the many French participants that "we live in a profoundly racist society," provoking increasing booing from agitated throngs in the audience. It seems to Catherine that the controversy in France, which had been conspicuous by its absence from the Paris Women's Day, has been exported here, given a platform in part because of the alliances that have been made between some sections of the Left here and British Muslims. When the chair, Milena

Buyum of the National Association Against Racism, opens the floor for interventions, people sprint to the microphone and many are incandescent with anger or near tears. The first to speak insists that most French people support the ban and he is shocked at the accusation of racism. British people in the audience shout "Algeria!" in response. Most of the younger women and men that intervene, many of whom are French, support the right to wear the headscarf: "We have to ask who is fundamentalist here," says one. By the end, a group of French women are singing with their hands in the air, surrounded by British people yelling "racist." The large plenary, "Women Struggling against Oppression," which follows, steers clear of the fundamentalism-racism divide and focuses instead on neoliberalism and patriarchy.

On the final day, October 17, we go again to the Assembly of Social Movements. Although the purpose here is to bring movements together around a common agenda, we are struck by the fact that it also provides a platform for the airing of disagreements. Of the many interventions that take place during the morning, two exchanges at the microphone particularly catch our attention. The first is a series of statements about an incident that occurred the night before, when a group of activists from the Wombles disrupted a session at which the mayor of London, Ken Livingstone, was invited to speak. The second is prompted by a spontaneous intervention from Sara and Anna of the Global Strike, who demand the inclusion of grassroots women and call for a Women's Day at every European Social Forum. Anne Kane responds from the floor seeking to defend the outreach efforts of the organizing committee, pointing to the Women's Assembly and to the plenary on Women and Oppression that have been held as well as to the strategy of integrating women across panels at the forum. Taken together, these interventions serve as a reminder of the contentious politics running through the organizing process for this London European Social Forum, not only in terms of the divide between the so-called verticals and horizontals, but also in terms of the disagreement among feminists and women's groups about the best ways of organizing in this political space.

RIO DE JANEIRO, SÃO PAULO, AND PORTO ALEGRE, JANUARY 2005

We have now secured further funding for our project from the Economic and Social Research Council which covers not only travel costs, but also allows us time away from our teaching responsibilities. We are, therefore, able to spend a longer period of time in Brazil than in other sites which allows us to interview feminist activists beforehand in Rio de Janeiro and São Paulo as well as in Porto Alegre where the forum is to take place. Prior research on the plentiful web-based material available on the several World Social Forums already held in Porto Alegre has enabled us to identify many prominent feminist players based around the country. Having only rudimentary Spanish and Portuguese, we arrange in advance for translators to help in all three locations. Magaly Pazello, Tati Wells, Adriana Veloso, and Carolina Schneider Comandulli are absolutely invaluable, aiding us in setting up and conducting interviews.

Soon after arriving in Porto Alegre, we attend the Feminist Dialogues (we had applied for permission to participate several months earlier and were successful this time around). At the registration for this event, we find the high proportion of academics and NGO professionals that we expect, along with a surprising number of young women. The first full day opens with a plenary of speakers analyzing the interconnections between globalization, militarization, fundamentalism, and feminist struggle. For the rest of the day and the next morning, we divide into smaller participatory workshops organized according to language capacity in order to continue our discussions on these themes. The presentations in the closing plenaries give us details about the history of the Feminist Dialogues and of the Campaign against Fundamentalism, about which we watch a short and visually powerful film juxtaposing a series of images, including those of the pope and George Bush. In the breaks, we conduct interviews with participants such as Sara Longwe of the African network FEMNET and Charlotte Bunch of the Global Center for Women's Leadership in the United States.

As the dialogues end, the fifth World Social Forum begins. We are unable to get our hands on a program early on the official opening day, January 26, defeated by the incredible queues. Later in the afternoon, there is a huge demonstration through the streets of Porto Alegre, ending in a party and concert. We miss the Campaign against Fundamentalism contingent, although we do glimpse their characteristic face masks, some sported by the Lilac Loonies, who are performing a striking piece of street dramatics about domestic violence in tattered bridal gowns. For most of the demonstration, we parade with the World March who are drumming and dancing, waving a multitude of banners and pennants inscribed with women's faces and words like *utopia*. Several are wearing purple World March T-shirts, shiny foil wigs, and plastic breasts and buttocks scrawled with slogans against commodification. Before leaving the opening ceremony in the evening, we manage to pick up a program which is by far the largest and heaviest yet.

The next day, forum workshops begin. They are all being held on one site which stretches along the banks of the River Guaiba in a series of themed "terrains." Long strings of stalls selling Che Guevara T-shirts, water, and Coke turn the space, as a whole, into a kind of hippie tourist market. This, along with the presence of multinationals, especially banks, and of impoverished people scavenging for the sellable detritus of those attending, serves as an uncomfortable reminder that the Forum does not transcend capitalist social relations. We are faced with our biggest fieldwork site yet so we decide to focus our energies on those terrains in which a feminist presence is more evident.

Although we separate on the morning of January 27 to conduct interviews, we meet up again in the afternoon for a workshop offering a "women's orientation" to the World Social Forum led by now-familiar faces associated with AFM and Feminist Dialogues. The English-language discussion about the history and dynamics of the feminist presence at the forum ends with an effort by members of Women Living Under Muslim Laws to organize a protest against the presence on site of a French Muslim intellectual, under the rubric of antifundamentalism. A debate ensues as to whether protest is an appropriate strategy. Bice makes a short intervention against the initiative, concerned about the hazy nature of the fundamentalist label and wanting more specifics about the nature of the problem posed by this individual. A few others speak up in agreement with her, but a decision is deferred until a meeting on the Diversity Boat the next day. Bice feels rather uncomfortable about shifting from an observer in the meeting to a full participant in the political debate and the taking sides that this entails.

The next morning, the meeting on the Diversity Boat proving impossible to track down, Bice attends a lively and interesting workshop organized by the Women's Global Network of Reproductive Rights (WGNRR). She then treks some distance to the Inter-movement Dialogues, a sequel to the session in Mumbai that Catherine attended, but finds it very hard to hear, given high noise levels and translation problems. She ends her day by going back to the Diversity Boat and interviewing Carole Barton of the Women's International Coalition on Economic Justice, who tells her about the history of feminist organizing against neoliberalism in the United States and at the transnational level. Catherine ends her day of workshops (she is restricted to those which are in English or which have operational simultaneous translation services) at a World March session on the relation of feminism to the global justice movement at which she has agreed to speak about our research as one of a number of panelists. It is packed with hundreds of people, men as well as women, despite the fact that problems with the translation booths mean that it starts about an hour late. Catherine is anxious not only because her participation may be construed as speaking for the World March but also because of the possibility that this audience will expect advice on strategy which, as an academic observer, she feels ill qualified to give. However, there seems to be considerable interest in our book project and in the feminist contribution to the global justice movement in general, and several people crowd around after the debate to talk to Catherine one-to-one.

The following day, January 29, Catherine goes to the "World Dignity Forum," where she is struck by the convergence in discourse between Indian Dalits and Latin American indigenous peoples, and by the number of women speaking. Bice interviews Monica Maher of the Catholic women's movement, the Grail, whom she met at the WGNRR session the previous day, before heading in the afternoon to a Spanish- and Portuguese-language session on biodiversity at which Via Campesina is a prominent presence. Meanwhile, Catherine attends the African Court of Women, where she sits through a series of haunting live and videotaped testimonies: a woman farmer from Chad talks of the impact on her livelihood of "economic war"; a woman from South Africa of the terrible effects of the privatization of utilities and health care; and a male poet chants a litany about the strength of African women, which meets with whooping, clapping, and cheering from the sweltering audience. Despite effort on both our parts, neither of us is able to secure interviews with the people to whom we have been listening—Bice makes contact with an English-speaking liaison for Via Campesina but this person leaves that night before an interview can be arranged. This is unfortunate because we are well aware that feminists working on ecological issues, on the one hand, and African women activists, on the other, are thinly represented not only at the Forum but also among our interviewees.

On the final day, Catherine spends some time in the Youth Camp. She attends a session held there at which representatives from the International Council acknowledge a striking discrepancy between the presence of young people at the front lines of the movement and their absence from the more high-profile panels and organizing processes of the World Social Forum. The question of generational hierarchies also surfaces in a workshop that Bice goes to on young women and the imminent *Encuentro* or gathering of feminists from across Latin America. There is considerable discussion here about how hard it is to be a feminist as a young woman, facing hostility, from both young men and other young women, as well as marginalization within groups dominated by older feminists. Although there are many different ideas here about how to push a distinctive young feminist agenda, there is a strong consensus from the start of the meeting that tackling such questions requires, among other things, women-only spaces in which feminist politics can be explored.

That evening, and in the days that follow, we sit in our hotel room typing up field notes late into the night. These notes contain our empirical observations, hastily jotted down during the forum events, as well as our reflections on what we have encountered. We continue to refine and augment these notes in the months that follow. They serve not only as additional factual sources for us but also as a continual reminder of our specific entry point and journey through our fieldwork sites.

CONCLUSION

In this chapter, we have told a story of our voyage through four fieldwork sites in search of feminist antiglobalization activism. In so doing, we have sought to highlight the remarkable heterogeneity of feminist antiglobalization activism that we witnessed across these sites. Some of the differences and conflicts between groups map onto national particularities. In the British context, for example, we heard a discourse in support of women's right to wear the Islamic headscarf, while among French groups there remained a militantly secularist opposition to the headscarf which, although not universal, was certainly more widespread than among their counterparts in the UK. Moreover, there are obviously some important differences in the ideological orientation of feminist groups, both within and across national borders. Thus, we found British feminist organizers on both sides of the divide between verticals and horizontals. Arguably a version of this divide may have been a factor in the withdrawal of NextGENDERation from the organizing of the Women's Assembly in France, given that this move was explained to us, at least in part, as due to a difference in approach between feminist anarchists and feminist Trotskyists. Perhaps more interestingly, in the Brazilian context, we saw some divergence in strategic choices, notably between the World March and associated groups, on the one hand, and those associated with AFM and the Campaign against Fundamentalism, on the other. The former seemed to prioritize popular education techniques and forging alliances with young women in the Youth Camp and with other groups through the Assembly of Social Movements; the latter mobilized complex academic-influenced discourses around fundamentalism and focused considerable effort on building networks in and around the Feminist Dialogues and Diversity Boat. Finally, we have charted some important differences in opinion within and across sites about the nature and purpose of autonomous feminist organizing within the Forum space. This can be seen, for example, in the Global Women's Strike support for a Bobigny-style Women's Assembly at the European Social Forum in London in the face of opposition from British counterparts.

As stated in chapter 1, we do not seek here to judge one set of protagonists in these debates as more correct than another. Rather, we simply want to highlight that feminist antiglobalization activism as a collective subject is not homogenous and unified but heterogeneous, fluid, contested, and continually in process. In this, as we have already pointed out, the subject of our study is not unusual, but rather typical of social movement activism more generally. In addition, this chapter has enabled us to emphasize the situated nature of our research and the partial vista it has afforded us of feminist antiglobalization activism. There are at least three ways in which situatedness plays out in the above account.

First, we have tried to show how our specific identities—our capacities, privileges, and limitations as individuals and researchers—shaped our access to information and our interpretation of it. We explored some of the resulting dynamics in chapter 1. In this chapter, we have drawn attention to several further factors. We have underlined, for example, the fact that we were lucky enough to obtain grant money to support our research. Without that financial support, we would not have been able to spend as much time in the countries we visited doing the supplementary interviews that turned out to be so essential given the difficulties of interviewing on site. We have also acknowledged the strengths and weaknesses of our linguistic capacities. In India we were obviously advantaged by the fact that English was the lingua franca for many: at panels, everything was translated into English on the spot and we were able to talk easily to activists. We could just about get by with our rudimentary French in Paris, but we undoubtedly missed some nuances in interviews and speeches. In Brazil, however, we were very reliant on translators. As we have pointed out, for interviews we were lucky enough to have help from several bilingual individuals, but the result is a set of particularly mediated interview transcripts. At the forum itself, the translation services provided were rather more limited and dogged by technical problems. We were thus constricted in what we could attend, what we could understand, and to whom we could talk, Catherine in particular. Contingent encounters could not lead, in the same way as at other sites, to lengthy and interesting discussions.

Second, we have sought to illustrate how the contours of the physical space and organizational infrastructure at each fieldwork site shaped our access to and encounter with activism. Thus, the more self-contained official venues in London and India were easier for us to navigate and to make connections within, although they were relatively isolated from the wider urban context. In Paris, the dispersal of the site across four different suburbs allowed political activism to be much more fully integrated into the diverse communities of the city, but made it much harder for us as researchers to cover the site systematically and to trace connections within it. We were simply unable to be physically present in all of the eleven terrains at the Brazilian forum and had to choose in advance which sites we were going to concentrate on. In addition, the fact that in no site was the program available before the start of the main events, and that panels were frequently rearranged and canceled, meant that we could plan only a day ahead and even then had to be flexible, reactive, and spontaneous in our effort to cover events and arrange interviews.

Finally, we have brought to the foreground the ways in which power hierarchies at the World Social Forum shaped patterns of visibility and absence in ways that are necessarily reflected in the story we tell about it and in our mapping of feminist antiglobalization activism in the rest of the book. We

argued in chapter 2 that the Forum is not power-free, but is rather stratified in various ways. Indeed, we conducted our fieldwork with the specific
intent of focusing on underrepresented feminist speakers. Our tale in this
chapter thus offers a deliberate corrective to the impression that feminists
are not an active presence at the Forum by showing them fighting their cor-
ner, in every nook and cranny of the site. But we have also drawn attention
to the fact that it was hard to find women from Africa speaking on panels,
for example, or younger women. Notably, Dalit women were also under-
represented as speakers in the Indian context. Consequently, these groups
remain less visible in our view of feminist antiglobalization activism.

Moreover, we want to acknowledge here that the methods we adopted
to gather information worked to reinforce rather than undermine some of
the patterns of dominance and marginalization at the Forum. Notably, our
approach to identifying interviewees, which largely entailed collaring those
speaking in feminist voices or from feminist groups on panels and then
asking them to recommend associates, meant that we necessarily privileged
individuals from more high-profile groups, key organizers rather than the
grassroots, and, in India, those with a class background that enabled them
to speak English. In addition, our strategy of collecting group documentation brought with it an emphasis on those groups that have the resources to
publish. In sum, if we had been able to deploy our methods differently (by
conducting interviews in Portuguese) or if we had used other ways of gathering information (such as ethnography with Hindi- and Urdu-speaking
groups in the streets of Goregaon), we would have had an alternative view,
one further undercutting some of the power relations on site and offering
a more inclusive representation of feminist antiglobalization activism. To
reiterate, then, this chapter strives to make explicit the ways in which our
view of feminist antiglobalization activism is a partial one, determined by
the space in which we saw it, what we did there, and who we are.

In part I as a whole we have shone a spotlight upon the presence of
feminist antiglobalization activism at the World Social Forum. To this
end, we have focused on efforts to contest gender hierarchies at the Forum
and to integrate feminist visions into struggles for a better world. While
arguing that feminist antiglobalization activism can be understood as a
distinct and significant form of collective action, we have also brought its
heterogeneous, complex, and contested character into relief. In part II of the
book we seek to map the wider terrain of feminist antiglobalization activism from our particular vantage point at the Forum, attempting to chart
its topography in a systematic and coherent way. In other words, in part
II we trace the contours and trajectories of the movement sector we have
identified as lying at the intersection of feminism and the global justice
movement. The following chapters, therefore, explore the origins of feminist antiglobalization activism, the beliefs and practices of its participants,

and the ways in which they forge solidarity with each other and with the broader global justice movement.

NOTE

1. A "quango" is a quasi-nongovernmental organization, one that is often set up initially by governments and to which governments delegate specific tasks but which are then usually granted operational dependence.

II

MAPPING FEMINIST ANTIGLOBALIZATION ACTIVISM

4

Uncovering Origins

Past and Present Sources of Agency for Feminist Antiglobalization Activism

> So the World Social Forum in 2001, in my personal experience, and I would say in the organizational experience of global women's networks, it was the culmination of something that was already there. . . . The world does not start with Seattle and the World Social Forum. (Sonia Corrêa, interview, Rio de Janeiro, January 10, 2005)

We begin part II by asking: what are the origins of feminist antiglobalization activism? For us, one way into this question is through the prism of agency, "defined as the capacity to determine and act" (Messer-Davidow 1995: 25). With this analytical move, we are aligning ourselves with those feminists who argue that it is necessary to recover past and present forms of women's and feminist agency given what they see as its general neglect. More concretely, feminists charge western political thought with conflating "agency" and "maleness" (Gardiner 1995: 2; see also Wilson 2007: 126) and depicting processes of social change in terms of a procession of Great White Men (e.g., National Women's History Project, n.d.). In response, feminist scholarship on politics, in general, and social movements, in particular, has given pride of place to women's and feminist struggles (e.g., Rowbotham 1977; Marchand and Runyan 2000b).

In terms of how we should study agency, feminists remind us to pay attention to both its collective and individual dimensions. As Patrocinio P. Schweickart puts it, feminism:

> necessitates *both* individual *and* concerted action—*both* my personal agency, *and* the collective agency of a political movement. Without other feminists, I am only a discontented woman. The "I" of each feminist is situated in the "we" of feminism. (Schweickart 1995: 229, emphasis in original)

In addition, whether individual or collective, agency should be treated as embedded within power relations rather than transcending them. On this point we agree with Chandra Talpade Mohanty that any attempt to make sense of feminist activism must not erase "material and ideological power differences within and among groups of women, especially between First and Third World Women," as this, "paradoxically, removes us all as actors from history and politics" (1998: 263; see also Mohanty 2003: ch. 1).

Following these imperatives, we develop two sets of arguments that map onto the two parts of this chapter. In the first part, we consider the collective dimension of agency by examining the movement forebears of feminist antiglobalization activism. In the second, we turn to individual agency, focusing both on its enabling conditions and on motivating factors.

MOVEMENT FOREBEARS

In order to frame our discussion of the collective agency that gave rise to feminist antiglobalization activism, we turn to feminist social movement scholar Sasha Roseneil, who uses an evocative family metaphor in her discussion of movement tributaries feeding into Greenham Common peace camp in England (Roseneil 2000). Acknowledging the influence of the "great aunts" of the suffragette movement, among others, and the "older cousins" of left-wing and peace movements of the 1960s and 1970s, Roseneil draws particular attention to the role of a "big sister" in the form of second-wave feminist agitation in the UK. As she explains, "Just as the women's liberation movement was formed out of and in reaction to the New Left, so Greenham was shaped and made possible by the ideas and agendas of the women's liberation movement" (Roseneil 2000: 32). We draw on Roseneil's metaphor to present our story of the movement forebears of feminist antiglobalization activism in a similar fashion, in terms of its great aunts, older cousins, and big sisters.

Great Aunts: First-Wave Feminism

Sonia Corrêa is certainly correct to state, in the quote opening this chapter, that the world did not start with Seattle and the World Social Forum for feminist antiglobalization activists. The roots of such activism, we suggest, can be traced back to first-wave feminism, if not before. First-wave feminists of the nineteenth and early twentieth centuries function as great aunts for our interviewees in two main ways.

On the one hand, they provide inspiration in the form of role models and past ideas and activities. Notably, Flora Tristán: Centro de la Mujer Peruana, founded in 1979, draws its title and mandate from a half-Peruvian, half-French woman writing in the 1830s and '40s. As founder member Virginia Vargas puts it, "The name of our organization . . . is a way of recovering a brave woman and . . . express[ing] the vision that we had (and still have) about our feminist commitments" (interview, Mumbai, January 18, 2004). Flora Tristán here is a symbol of the fusion of two crucial struggles, "for women's rights and . . . for economic justice" (interview, Mumbai, January 18, 2004). As Corrêa elaborates, Tristán can be seen as part of a wider feminist network, the legacy of which is still felt today:

> Latin American feminism can be traced back to the nineteenth century with Flora Tristán and even anarchists. . . . They were . . . connected across countries . . . between Argentina, Brazil and Uruguay. . . . It is something that we cannot erase. (Interview, Rio de Janiero, January 10, 2005)

On the other hand, this first wave of feminism is the mobilizing context within which two of our "core" groups listed in chapter 1 (textbox 1.1) were founded. The Women's International League for Peace and Freedom (WILPF) emerged in the maelstrom of the transnational activism of suffragettes and peace campaigners from Europe and North America who came together in 1915 in the Hague, the Netherlands, to protest against the war that was by then raging across Europe (see, e.g., Rupp and Taylor 1999: 369; WILPF n.d.a). Another example is the international Grail organization of Catholic women, started soon after the First World War by a priest named Jacques van Ginneken. His assumption that "many new possibilities were opening up for women" and that they could "make an immense contribution to the transformation of the world" bears the mark of first-wave feminist discourse (Grail n.d.).

Older Cousins: Left-Wing Organizing

More recent antecedents can be found in the form of Left mobilizations which we characterize as the older cousins of feminist antiglobalization activism. We are using "left-wing" here in a broad sense to mean a critical analysis of capitalism as generating structural inequalities and instabilities. As we shall see, movements informed by such an analysis have functioned as sources of inspiration for feminists and also as sites of gendered marginalization, pushing them into autonomous organizing.

In all of the countries of our fieldwork, the Left has inspired extensive numbers of women to become active, providing them with an organizational home and functioning as fertile ground for the development of feminist views. In India, for example, the anticolonial struggle against the British had important left-wing elements. This was the milieu in which innumerable women, as well as men, came to activism (e.g., Jayawardena 1986: 93–108; Jagori n.d.; Madhok n.d.) and from it emerged analyses and agendas that have continued over the decades to exert a profound influence on women's organizing (see Karat 1997, 2005: 3). After independence in 1947, social, economic, and legal change was slow to come (Kumar 1993: 97; Gandhi and Shah 1991: 18). It was in this context that women associated with the Communist Party of India founded the National Federation of Indian Women, at least in part because of the realization that "all women's groups and movements must come together and have a fighting organization, otherwise even in a sovereign independent India, your gender justice will not get realized" (Amarjeet Kaur, interview, Mumbai, January 20, 2004). In the other countries of our fieldwork, left-wing organizing also provided a platform for women's mobilization, albeit years later, at the end of the 1960s. This was a period of political ferment in France and the UK (e.g., Duchen 1986: 5; Jenson 1996: 73) and of militant armed struggle against the dictatorship in Brazil (Alvarez 1990: 70).

In addition to being an important influence upon women, left-wing mobilizations have been stratified by power relations in the form of gendered hierarchies, similar to those in operation at the World Social Forum as documented in chapter 2. These have led to anger and frustration for women and triggered autonomous feminist organizing. In France and the UK, for instance, women bridled at the sexism of their comrades and the treatment of feminist arguments as a "bourgeois diversion" (Lovenduski and Randall 1993: 62; see also Allwood and Wadia 2002: 218; Duchen 1986: 7–8). As a consequence, by the early 1970s feminists in both countries had begun to mobilize largely within their own, independent organizations and to develop radical feminist traditions of thought that prioritized analyses of patriarchy and male domination (e.g., Duchen 1986: 40; Jenson 1996: 79). In Brazil, women within the armed resistance were pushed into subordinate roles that they often felt unable to challenge within the terms of Marxist discourses. From the mid-1970s onward, in the context of a shift away from armed struggle toward mass mobilization, leftist women began to openly question the priority of class struggle and to set up their own autonomous networks (Alvarez 1990: chs. 3, 4).

In Brazil, as in all of the countries of our study, the Left was never abandoned completely. Instead, in the Latin American context, the practice emerged of "'double militancy'—whereby many feminists participated both in a party or class organization to advance the general struggle *and* in feminist and women's groups to promote changes of specific concern to women" (Alvarez 1998: 298, emphasis in original). Moreover, women in both Brazil and the UK developed a "socialist feminist" paradigm that sought to integrate Marxist and feminist frameworks by giving equal weight to both class and gender (Lovenduski and Randall 1993: 61; Alvarez 1990: 101–7). And in France, there were efforts to combine Marxism with psychoanalysis (Duchen 1986: 40; Jenson 1996: 79), alongside a syndicalist feminist tradition striving to develop feminist agendas within trade unions (Jenson 1996: 82–84). As we will see below, feminist efforts to work within, to challenge, and to build alliances across the Left continue today, as do struggles to establish and defend feminist organizational autonomy.

Big Sister: Second-Wave Feminism

An autonomous, second-wave feminist movement had emerged around the world by the 1970s. From the outset, this took the form both of a transnational layer of organizing and of diverse national movement formations. In our view, it is second-wave feminism that is the most important collective antecedent of feminist antiglobalization activism in terms not only of providing personnel and ideas, but also of generating its organizational infrastructure. We focus on the latter here, after a short discussion of the reasons behind feminism's reemergence as a political force.

We want to draw attention to three factors, other than dissatisfaction with the Left, that helped to precipitate this second wave. To begin with, long-term socioeconomic trends played a role. It has been widely remarked that the expansion of education and changing patterns of employment in many places around the world in the decades after the Second World War simultaneously empowered women and left them frustrated at the limitations they faced in terms of their integration into the workplace and public life (Charles 2000: ch. 4; Friedan 1963). This trend is particularly visible in Brazil, where the military regime presided over an "economic miracle" with highly polarizing effects. While raising the living standards of middle-class women and men, enabling many more women to gain access to education and work, it also dramatically lowered the living conditions of the working classes, bringing with it the collapse of public services and declining wages. In this context, the paths of radicalization for working-class and middle-class women diverged, with the former mobilizing around their roles as mothers and wives and the latter developing a feminist consciousness in response to their lack of advancement in the workplace (Alvarez 1990: 50–53; Corcoran-Nantes 2000: 87).

Another set of factors that merit attention are the context-specific and contingent political opportunities at the national level that enabled politicized women to develop and consolidate their autonomous movement networks.[1] In India, for example, it was not until the late 1970s that what is widely referred to as the contemporary Indian women's movement emerged (Ray 1999: 3; Calman 1992: 22; Kumar 1993: 96). This is in part because the imposition of a national emergency in 1975 had constrained much domestic political activity and its lifting in 1977 was "like a soda bottle opening— right across the country" (quoted in Calman 1992: 35). There was a more gradual political thaw in Brazil. The 1973 oil crisis put the economic miracle into jeopardy and the military government was forced into a policy of political liberalization, accelerated in 1979. This prompted many of the middle classes to join the ranks of the opposition and allowed for the proliferation of feminist associations and activities (Alvarez 1990: 79). Their political influence was enhanced as a growing number of parties in the newly liberalized political system began to compete for women's votes (Alvarez 1990: 238). By the mid-1980s, Brazil had an elected civilian government that embarked on a process of constitutional review. The involvement of feminists was actively sought in this process, as evidenced by the establishment of a National Council on Women's Rights (Jacqueline Pitanguy, interview, Rio de Janeiro, January 12, 2005; see also Alvarez 1990: 219–22).

Last but not least, we want to emphasize the role of political opportunities presented to feminists at the international level. The UN declared 1975 to be "International Women's Year," requiring reports from every country on the condition of women citizens. In India, this led to the production of a government-sponsored document that "blew apart the myth that post-Independence Indian women were gradually 'progressing'" (Madhok 2004). This is seen by many commentators as another important trigger of the Indian women's movement (Calman 1992: 51; Gandhi and Shah 1991: 19; John 1998: 542). The UN launched its "Decade for Women" shortly afterward, punctuated by a series of conferences and parallel NGO forums in Mexico City in 1975, in Copenhagen in 1980, and in Nairobi in 1985. These events gave feminists an international stage and an international focus for their organizing.[2]

It is in this context that we see the emergence of a transnational layer of feminist organizing, which included from the start several of the feminist antiglobalization groups listed in textbox 1.1. For many commentators, the Mexico City conference may have resulted in few substantive agreements, but in convening up to 5,000 delegates from 138 countries, it was important because it "established a network."[3] This network had expanded exponentially by the time of the third conference in Nairobi. As Sonia Corrêa puts it: "We were 13,000, 14,000 in Nairobi, we had taken over the town. . . . So it is not minor. . . . I want to stress that, long before the World Social Forum, this has been going on" (interview, Rio de Janiero, January 10, 2005). The Development Alternatives with Women for a New Era (DAWN), of which Corrêa is a member, is one of several groups from textbox 1.1 that was founded during this period specifically in order to coordinate the activities of southern feminists for Nairobi (Peggy Antrobus, interview, July 10, 2004). To take another example, Sara Longwe told us how FEMNET, the African Women's Communication and Development Network, was launched by the same women who had organized the Nairobi event (interview, Porto Alegre, January 25, 2005).

The transnational layer of feminist organizing continued to expand and consolidate into the 1990s under the auspices of a series of conferences called by the UN on development-related issues in the wake of the end of the Cold War. As Corrêa describes:

> the incredible cumulative process . . . of the conferences of the nineties, where we were threading from one to the other, it wasn't just the business anymore of women's issues but the whole [remit] of the UN. We had 30,000 people in Rio [at the UN Conference on Environment and Development, 1992], which was another big chunk. So we are moving from environment to human rights to population to social development . . . and carrying people and understanding and analysis of global processes. (Interview, Rio de Janeiro, January 10, 2005)

This process spurred on the creation of more feminist antiglobalization groups. For example, the Centre for Women's Global Leadership (CWGL) and the Women's Environment and Development Organization (WEDO), both U.S.-based organizations founded respectively in 1989 and 1992, quickly assumed the role of coordinating women's caucuses at UN conferences (Stienstra 2000: 24–25). Further, it was at the UN Women's Conference at Beijing in 1995 that Articulacíon Feminista Marcosur was born (Vargas 2003: 914) and that the proposal was made to launch the World March of Women (begun as an initiative in Quebec) as a global network (World March of Women n.d.a).

While the transnational layer of second-wave feminist organizing was expanding and consolidating, the picture was more complicated with regard to national feminist formations. In many northern countries, feminist movements were undergoing processes of decentralization and institutionalization by the end of the 1970s. In France, national-level organizing fragmented under the weight of ideological and personal differences (e.g., Duchen 1986: 27–30) while British feminists pursued a preference for non-state, small-scale, decentralized initiatives in the form of clinics, nurseries, rape crisis centers, and the like (Roseneil 2000: 30, 33; Caine 1997: 266; Walby 2002: 537). At the same time, feminists working with center-left parties in both countries became increasingly institutionalized (e.g., Beckwith 2000: 456; Lovenduski and Randall 1993: 12, 191–93). In the South during this period, feminist organizing underwent processes of "NGOization" and transnationalization. In both India and Brazil, previously informal, voluntary, self-funded groups became formalized, professionalized, and externally funded (Khullar 1997: 112; Rajan 2003: 31–36; Alvarez 1998).[4] The closely connected process of transnationalization was an especially salient trend in Brazil, aided by regional Latin American *Encuentros* and participation in UN conferences. The 1992 UN Conference on the Environment and Development held in Rio de Janeiro, for instance, afforded thousands of Brazilian feminists and women's groups an astonishing networking opportunity. Preparations for the Beijing conference a few years later reinforced this process and also functioned to consolidate national-level coordination. The Articulação de Mulheres Brasilieras was founded in this context, linking over 800 women's groups in Brazil (Alvarez n.d.: 19) and helping many Brazilian women to make their way to the NGO forum outside Beijing (Alvarez 1998: 309–14).

Reconfiguring Sisterhood: Toward the Global Justice Movement

Feminist organizational expansion, diversification, and transnationalization all provide part of the story of why and how feminist antiglobalization activism emerged. But another factor that should be taken on board is the reconfiguration of feminism in the 1980s in the face of challenges posed by shifting power relations. More specifically, feminists during this period were increasingly forced to confront the impact of racist and geopolitical hierarchies on their organizations and agendas and to respond to the imposition of neoliberalism around the world.[5] The resultant shifts in the contours of feminism have played a crucial role in facilitating its convergence with the emergent global justice movement.

The 1980s saw the widespread rise of autonomous organizing by racialized minorities of women. In the UK, black women set up their own groups because they were angered not only by racism in education and health and high levels of unemployment, but also by their marginalization within black and feminist struggles (Sudbury 1998: 5, 7; Lovenduski and Randall 1993: 80; Patel 2001: 153). As Sarah of the Global Women's Strike put it to us, "racism in the feminist movement was very, very heavy," while Milena Buyum of the National Association Against Racism declared, "My personal view is that the women's movement historically in the West has neglected issues of racism, and the way that black women experience being women, which is not the same as being a white woman" (interviews, London, January 12, 2004 and November 5, 2004). Similarly, Dalit women in India have accused the Indian women's movement of failing to challenge distinctions of caste that operate within it and that, arguably, are imbued with racist overtones (Grey 2005: 132). As a consequence, the first separate national meeting for Dalit women was organized in 1987 and in its wake separate Dalit women's organizations began to emerge (Hardtmann 2003: 193).

In all cases, the autonomous organizing of marginalized groups of women has generated a platform from which efforts have been made to shift the agenda of the larger feminist movement. It is our impression, however, that this has been most successful in Brazil. By the late 1980s it was becoming apparent that black women in Brazil lived very different lives, and had very different needs, from most white women (Caldwell 2004: 5).

These stark inequalities, and the failure of mainstream feminist organizing to challenge them (Duke 2003: 363), led to the proliferation of black women's groups and, ultimately, to the launch of a national coalition, the Articulação de Mulheres Negras Brasileiras, in 2000. According to member Lúcia Xavier, the conference at which the launch took place was "the first time that all feminists, as a movement, expressed very clearly that the feminist movement was also engaged in antiracist struggle" (interview, Rio de Janeiro, January 12, 2005).

Racist hierarchies were not the only challenge to which feminist movements were responding. In the 1980s and 1990s, global processes of neoliberal restructuring enforced through interstate institutions and the policies of individual states were taking a toll on women worldwide and granting new relevance to long-held Left critiques of capitalism within feminist circles. As a consequence, some strands of the feminist movement began to realign themselves with left-wing forces. Thus, for example, the Indian women's movement faced increasing urban unemployment, skyrocketing levels of debt and food production costs, and rising levels of suicide and domestic violence.[6] It was also grappling with the rise of communalist tensions that both mobilized women and targeted them for violence (Karat 2005: 13; Sarkar and Butalia 1995: 3; Cochrane 2004: 17). This dual onslaught brought renewed efforts among autonomous women's groups to cooperate more extensively with secularist, left-wing organizations (Sarkar and Butalia 1995: 3). As one of our interviewees told us, the issue of communalism "definitely makes you identify the Left as your allies" (Kalpanna Kannabiran, interview, Hyderabad, January 10, 2004).

Or consider France, which saw the return of the Right to power in the 1990s and the intensification of neoliberal policies such as employment laws requiring flexible, variable working hours and allowing short-term contracts. As Allwood and Wadia state, "Women . . . were mainly at the receiving end of changes in working patterns and felt that they were being pushed back into the home" (2002: 216). In reaction, a wave of public sector protests erupted in 1995, heralding the revitalization of oppositional leftist forces and the formation in 1998 of the Association pour la Taxation des Transactions pour l'Aide aux Citoyens (ATTAC), an organization that would become a pivotal player in French *alter-mondialiste* politics as well as in the World Social Forum (Waters 2004: 85; Sommier and Combes 2007: 108). It is in this environment of general foment and the emergence of a broader opposition movement that feminist groups experienced a resurgence (Allwood and Wadia 2002: 216; Sommier and Combes 2007: 114). The Collectif National pour les Droits des Femmes (CNDF), for instance, "is a grouping of feminist associations, of unions and of political parties, constituted on January 24, 1996" (CNDF 2007, our translation; see also Allwood and Wadia 2002: 217). As one interviewee put it:

> In France in these last years it is not really a separate movement as in the 1970s. There is a form of autonomy but there are many alliances with social movements and with the *alter-mondialistes*. . . . I think this is particular to France and it helps us a lot. (Sophie Zafari, interview, London, October 13, 2004)

The transnational layer of feminist organizing has not been immune from these complex dynamics. On the contrary, racist stratifications and processes of neoliberalism have been central to propelling changes to the agenda and composition of transnational networks. We would add that geopolitical divisions between North and South, by which we mean the ways in which the interstate system still reflects the hierarchical patterns of past imperialism, have posed their own distinctive challenges to feminist organizing across state borders. Right from the start of the UN Decade and the meetings in Mexico City and then in Copenhagen, southern women accused their northern counterparts of reproducing racist, imperialist attitudes (e.g., Miles 1996: 109). White northern women dominated the early conferences, as did the dominant development paradigm known as "Women in Development." Proponents of this framework argued that the salience of women's productive role in development had been ignored and that their advancement depended on their full integration into economic life (see Boserup 1970; also Newland 1988). But this approach, along with the hegemonic role of northern women at the conferences, were increasingly resisted by their southern counterparts, who began to articulate an alternative analysis—what Peggy Antrobus (2004: 46) terms the "socialist Southern view." This perspective took issue with the portrayal of capitalist development as a benign process and asserted that women were not only already part of the process, but were being systematically exploited by it.

The Nairobi conference proved to be a breakthrough moment in terms of the negotiation of this standoff. As Antrobus explains it:

> In Nairobi the Third World women were clearly an overwhelming majority. Third World women were setting the pace, defining the issues, proposing solutions, taking initiatives. The polarization between "developed" and "developing," North and South, which was evident in Mexico, was absent. The growing feminist movement has helped women from the North and the South to find a basis for solidarity which respects and celebrates cultural and ideological differences. (Antrobus, quoted in Miles 1996: 117)

In other words, a decade of interaction and face-to-face meetings in international fora had enabled feminists "to create solidarities based not on preconceived identities but on historically specific circumstances of the global economy that were constraining the lives of women around the world" (Desai 2002: 29).

A corresponding shift in the transnational feminist agenda was exemplified in the presentation of a DAWN report titled *Development, Crisis and Alternative Visions* (Sen and Grown 1987) at the NGO Forum at Nairobi. This document encapsulated, for the first time, a distinctive, fully formulated southern feminist perspective (Miles 1996: 114; Antrobus 2004: 77). Arguing that the prevailing economic model perpetuated women's poverty and subordination, it introduced neoliberal structural adjustment programs, and the international financial institutions that impose them, as crucial foci for feminist research and advocacy in the international arena (Miles 1996: 114; Antrobus 2004: 77). Moreover, its critique of capitalist economic development, while influenced by Marxism, was framed in explicitly feminist terms (Antrobus 2004: 57). As a number of southern networks, including DAWN, became increasingly integrated into feminist lobbying efforts, this kind of analysis gained prominence within feminist circles and debates during the UN conferences of the 1990s. As Carole Barton of the Women's International Coalition for Economic Justice (WICEJ) describes it:

> a number of women's groups internationally, building on Nairobi, wanted to have a stronger voice around globalization and economic justice issues in several UN fora. . . . [I]n Beijing they organized an economic justice caucus . . . It was a coalition of several groups that also ended up being part of WICEJ including DAWN, WEDO, the Centre for Women's Global Leadership. . . . [T]hey were active in bringing that kind of presence into workshops etc. in Beijing around gender and economic justice issues. (Interview, Porto Alegre, January 28, 2005)

By the time of Beijing, then, southern groups had successfully created a consensus in the transnational layer of feminist organizing around the idea that globalized neoliberalism was highly salient in shaping women's lives and thus should be central to feminist analyses and agendas (Stienstra 2000: 213).[7]

In sum, the second-wave feminist movement has been the most important general influence upon feminist antiglobalization activism, providing ideas and organizational infrastructure. Moreover, endeavors to overcome critiques of racial and geopolitical hierarchies within feminism and to respond to the predations of neoliberal capitalism have resulted in the emergence of more radical agendas and more inclusive alliances among feminists, as well as new relationships with the Left. All this means that, by the late 1990s, feminists around the world were sympathetic to the concerns of the emergent global justice movement and predisposed to link up with it. As Corrêa states, "when Seattle happened, lots of women's networks

. . . were attentive and prepared to be there and to connect" (interview, Rio de Janeiro, January 10, 2005).

To avoid giving the impression that feminist antiglobalization activism has emerged in an automatic way from past collective mobilizations, however, the reasons for the mobilization of individual activists within it need consideration. It is to individual agency, therefore, that we turn to in the next part of the chapter.

BECOMING A FEMINIST ANTIGLOBALIZATION ACTIVIST

The work of Cheryl Hercus on feminist motivations suggests that any answer to the question of what brings individuals into feminist antiglobalization activism should pursue at least three lines of inquiry. First, influenced by resource mobilization theory, Hercus acknowledges the need to explore the "microstructural conditions necessary for recruitment and participation in collective action" (2005: 7), that is, the economic resources and social relationships that enable individuals to become activists.[8] Going beyond what she sees as the instrumentalist and rationalist assumptions implicit in resource mobilization theory, however (see also Crossley 2002; Goodwin, Jasper, and Polletta 2001a), Hercus points to two further lines of inquiry. On the one hand, she highlights knowledge of power relations, or what she calls "injustice," as a precipitating factor:

> The process of becoming and being feminist . . . involves thinking about or knowing the world in a certain, feminist way. . . . [R]eferred to as feminist consciousness, [this is] a shared way of understanding or *knowing* the world that includes an awareness and rejection of gender inequality as being unjust, unnecessary, and worth fighting against. . . . This does not imply a lack of recognition of other axes of injustice but to be feminist there must be an awareness of gender-based injustice. (Hercus 2005: 10–11)

On the other hand, Hercus argues that the influence of what she calls "agentic emotions" should be explored (2005: 11).[9] She is not alone in her interest in the relationship between feelings and political agency, for feminists have long critiqued the association of women with emotion and passivity and men with rationality and action (see, e.g., Jaggar 1989; Jasper 2003: 160).[10] As our interviewee Sian Sullivan put it, "emotion is so written out of political engagement, and it's so written out of formal institutions" (interview, London, November 4, 2004). It is precisely for this reason that feminist attention to the emotional factors influencing the agency of both women and men is important. The ensuing analysis therefore inquires into the economic resources and social relationships enabling individuals to become feminist antiglobalization activists as well as into their consciousness of injustice and emotional responses.

Economic Resources and Social Relationships

In terms of the "microstructural conditions" that facilitate activism, our interviewees conform to the expectations of resource mobilization theory in being relatively well-off individuals, well integrated into society. They have had access to high levels of education, with more than half having obtained or working toward postgraduate university qualifications. Connectedly, all of our interviewees who are in work have professional-status jobs. There are no clerks among them, let alone blue-collar workers, and none rely on physical labor or survive in the informal, semilegal or illegal economy. Those who are retired have left jobs as librarians or academics. It is important to acknowledge, however, that we do not have details of their income and several interviewees alerted us to the precarious and financially unstable nature of their employment, drawing parallels with the conditions faced by other women in conditions of neoliberal globalization. For example, NGO professionals often hold their jobs only as long as a particular grant lasts. Nonetheless, it is clear that these individuals are, in general, relatively privileged in terms of what could be called their class positioning in neoliberal capitalism. In this sense, they have access to the social, if not the economic, capital, that is, to the lifestyles, information, status, and people, which resource mobilization theorists see as making activism more likely.[11]

Feminist antiglobalization activists also conform to the expectations of resource mobilization theory in being very well connected within activist circles. These associations generally take two forms. First, activists may come from what one interviewee called a "political family" (P. Pavana, interview, Mumbai, January 18, 2004). Such families offer concrete, interpersonal connections into an activist milieu as well as provide inspiring role models, as Subhashini Ali of the All India Democratic Women's Association (AIDWA) illustrates graphically:

> I come from a very privileged family, not just in terms of economics but it is a very, very progressive liberal family. My grandmother was a political activist, she was in every kind of elected position [and] . . . she was also a women's rights activist. . . . And my mother and my father were both freedom fighters. . . . My mother was a big national heroine. (Interview, Mumbai, January 20, 2004)

Growing up in a political family also fundamentally shapes and sustains the worldview and political outlook of an individual. Thus, Nadia De Mond of the World March of Women said of her father that he "taught me to look

behind things and not just take in everything I heard from television news
. . . that sort of critical awareness" (interview, Paris, November 14, 2003).
For Kaarina Kailo of ATTAC in Finland, it was the radical Christian values
of her parents and the consequent "strong ethical background in my home.
. . . So from that premise I was always questioning anything that I found to
be unjust" (interview, Paris, November 15, 2003).

Second, we found that our interviewees frequently have innumerable
informal, social links with other activists. So, Charlotte Bunch, founder of
CWGL, for instance, told us: "I have been working with women globally
for many years and have very strong connections" (interview, Porto Alegre,
January 26, 2005). Bunch highlighted the fact that many of the women
with whom she networks are close friends, emphasizing that the "personal
and political" for her are intertwined (interview, Porto Alegre, January 26,
2005). Similarly, Jacqueline Pitanguy in Brazil told us that she founded the
organization CEPIA (Cidadania, Estudo, Pesquisa, Informação, Ação) with
a woman who has been one of her best friends ever since they met in a
feminist consciousness-raising group (interview, Rio de Janeiro, January 12,
2005). Clearly, our interviewees attach great normative value to their relationships with others. As Sonia Corrêa emphasizes, friendship plays a key
role not only in the factors enabling individuals to become activists but also
in sustaining that activism: "being able to reconnect and reconnect again
and go through difficult circumstances, the politics of friendship is just vital,
you cannot do without it" (interview, Rio de Janeiro, January 10, 2005).

In sum, feminist antiglobalization activists tend to be relatively class
privileged and very well connected. While this goes some way to explaining
how it is possible for them to become politically active, it is not the end of
the story, however, since it does not explain what motivates them to act. For
this, we turn to their claims about power relations and injustice, and their
emotional responses to both.

Knowledge of Injustice

As we have discussed, Hercus argues that knowledge of injustice is a
principal motivating factor for feminists. This is strongly confirmed in the
narratives of politicization offered by our interviewees, which make many
claims about personal experiences of injustice and about the injustices suffered by others. With regard to the former, a wide array of experiences is
recounted. Given what we argued above about the relative class privilege
of interviewees, it is not surprising that suffering in terms of economic
deprivation rarely features. However, consciousness of relative economic
inequality with men is discussed. Kaarina Kailo, for example, was shocked
to realize as a young woman that one of her colleagues received "twice the

salary that I got, as a student doing correspondence-related work . . . just because he was a man. That was ridiculous to me" (interview, Paris, November 15, 2003). At the same time, Kailo was wrestling with inequality in the domestic division of labor in her first cohabiting relationship:

> slowly I realized that . . . I was supposed to be an underling you know . . . almost like a maid. . . . That's where I started becoming a feminist, when I noticed that we were sharing the bills and . . . then all of a sudden I was supposed to be taking on a lot of jobs . . . like ironing his shirt but he wasn't ironing my shirt! And we both had jobs [outside the home]. (Interview, Paris, November 15, 2003)

Marginalizations and exclusions in left-wing mobilizations, highlighted in the first part of this chapter as triggering collective feminist organizing, also feature in individual narratives. In the same way that many women in the 1960s and '70s became feminist through their frustrations with the male-centered character of what has been widely termed New Left politics, a number of our younger interviewees explain that they became feminists as a response to their experience of sexist practices within strands of the global justice movement. Gail Chester suggests as much in her analysis of the factors bringing young women into Women Speak Out in the UK. This network has drawn its participants from the "direct action movement" against road building, genetic modification of food, airport expansion, and the like, all key strands of British antiglobalization politics (see also McKay 1998; Seel, Paterson, and Docherty 2000). As Chester explains:

> what struck me when I went to the first couple of Women Speak Out gatherings was how similar in some ways it was to the early women's liberation movement, which is that what had brought a lot of the women there was complete frustration with trying to work with the men in the direct action movement. (Interview, London, November 8, 2005)

Daniela Pamminger of the group Feminist ATTAC in Graz, Austria, gives another example, emphasizing her unpleasant experience within the local mixed ATTAC group:

> when they started talking I had to leave because they were so . . . [groans] very tiring. . . . [T]hey want to come to *this* point but they start *here* and they keep telling stories for half an hour. . . . If you want to talk they are interrupting you all the time. . . . And if you had a proposal, they would say, "Ah, but this would be better," and . . . if you are a young person they just don't even listen. So . . . we founded Feminist ATTAC. (Interview, Paris, November 13, 2003)

Similarly, Julia Di Giovanni was active in ATTAC in São Paulo, Brazil when she had a "crisis . . . I was the only woman and I was the only person who was younger than forty years old, it was difficult. . . . [W]hen you realize that sexism exists, it is a little bit of a shock! You get tired of being treated like a child" (interview, Porto Alegre, January 26, 2005).

Our Brazilian interviews in particular point to a wide range of injustices in the past lives of activists that motivate activism. Glaucia Matos from black Brazilian NGO Fala Preta! told us how she "revolted" against gender-stereotyped behavior as a young girl: "I would play with the boys' toys, didn't like dolls. . . . I didn't understand. . . . My first consciousness when I was younger was that I was poor and my second consciousness was that I was a feminist" (her "third consciousness" around black identity came much later as an adult through discussions with another black woman; interview, São Paulo, January 18, 2005). Greice Cerqueira of the Women's Global Network for Reproductive Rights (WGNRR), on the other hand, became active around issues of race and self-expression at school, growing "black power hair": "the psychologist at school told me . . . and my other friends, that she wanted us to cut our hair. . . . It was about oppression and for me at that time was not only about black women, but . . . women in general" (interview, Amsterdam, December 22, 2004). A final, moving example is provided by Telia Negrão of the Coletivo Feminino Plural, who confessed that:

> my mother suffered from domestic violence. . . . [W]hen I left home I carried this past with me. This is a personal thing. I wanted to fight against it. . . . I started my activism really young. . . . I always tried to fight for ideas of nonviolence and to make people believe that there are other ways to behave with each other. That was a way I found to overcome my own problems, thinking that I was not the only one who suffered from this, but many people did. (Interview, São Paulo, January 22, 2005)

It is not just personal experience of injustice that motivates activism, however, but also knowledge about the injustices suffered by others. It may be the witnessing of such suffering that triggers activism, or the fact that it happened nearby. For Anne Kristin Kowarsch of the International Free Women's Federation, police violence toward protestors in Germany was the final push to political involvement: the pivotal event was the death of a young woman at the hands of police "in a fight between fascists and antifascists near the town where I lived. . . . And it was quite a heavy incident that . . . made me . . . get involved to do something to prevent other things like that from happening" (interview, London, October 16, 2004). This resonates with the story told by Pennie Quinton of Indymedia in the UK about her "first-ever demonstration":

> we all went outside Parliament, and I was with somebody there that was Irish, this man, and this policeman said, "What are you doing on this march, you

fucking Irish paddy?" . . . And I was really shocked by that behavior. . . . So for me, yeah, people just didn't really have a voice. . . . I believe that people should have a voice to express [themselves] and be involved with the making of their society. (Interview, London, November 10, 2004)

The injustices faced by others may also be learned about through formal, social scientific research. Several of our interviewees, for example, first encountered claims about the gendered injustices faced by women through postgraduate-level study. For Jacqueline Pitanguy, "my entrance into the feminist world was kind of intellectual," stemming originally from her research into women's economic status (interview, Rio de Janeiro, January 12, 2005). Similarly, fellow Brazilian Wania Sant'Anna "was invited by my teacher to work on . . . a profile of the Brazilian women's movement, what had happened during the UN Decade on Women, since 1975. . . . I interviewed many women who were in the feminist movement, in groups and so on, and that is why I became involved, doing research" (interview, Rio de Janeiro, January 14, 2005). For Virginia Vargas, too:

> it was a more theoretical than practical issue. I was in charge of organizing a workshop for three months in Peru about women's issues. . . . [At the time I was asked to do this] I was working . . . in the Institute of National Culture in Peru, doing research . . . [into] cultural public policies. . . . I said . . . "That's a boring thing to be here making things up for women when I should be doing my research that I like." Still, I began. . . . When we were finished, my life changed totally. Because then I realized that there really was a big issue there. (Interview, Mumbai, January 18, 2004)

Vargas goes on to indicate that there is an important process at work here, whereby someone learning about the suffering of others from social scientific sources may ultimately come to understand their own experience differently, drawing parallels between distant lives and their own. As Vargas puts it:

> still in that moment I was thinking that the problem . . . was the others, the poor women, because I was a very liberated woman. . . . I thought that I was free. When we began to organize as women . . . my partner at that moment and my friends, my male friends, began to say, "How is it possible that you who are so intelligent . . . use your time in stupid things like this?" So—*wow!* Then the thing was also about us. (Interview, Mumbai, January 18, 2004)

In this way, our argument that activists mobilize on the basis of formal knowledge about oppression should not be taken as drawing a sharp distinction between cognition and personal experience. It is precisely through cognitive processes, after all, that we make sense of our experiences in particular ways. Moreover, as will become clear below, emotional responses are also part of the picture.

Emotional Responses

Turning finally to the emotions or feelings of our interviewees, it is not surprising that anger at injustices, whether learned about or experienced, is the emotion most frequently mentioned by our interviewees as precipitating their activism. This is not unique to our data. Hercus argues (2005: 11) that of those emotions that have received scholarly attention in analyses of why women become feminist, "anger is the most prominent." In this vein, Maureen O'Mara of the National Association of Teachers in Further and Higher Education in the UK expressed her rage upon her discovery that she was paid less than a colleague: "Just because men do jobs that are in short supply or have value, whereas women's jobs have less value, that then becomes a material factor in the differential of pay. And that made me very angry" (interview, London, November 4, 2004). In addition, several of our interviewees talked about being angered by their exclusion or marginalization from decision making within mixed activist groups or spaces. Helen Lynn of the Women's Environmental Network (WEN), also in the UK, declares that "the overriding emotion usually at things is anger at [being] silenced, because you don't get your point across, or they go 'yeah yeah' but they don't really take it on board" (interview, London, October 29, 2004). Lynn talked eloquently about the rage articulated by women with whom she campaigns on the issue of breast cancer:

> so many people have been so affected by it, so it's a very emotional issue. . . .
> They were bloody angry, the women with breast cancer. They were really angry.
> I attend the world conference on breast cancer when it's on, usually in Canada,
> and the women activists there are angry and will not be silenced. (Interview,
> London, October 29, 2004)

Anger is also a common response to consciousness of injustices suffered by others. Thus Pennie Quinton talks of the Paddington rail crash in London, which triggered her reinvolvement in activism after a period of withdrawal: "I was just really angry that people traveling to work were . . . killed in this way" (interview, London, November 10, 2004). Perhaps more surprisingly, interviewees also responded to academic research into injustice with anger. Pitanguy's findings about unequal income left her feeling "enraged. . . . [T]hat is when I looked for a women's group" (interview, Rio de Janeiro, January 12, 2005).[12] Isabelle Fremeaux of the Lab of Insurrectionary Imagination concludes that "being political for me is to never lose that sense of analysis and anger" (interview, London, January 9, 2004), a point echoed by Nadia Van der Linde of the WGNRR:

> Being an activist for me means being passionate about something . . . and that
> passion is definitely fed by anger and frustration at, you know, unfairness,

injustice. . . . I mean all those issues [about women's lack of access to health care and reproductive rights] . . . make me greatly, greatly upset and that for me is a big fire to make sure that we do something. (Interview, Amsterdam, January 19, 2004)

Anger on its own, however, may not be sufficient to mobilize activism. As Milena Buyum points out, when describing her rage at the killing of a black man in police custody, that "anger could just make you apathetic, and [make you] just get out of it and say, 'Well, there's nothing I can do about it'" (interview, London, November 5, 2004). Quinton makes a similar argument:

My mum worked as a teacher and as a secretary, and she'd be very angry about things. I think my family feel a sense of injustice about things but they're afraid to act. They'll moan about things, and they'll rant at the television, but they won't actually take action. . . . And I really felt that anger, but actually wanted to do something as opposed to just be shouting at the television. (Interview, London, November 10, 2004)

While Quinton hints that courage is a necessary additional emotional ingredient, other interviewees direct us to feelings of affection for other women and to empathy with them, sentiments that feminist scholarship on social movements has foregrounded (Hercus 2005: 11). Affection is evident, for example, in Pitanguy's insistence that she became a feminist "out of love: love for women" (interview, Rio de Janeiro, January 12, 2005) and in Mahe Jabeen's description of her decision to set up her NGO Phoenix in Hyderabad: "I developed some kind of attachment with the slum women and they used to call me . . . Beloved Sister" (interview, Hyderabad, January 7, 2004). Empathy is almost impossible to disentangle from this, but is obvious in Nadia De Mond's summary of what brought her to activism: "a feeling of being on the side of the oppressed" (interview, Paris, November 14, 2003). It is also an ingredient in Kowarsch's articulation of her response to witnessing a violent death at the hands of the police: "it was important for me to say . . . 'I don't want anybody to live through the same'" (interview, London, October 16, 2004). We are left, ultimately, with a picture in which knowledge of oppression and emotional responses to that knowledge are interlinked in complex ways.

CONCLUSION

In this chapter we have explored the origins of feminist antiglobalization activism. Our starting point was the assertion that the question of origins is best pursued from a feminist perspective by focusing on agency at both the collective and individual levels. In terms of the former, we argued that there are long-term collective roots to feminist antiglobalization activism in the form of first-wave feminism and left-wing organizing, but it is second-wave feminism that we see as the most important influence. In this regard, we drew particular attention to the reconfigurations of feminism during the 1980s that encouraged its convergence in the 1990s with the emergent global justice movement. In terms of the latter, we argued that feminist antiglobalization activists are enabled to act by the economic resources and social networks to which they have access, and motivated to do so because of their knowledge of injustice and the emotional reactions this evokes.

We asserted at the outset of the chapter that a feminist story of movement origins must treat agency as constituted within and by power relations. In this connection, our account of the emergence of feminist antiglobalization activism has sought to foreground the ways in which movements themselves are stratified by hierarchies and the ways in which such hierarchies galvanize individuals into action. In the next chapter, the question of power relations becomes more central to our analysis as we turn to "the enemy" that feminist antiglobalization activists are mobilizing against.

NOTES

1. The concept of "political opportunity structures" was developed by social movement theorists in an effort to bring shifts in state structures and political alignments into analyses of why movements emerged. See Tarrow 1998 for a classic articulation, or Costain 1992 for an application to second-wave feminism.

2. See, e.g., Antrobus 2004: ch. 4; Keck and Sikkink 1998: ch. 5; Hawkesworth 2006: 117–31; Desai 2002: 25–30.

3. Mair quoted in Keck and Sikkink 1998: 169; see also Hawkesworth 2006: 119–22; Desai 2002: 27; Antrobus 2004: 42.

4. Also important here, of course, is the retrenchment of the state in the context of the implementation of neoliberal policies, which will be discussed shortly.

5. We do not mean by this to suggest that other hierarchies and renegotiations around them are not in themselves important, but rather that we do not see them as having made such an extensive impact on the attitudes of feminist antiglobalization activists today. In all the countries of our study, for example, there have been significant divisions around class: between educated, middle-class elite women who tended to adopt feminist identifiers and join autonomous organizations and the urban and rural working class and poor. In Brazil, notably, in the 1970s, poor working-class women increasingly joined militant trade unions, created self-help community groups, and allied themselves with popular movements. As Sonia Alvarez says, motherhood, not citizenship, provided the principal mobilizing concept for these women, and the Catholic Church often played a key role (Alvarez 1990: 50; Corcoran-Nantes 2000: 88; Stoltz Chinchilla 1992: 40; Burdick 1992: 176). In the very different context of the UK, working-class women were becoming increasingly politically active by the mid-1980s, with the creation of the national

coordination of Women Against Pit Closures, for example, set up in 1984 to help mining families, with its first national conference taking place a year later. As in Brazil, class tensions worked against the forging of alliances with middle-class, self-identified feminists (Beckwith 2003: 176; Lovenduski and Randall 1993: 122–24). In these two countries, as elsewhere, it seems to us that feminism itself has not been transformed by the phenomenon of separate working-class women's organizations; moreover, feminist antiglobalization activism remains led by middle-class women, as we will see in the second part of the chapter.

6. See Calman 1992: 25, 35–36; AIDWA 2002: 16–17; AIDWA n.d.b; Karat and Sangwan n.d.: 3.

7. We note in this context the parallel shift in the late 1990s to the use of the terminology of globalization in academic feminist critiques; see Eschle 2004a for a more detailed discussion.

8. Resource mobilization theory (RMT) was developed as a response to scholarship which argued that social unrest, a symptom of social strain and breakdown, tended to come from poor and socially marginalized groups in society who were motivated by rage at grievances (see discussions in Beuchler 2004; Crossley 2002: 11). In contrast to this, RMT theorists perceived activists as "rational agents who weighed the costs and benefits before choosing to join social movement organizations" (Hercus 2005: 6; see also Mayo 2005: 56; Canel 2004; Crossley 2002: 56–104). Connectedly, the theory emphasizes that activists, particularly organizational leaders, are "entrepreneurial" individuals able to mobilize not only economic funds but also "relational resources" or social networks (della Porta and Diani 2006: 119; see also Canel 2004; McCarthy and Zald 1973; Jenkins 1983: 530–31). For feminist applications of this approach, see Freeman 2003; Costain 1994: 6–11.

9. In addition, Hercus draws attention to processes of individual identification, "identifying yourself as *belonging* or claiming to belong to the group or category of people called feminists," and also argues for the need for analysis of "*doing* feminist types of things" (2005: 10–11). We touch upon both of these themes in subsequent chapters, so we do not include them here.

10. The feminist emphasis on and analysis of emotions in politics has been influential on an emergent view in social movement scholarship that emotions are culturally and socially constructed, that they involve differing degrees of cognitive processing, and that activists may draw on them quite deliberately and, indeed, reflectively (Goodwin, Jasper, and Polletta 2001a: 12–16; see also Jasper 2003).

11. As we argued in chapters 2 and 3, this relative class privilege is also reflective of hierarchies in play at the World Social Forum where we conducted our fieldwork, and its prevalence in our sample is likely reinforced by our strategy of targeting speakers on panels for interviews.

12. All of these examples resonate with James M. Jasper's concept of "moral shock," which indicates that the strength of reaction to an experience of injustice is very important; it may serve to catapult an individual into activism with or without the existence of preexisting networks (discussed in Goodwin and Jasper 2003: 54; della Porta and Diani 2006: 122). We suggest that injustice that is personally experienced or witnessed firsthand, especially that perpetuated by those in previously trusted positions of authority (della Porta and Diani 2006: 112), is likely to be a particularly strong source of moral shock.

5

Naming the Enemy

Feminist Antiglobalization Activists Confront Oppression

> Neo-liberalism and patriarchy feed off each other and reinforce each other in order to maintain the vast majority of women in a situation of cultural inferiority, social devaluation, economic marginalization, "invisibility" of their existence and labour, and the marketing and commercialization of their bodies. (World March of Women 1999a)

> In a transnational world . . . feminists need detailed, historicised maps of the circuits of power. (Kaplan 1994: 148)

We ended the previous chapter with the claim that individuals become feminist antiglobalization activists in part because they become conscious and angry about the power relations and the injustices that they and others face. In this chapter, we turn to their collective analysis of the nature of these relations, their "naming of the enemy," to paraphrase Amory Starr (2000). In other words, we ask what are feminist antiglobalization activists fighting against?

Feminists of many stripes have long characterized "the enemy" in terms of *oppression* and here we follow their lead.[1] We find oppression a helpful concept because it connotes a type of "power-over," that is, power exercised over the actions and choices of an actor, constraining them in some "non-trivial way" (Allen 1998: 33). What is more, invoking the term indicates a normative, subjective judgment that the constraint involved is damaging, harmful, or wrong (Allen 1998: 34).[2] Drawing on the feminist theorist Iris Marion Young, we understand oppression as having two further defining features. First, it is structural. This means that, rather than being agentic or intentional, "the result of a few people's choices or policies" (Young 1990: 41), oppression is reproduced, unconsciously as well as consciously, through social institutions and assumptions.[3] Second, "[o]ppression refers to structural phenomena that immobilize or diminish a group," specifically social groups such as women, black people, and the like (Young 1990: 42). While recognizing that not all groups are oppressed and, moreover, that group membership and identity can be fluid and shift (Young 1990: 43–48), Young's point remains that oppression shapes the experiences of individuals in a range of groups in ways that are constraining, harmful, and wrong.

In terms of how we study what feminist antiglobalization activists are fighting against, foregrounding oppression leads us to pursue two lines of inquiry. On the one hand, given that Young points us to a structural understanding of oppression and, in fact, argues that social movements increasingly see their enemy in these terms (1990: 41), we seek here to investigate the precise ways in which feminist antiglobalization activists develop this structural critique. On the other hand, we are prompted to examine the claims of our interviewees about the ways in which oppression impacts upon the social groups to which they belong and to which they speak. In other words, how do feminist antiglobalization activists characterize the harmful, damaging effects of oppression on the daily lives and experiences of women around the world?

In what follows, then, we begin with the structural underpinnings of the critiques of feminist antiglobalization activists. We argue that the enemy is perceived in terms of multiple systems of oppression, specifically patriarchy, racism, and globalized neoliberalism. These systems are seen as global in scope, socially embedded, internalized, and state mediated—and moreover, as intertwining with each other and mutually reinforcing. Turning to the question of impact, we distill from our activist accounts five nodal points of oppression in women's lives, conceptualizing them as economic inequality, exclusion from decision making, environmental degradation, bodily "nautonomy," and violence.

SYSTEMS OF OPPRESSION

We propose that feminist antiglobalization activists tend to perceive their enemy in terms of systems of oppression.[4] We understand a system in basic terms as a set of connected parts that function together to make a complex whole; the use of this terminology is intended to convey a macro-level cohesiveness and internal patterning to the way in which oppression works in society. Allusion to a system in this sense is widespread in our data. "What feminism is to me," states one anonymous interviewee, "is a critique of the system" (interview, Porto Alegre, January 26, 2005). The All India Democratic Women's Association (AIDWA) agrees that "women's concerns" are "an integral part of a larger socio-political and economic system" (AIDWA n.d.b) and the feminist caucus in the Association for the Taxation of Financial Transactions for the Aid of Citizens (ATTAC) in Austria echoes this view in its call for a "genuine, emancipatory alternative to the present economic and social system" (Feminist ATTAC n.d.). For Nalu Faria of Sempreviva Organização Feminista (SOF) in Brazil, to take a final example, the problem is "capitalism. . . . The global fight against this system is the priority" (interview, São Paulo, January 17, 2005). Although Faria underlines capitalism as the fundamental source of oppression, most of our interviewees mention more than one system and treat them as equally important. Some emphasize "heterosexual and heteropatriarchal systems" (Kaarina Kailo, interview, Paris, November 15, 2003), for instance, and others talk in terms of "religious, economic, cultural and political fundamentalisms" (AFM 2002) While many systems of oppression are name-checked across our interviews and group documents in this fashion, three receive the most attention overall.

The first is patriarchy. The Andhra Pradesh Chaitanya Mahila Samakhya (APCMS), for example, proclaims that it fights for "the end of patriarchal oppression and against . . . patriarchal family systems" (APCMS n.d.b: 11), while Kaarina Kailo of the Finnish branch of ATTAC insists, "If you don't theorize . . . the whole patriarchal system . . . then you are not getting to the deep core, the hard core of the problem" (interview, Paris, November 15, 2003). Patriarchy is a widely used concept in feminist circles, but also a highly contested one. Intended to convey a relationship of power-over hinging on and working through gender categories and identities (Allen 1998: 23–25), it has been adopted by feminists precisely because it captures the fact that this form of power works as a system of oppression, that is, that gender relationships function together to make a complex whole in which women are systematically disadvantaged relative to men. And while the system-level character of the concept is one of the key reasons it is controversial within feminism (particularly with regard to the scope of the system and the rigidity of relations within it; e.g., Ramazanoğlu 1989: 34–36), it is also the reason why others argue for its retention (Walby 1990: 20; see also Bryson 1999)—and why, we suspect, just over half of our interviewees use the term (51 percent).

Interestingly, *patriarchy* has rather more discursive currency among our interviewees than *gender*. Part of the reason for this is that gender, as a concept, does not translate well into all languages, particularly French, as several Francophone interviewees pointed out. Highlighting another problem, Greice Cerqueira from Brazil told us that gender is "abstract and . . . very easy to . . . manipulate. Governments say 'we are taking gender issues very seriously, and we are mainstreaming gender issues.' And exactly what are they doing in terms of women?" (interview, Amsterdam, December 22,

2004). Cerquiera is drawing here on a deeper wellspring of criticism of the concept of gender for marking a depoliciticizing move away from "women" (see, e.g., Marshall 2000). Given these concerns, it is perhaps not surprising that our activists focus on *"women's oppression* and exploitation" (Mahila Jagruthi n.d., emphasis added) or on "all the terrains where *women suffer discrimination* and unequal treatment" (CNDF, n.d.a, our translation, emphasis added), or that they prefer to use the concept of patriarchy to convey the system of oppression that women face.

What, more substantively, do feminist antiglobalization activist groups tell us about patriarchy? The World March of Women offers perhaps the most developed analysis:

> [We face] domination over women through a social and political system: patriarchy . . . a system whose values, rules, standards and policies are based on the supposition that women are naturally inferior as human beings. It is based on the hierarchy of the roles that societies define for men and for women [and] can be seen in all spheres of life. . . . At the dawn of the third millen[n]ium, we are still living in a world dominated by this system which enshrines male power. (World March of Women 1999a)

This quote highlights several important aspects of patriarchy. To begin with, the drafters of the World March document confirm that there is a relation of power-over at work here: one that grants men status and subordinates women. Furthermore, they see it as reproducing gender categories that are social rather than biological, "based on the hierarchy of the roles that societies define for men and for women." This is in line with the assertion of feminist scholar Sylvia Walby that conceptualizing patriarchy as a system composed of social structures and practices enables an avoidance of biological determinism (1990: 20). Another dimension of patriarchy is its relation to state institutions. The World March analysis above asserts that patriarchy is a "political" as well as social system in the narrow sense of shaping and being shaped by states and state agencies. AIDWA put it thus: "The Indian State, representing as it does the narrow interests of powerful elites of the capitalist and landlord classes, strengthens patriarchy as an ideology intrinsic to its interests" (AIDWA n.d.b). In the very different context of Africa, the NGO network FEMNET also identifies "the patriarchial state" as failing to challenge the gender hierarchies that are in its interests (FEMNET 2009).

The second system of oppression highlighted by our interviewees is racism, by which we mean the patterned ways in which categorizations based on race, or notions of inherited characteristics, descent, or ways of life, are used to justify unequal relations between people (Frankenberg 1993: 81, n. 4). This involves, according to social movement theorist Steven Beuchler, "material discrimination and ideological oppression between dominant and subordinate racial groups that are interwoven throughout society's major institutions" (2000: 112). Thus, the Women's International League of Peace and Freedom (WILPF) declares that it "continues to work for the elimination of racism in all its forms on national and international levels, as well as within the organization" (WILPF n.d.b) and the World March of Women challenges "racism, which generates intolerable inequality" (2004c).

As we discussed in the previous chapter, racism has drawn particular ire in both the UK and Brazil. Milena Buyum of the National Association Against Racism in London expounded on the scope of the problem when she told us that "women, black women, are at the forefront, they bear the brunt of racism, they experience it on a daily basis, and they often have to deal with the most horrendous consequences of racism" (interview, London, November 5, 2004). In parallel, Lúcia Xavier of CRIOLA explains the importance of addressing "racism in the [Brazilian] health system. This is a real problem in Brazil because the health system is very racist. It has a very bad understanding of black people and especially black women. So we are trying to change this" (interview, Rio de Janeiro, January 12, 2005).

Taking a different form in India, it is at least arguable that racism infuses caste discrimination (see debates in Hardtmann 2003: 217–18; 222–24) as well as playing a role in communalist rhetoric and violence. Certainly activists associated with targeted groups make it clear that they see a distinct system of oppression at work. Thus, as Sujatha Surepally of the Dalit Women's Federation pointed out:

> whether it is the university, whether it is a teaching institute, whether it is an organization, whether it is a family, whether it is a friend's circle . . . whether it is the movement . . . Dalit women are always treated differently . . . facing thrice oppression: caste [as well as] class and gender. (Interview, Mumbai, January 17, 2004)

Or take Mahe Jabeen of Phoenix. "As a Muslim, I belong to a minority community. My second [class] citizenship as a Muslim brought me to struggle," she asserts, before identifying the "growing communal violence on Muslims, Christians and other religious minorities" as a major problem in India (interview, Hyderabad, January 7, 2005).

The phenomenon of the racialized subordination of Muslims is not unique to India. As Milena Buyum claimed, "there's a rise in Islamaphobia across the world . . . particularly after September 11th. The way Muslims are viewed . . . is tainted by a lot of racism and hostility" (interview, London, November 5, 2004). A link with state power and its mediation of racism is implicit in this analysis in that states like India as well as hegemonic states in the West are accused of colluding in and reproducing discourses that racialize and subordinate Muslims. It is in this light that Women Living Under Muslim Laws works to protect "Muslim minorities facing discrimination, oppression, or racism" around the world (WLUML 2005). This is not to deny the disagreement among feminists on the relationship between racism and Islam, which we showed in our discussion of the European Social Forums in chapter 3. Interviewee Sophie Zafari, for instance, argues that there is a distinction among French activists between "'integrationalists' and those fighting racism." The former pay "more attention to religious fundamentalism as an enemy to women's rights"; the latter prioritize the struggle against racism and are prepared to work with some Muslim groups (interview, London, October 13, 2004). The fact remains, however, that racism is widely acknowledged as a key system of oppression among our interviewees, and Islamaphobia is seen by some as an important contemporary aspect of it.

The third and final system of oppression underscored by activists is neoliberal globalization. While a handful of our interviewees, including Nalu Faria as indicated above, insisted that it is the underlying capitalist system on which we should focus, a much larger majority (86 percent) invoked some kind of globalization label to describe what it is they oppose, albeit with some serious reservations about this terminology.[5] When using the term in a critical way to articulate their understanding of the enemy, our interviewees specify that it is the economic or neoliberal dimension of globalization to which they are opposed. As interviewee Nadia De Mond sums up:

> when others talk about globalization as this wonderful thing and they refer to having more communication and solidarity, of course that is not what we are "anti," that is obvious. So maybe it is not correct to say we are antiglobalization but for us it means anti–neoliberal globalization. (Interview, Paris, November 14, 2003)

More substantively, neoliberalism is understood as "a political project . . . headed by the multinational companies, by [international] financial organizations" (Guacira Oliveira, interview, Porto Alegre, January 26, 2005) and by "states or international institutions" (Giselle Donnard, interview, Mumbai, January 17, 2004). As one interviewee elaborates, "the world is a village now. But this village is controlled . . . by multinationals, by political powers and so on" (Giselle Donnard, interview, Mumbai, January 17, 2004). These forces together constitute "a system governed by unbridled competition that strives for privatization, liberalization, and deregulation" (World March of Women 1999a)—an allusion to policies that have restructured the relationship between the state and the economy, cutting back state control and allowing market mechanisms into more areas of social life. As the World March concludes: "neoliberal capitalism . . . is a system entirely driven by the dictates of the market and where full enjoyment of basic human rights ranks below the laws of the marketplace" (1999a).

In more concrete terms, in the North this has meant an "attack on the resources that have hitherto been allocated to working populations like public services, the welfare state and so on, by privatizing these, by reducing wages in absolute terms, by cutting pensions and raising the retirement age" (Anne Kane, interview, London, October 12, 2004). In the South, as the same interviewee continues, the neoliberal agenda is seen as involving "much more dramatic measures." It is exemplified by structural adjustment policies or programs (SAPs), the main goal of which has been to spur on economic growth by promoting export-led trade and integration into the global market. As is well documented, these policies have involved the privatization of social services and land, cuts in social spending, the withdrawal of subsidies for consumers and producers, and the reorientation of land and other economic resources to export production (e.g., Earth 1996: 123; Moghadam 2009: 94; Burbach 2001: 4–5). In this context, AIDWA attacks the obfuscation of neoliberal terminology:

> "Globalisation of markets" means globalisation of poverty, inequality, malnourishment and unemployment. . . . "Free market forces" means rising prices of food and essentials and a dismantling of the public distribution system. . . . "Structural adjustment programme" means increase in indebtedness. . . . "World trade organisation" means loss of national sovereignty. . . . "Trade liberalisation" means dumping of cheap goods by the rich developed countries and trade barriers for Third World countries. (AIDWA Maharashtra State Committee n.d.)

These three systems of oppression—patriarchy, racism, and neoliberal globalization—are understood as structuring lives in the sense outlined at the start of this chapter. In other words, oppression is characterized less in terms of the actions of individuals or groups and more as functioning through systems that position certain individuals and groups as dominant over subordinates.[6] It is these systems, then, that determine whether individuals acquire or lack power and status. Such a view is implied in the acknowledgment that "men in general are not the enemy," as Brazilian academic Moema Toscano states (interview, Rio de Janeiro, January 13, 2005) or, as Isabelle Fremeaux in London puts it, "I don't see enemies in individuals" (interview, London, November 9, 2004). There is still space here for a critique of male, white, upper-class privilege, however, and the conduct of those who uphold that privilege. As Toscano confirms, "there is a kind of man who reproduces . . . this patriarchal system and extends it to his sons, his workplace and his political behavior. I am not very happy with that, it needs to change."[7] Nonetheless, our interviewees agree on the need to go beyond a focus on "individual men" who may engage in oppressive "practice" (Mahila Jagruthi 2001) and to look instead at the wider structural dynamics underpinning their actions.

Drawing on the analyses of feminist antiglobalization activists, we identify four main structural features shared by the systems described above.
To begin with, patriarchy, racism, and neoliberal globalization are seen
as large scale, even global in scope. It is this dimension to which Nancy
Burrows of the World March refers when she asserts, "the feminization of
poverty is universal all around the world . . . regardless of the different
shapes and forms and the diversity, the ways in which our experiences of
poverty are different in one country or another" (interview, Paris, November 14, 2003).

These systems of oppression also reach deep into society. As several interviewees note about patriarchy, in particular, it "can be seen in all spheres
of life" (World March of Women 1999a); "it is everywhere, in revolutionary
movements and in our own organizations" (P. Pavana, interview, Mumbai,
January 18, 2004). Patriarchy is also in the home, leading one interviewee
to conclude "there is no environment, no opportunity, no independent
existence [outside of it]" (Sushma, interview, Mumbai, January 17, 2004).
For another, "patriarchal social organization is at the heart of the sorts of
institutions and the ramifications of these institutions that . . . we try to
contest" (Sian Sullivan, interview, London, November 4, 2004).

This brings us to the fact that patriarchy and the other systems are seen
as internalized, that is, as unconsciously reproduced, by women as well as
by men, operating so deeply in our psyches that we become self-policing,
colluding in our own oppression. Take the assertion of P. Pavana of
Andhra Pradesh Mahila Samatha Society (APMSS) that patriarchy is so pervasive, it is "in women also" (interview, Mumbai, January 18, 2004) and
Toscano's belief that "machismo can be represented either by men or by
women, these women that bring up their sons to be the head of the family
and so on" (interview, Rio de Janeiro, January 13, 2005). Moving on from
patriarchy, Isabelle Fremeaux insists that neoliberal capitalism is "this all-
pervasive, intrusive system that defines our social relations and our sense
of identity," and concludes that "capitalism is really inside all of us" (interview, London, November 9, 2004). Jutta Ried of ATTAC in Germany sums
it up this way: the "main problem" today is the "internalised system . . . in
both men and women" (e-mail interview, November 26, 2004).

The final structural feature perceived to characterize all three systems is
that they are mediated through the state and interstate system. References
have been made to this feature in the discussion above. The state can be
seen variously as a conduit for the operations of oppression; as a more
or less bounded space that gives distinctive form to these relations of oppression; and, as we shall see in the next chapter, as an actor that not only
sustains oppressive relations, but also provides a focus for struggles for
change. Debates about the character of the state and interstate system and

their role in upholding and contesting patriarchy, in particular, are widespread within feminism.[8] The critique articulated by activists above makes it clear that the patriarchal state is also a racialized and neoliberal one—it is at least partly in and through the state that these systems of oppression congeal. Moreover, the interstate system more generally should be seen as producing its own stratifications and hierarchies, which map onto and complicate other systems of oppression. It is a factor, for example, in the division between the third world and the first world or between the North and the South (Charlton 1997: 9).

The last point we want to make is that patriarchy, racism, and neoliberal globalization may be analytically distinguishable systems for our activists, but they are also recognized to be systematically intertwined with each other (as well as, in some cases, with other systems of oppression). Thus, the Women's International Coalition for Economic Justice (WICEJ) affirms an "integrated feminist analysis" that addresses "the *intersectionality* of the cause of inequalities . . . the *collision* of multiple oppressions" (WICEJ n.d.b, emphasis added). "A crucial point" for members of NextGENDERation, the European network of feminist students and scholars, "concerns the *interlocking* character of systems of oppression, along lines of race, gender and class" (Andrijasevic and Bracke 2003, emphasis added). For the World March, capitalism and patriarchy "*reinforce one another*" (World March of Women 2004b, emphasis added). In this, activist accounts resonate with, and often explicitly draw on, an increasingly influential approach in feminist scholarship known as "intersectionality."[9] In our view, the intersecting character of systems of oppression is brought into sharpest relief in activist accounts of their context-specific impact on women's lives, and it is to these we turn in the next part of the chapter.

NODES OF OPPRESSION

So how are these systems of oppression seen to impact upon women's lives and experiences on the ground? In what follows, we suggest that five main nodal points of oppression—economic inequality, exclusion from decision making, ecological degradation, bodily nautonomy and violence—can be distilled from feminist antiglobalization activists' claims. Each of these is seen as produced or exacerbated by the interplay of the systems identified above and as taking very different forms in different contexts. In this, the critique of our interviewees overlaps with many other feminist analyses of the operations of globalized oppression.[10] Taken together, they amount to a thoroughgoing and scathing indictment of the way in which women's lives are damaged and constrained worldwide.

Economic Inequality

The first node we identify is economic inequality, which has two analytically separable aspects to it: pay and conditions at work, on the one hand, and deprivation, on the other. We begin with feminist complaints about exploitation and inequality in the labor market. Jacqueline Pitanguy of the Brazilian NGO CEPIA (Cidadania, Estudo, Pesquisa, Informação, Ação) claims that "all the statistical evidence" on her country "shows that women earn less than men" of equivalent professions and class (interview, Rio de Janeiro, January 12, 2005). Fleshing out this claim, Wania Sant'Anna insists that such "inequality is the result of decisions—decisions to have certain groups excluded, [others] involved, productive or not" and, moreover, that gender discrimination and class inequality in the Brazilian labor market is overlain with racism:

> The elites in Brazil are against black people. . . . After slavery, we had nothing for former slaves, nothing. In fact, we had an immigration policy that took place at the end of the nineteenth century and beginning of the twentieth century, for the forms of work developed for black people, as former slaves. . . . They were replaced by people who came from Europe. . . . So that explains why black people in Brazil have such low status, economically, politically and so on. (Wania Sant'Anna, interview, Rio de Janeiro, January 14, 2005)

These views are given statistical support by researchers who have shown that white women were the main beneficiaries of the occupational diversification that began in Brazil during the so-called economic miracle of the mid-1960s, enjoying more access to education and the labor market (Carneiro and Santos, cited in Caldwell 2004: 5). Despite these expanding opportunities, however, economic inequality has continued (Mollo and Saad-Filho, n.d.), with women's salaries in general lagging 36 percent behind men's by 2000 and with Afro-Brazilian women the most disadvantaged of all—notwithstanding the fact that both white and black women tend to complete more years of education than their male counterparts (Lovell 2006: 65).

In India, also, neoliberalism has led to the incorporation of women into the labor market in exploitative and unequal ways. For AIDWA the "[f]eminisation of labour means informal, piece rated, low paid work for women in free trade zones and export processing zones" (AIDWA Maharashtra State Committee n.d.). This kind of work is also "increasing in [the] home-based sector" as Amarjeet Kaur of the National Federation of Indian Women (NFIW) reminds us, and "the home-based sector is on the increase. . . . [F]or many factories the work is outsourced and given on contract . . . 90 percent [of the total home-based workforce] is women" (interview, Mumbai, January 20, 2004). In this context, "[w]omen work from their homes bearing all infrastructural costs and get paid one third of what they would earn in a regular job for the same work" (AIDWA 2002: 17). Feminist scholarship substantiates these claims with evidence that companies have for some decades been shifting their production sites to developing countries and outsourcing their production processes in order to take advantage of lower labor costs, with poor, lower class, lower caste women bearing the burden of meager wages, long hours, and job insecurity (e.g., Naples 2002: 10–12; Moghadam 1995, 2000).

Inequalities in the labor market are also identified by activists as a problem in the North. In the UK, Maureen O'Mara of the National Association of Teachers in Further and Higher Education claimed in her interview that the seven lowest paid of the seventy occupational groupings are dominated by females (interview, London, November 4, 2004). This claim finds support in recent UK survey evidence that the lowest paid sectors of cleaning, health care and related personal services, and retail cashiers are all over 64 percent women (Office for National Statistics 2005). Part of the reason for low pay is because women are more likely to work part time. By 1986, for instance, 42 percent of British women's employment was part time, which meant low hourly wages with little security (Randall 1992: 83), and the situation has not improved significantly since with 38 percent of women working part-time hours at the time of writing (Office for National Statistics 2009). O'Mara argues that an additional factor is "vocational segregation . . . how girls perceive themselves in what they can do at school." She also emphasizes the role of market forces: "men do jobs that are in short supply or have value, whereas women's jobs have less value; that then becomes a material factor in the differential of pay" (interview, London, November 4, 2004).

For activists from around the world, the underlying source of the problem lies in women's responsibility for caring work in the home. Thus, one claims that "the present sexual division of domestic work is still the main origin of . . . gender inequalities in the world of paid work" (ATTAC member, e-mail, November 14, 2004), while another asserts that "for a woman that has got children, who has got work, it's still very, very difficult to become part of . . . society" (Mariangela Casalucci, interview, London, October 16, 2004). As one transnational network insists, "special attention" needs to be paid "to the world of social reproduction for which women worldwide are primarily responsible" and which is "unpaid and undervalued" and ignored in discussions about production and trade (International Gender and Trade Network 2005).

Economic deprivation is identified as a second problem, given that it seriously restricts the life choices and life chances of poor women and men. Unsurprisingly, there is particularly deep concern on this point in the South. Thus, Sant'Anna argues that Brazil "is the most unequal country in the world; the rich are very rich and the poor are very poor . . . with nothing to eat, no work and so on" (interview, Rio de Janeiro, January 14, 2005). Many of our interviewees claim that deprivation has worsened in recent decades due to the deliberate economic policies pursued under neoliberalism. "In the Indian patriarchal family," AIDWA declares, "women usually eat only after all other members are fed. In a period of scarcity they eat less" (2002: 49). According to the same group, scarcity has been exacerbated by government policies that have driven up the prices of basic commodities and slashed food subsidies and ration distribution systems, as well as privatizing water (AIDWA 2002: 48–49, 51). One Indian interviewee reminds us that not all women in the South are equally deprived by neoliberal policies, insisting "it is really a dead end for the poor"; "capitalism," she concludes, "doesn't offer anything to marginalized women" (Rukmini Rao, interview, Hyderabad, January 6, 2004).

Exclusion from Decision Making

Exclusion from decision making is our way of characterizing a second node of oppression to which our activists draw attention in both the state and society more generally. In terms of the former, we find a claim that women, and especially poor women facing racial or caste discrimination, have restricted access to state decision-making processes. Interestingly, this is not a prominent argument among British and French feminists. Only one British interviewee, Emma Dowling of ATTAC, expressed a worry that "political abstention is widespread" and that we need to find "ways to make our societies more democratic" (interview, Dublin, September 19, 2004). Also, the French group Femmes Solidaires, as we shall see in the next chapter, argues for greater access for women to political institutions.[11] Among Brazilian and Indian interviewees, however, political exclusion is a much more widespread concern, reflecting the recent history of these countries. As one Brazilian interviewee reminds us, "I belong to the generation that still remembers the bad spell of totalitarianism. I had in my young adulthood the experience of living under dictatorship" (Sonia Corrêa, interview, Rio de Janeiro, January 10, 2005), while another talks of "political persecution" under the dictatorship and how her "party was illegal at that time" (Telia Negrão, interview, Porto Alegre, January 22, 2005). Indeed, Wania Sant'Anna asserts that even into the 1980s in Brazil "state control of social movements was still quite extensive. And the women's movement also suffered this kind of control" (interview, Rio de Janeiro, January 14, 2005).[12] In parallel, India, as we saw in chapter 4, suffered the imposition of martial law in the mid-1970s, which constrained much domestic political activity, including that of women.

Although both Brazil and India now have formal democratic procedures and processes in place, there are still pronounced complaints of the continued marginalization of many sectors of society in state decision making. Thus, Virginia Feix of Themis, a legal advice and campaigning group in Porto Alegre, warns that a "big majority of the people in Brazil are excluded from all rights . . . and they don't know they are citizens" (interview, Porto Alegre, January 14, 2005). In the Indian context, Subhashini Ali worries that access to decision makers has worsened greatly in the context of the War on Terror: "they are all so well protected that you can hardly get near a democratically elected leader anymore" (interview, Mumbai, January 20, 2004). Offering a more elaborated example of how the Indian state conspires to restrict political participation, Amarjeet Kaur told us about the impact of the two-child policy, which bars women with more than two children from contesting elections:

> On the one hand . . . discourse for political participation is increasing, the issue of 33 percent reservations into the Parliament and assemblies is growing, and all over the world governments sit together and they say, yes, they are increasing [the] political participation of women. And on the other hand . . . [they are] creating structure and . . . formats that [mean] the women will be excluded. . . . [O]nly the women [who are] educated and who know how to have only two children, [who can guarantee] child survival . . . [can enter] into politics . . . [not] a poor woman, a Dalit woman, a tribal woman, an illiterate woman. (Interview, Mumbai, January 20, 2005)

Without any access to the state, poor, lower caste, lower class women consequently have no chance of shaping the policies that impact on their lives.

The concern about exclusion from decision making is not limited to state institutions at the national level, but extends to interstate institutions. Thus, Jacqueline Pitanguy argues for the need to fight against a global "oligarchy" (interview, Rio de Janeiro, January 12, 2005). Sant'Anna concurs, identifying the chief problem since the 1990s as the lack of democratic accountability for "international corporations, governmental agents, private agencies, bilateral agencies and so on, working against the broad agenda of women" (interview, Rio de Janeiro, January 14, 2005).

In addition, criticism is leveled at the fact that women, particularly poor women, are not able to participate fully in decision making in the wider society. Our interviewees highlight two dynamics in this context. First, they claim that women are frequently not able to be fully self-determining in their daily lives. Again, we are struck by the prevalence of Indian and Brazilian commentary on this issue. See, for example, the argument of Mahe Jabeen that "the women and girls in these [Hyderbadi] slums are totally marginalized and excluded, . . . deprived of the opportunity to . . . engage with other women," which "weakens their capability and determination to organize [them]selves" (interview, Hyderabad, January 7, 2004). Amarjeet Kaur's indictment of the two-child norm is based, in part, on the fact that "women are not the deciding factors of the family's size. In our Indian conditions, the kind of traditions and culture [we have] . . . she is not able to decide about it" (interview, Mumbai, January 20, 2004). The forces of fundamentalism are also lambasted, seen as seeking to control women's sexuality and defend the traditional family. In this light, AIDWA indicates that phenomena as disparate as the firebombing campaign against abortion clinics in the United States, the Vatican campaign against reproductive rights, the Taliban's attacks on women "in the name of Sharia," and the insistence by Hindu communalist forces in India that women "have only one major task which is to produce sons and bring them up as warriors," all serve to limit women's capacity to make their own choices and determine the direction of their daily lives (AIDWA 2002: 43, 19–21).

Second, we find anxiety across both North and South about the way women have been marginalized in the decision-making processes of ostensibly progressive forces for social change. As we saw in chapter 4, activists have often organized themselves into feminist groups precisely because of the discrimination they have faced within mixed-gender groups on the Left. An example is provided by an anonymous interviewee from the Association for Women's Rights in Development (AWID), who told us about being a young woman involved in mixed environmental groups: "we had to do a lot of work but we were excluded from the decision making in the organizations and also . . . there were not many spaces for women to speak about the particular issues that we were facing" (interview, Porto Alegre, January 27, 2005). Or as the peace network Women in Black (n.d.a) asserts, "Women's voices are often drowned out in mixed actions of men and women."

Ecological Degradation

The third node of oppression we identify hinges on ecological degradation and particularly the risks it poses to women's health and livelihoods. For feminist antiglobalization activists, the danger here is stark:

> In many parts of the world people, especially those living in poverty, are exposed to toxic substances and radiation; lack clean, safe water and sanitation; or live in disaster-prone areas. Global climate change contributes to these dangerous situations . . . women and men have different susceptibility to various environmental hazards. (WEDO, REDEH, and Heinrich Boll Foundation 2002)

In the South, especially, environmental hazards can result in displacement and destitution. In this regard, several interviewees drew particular attention to the mass suicides in India among failing cotton farmers and weavers due to drought and bad soil conditions and, thereby, increased indebtedness to multinational corporations. In response to this, the organization of interviewee Rukmini Rao, the Deccan Development Society, sent a group of rural women to London to campaign against British government funding for "the vision of agriculture which kills all the farmers, you know some 3,000 of them have committed suicide" (interview, Hyderabad, January 6, 2004). As Kalpanna Kannabiran of the NGO Asmita describes it: "The suicides are . . . mainly young men in their twenties and early thirties. It's just a collapse of no crop, no food. And what the mass suicide results in is the large-scale destitution of women" (interview, Hyderabad, January 10, 2004).

In the North, women may be sheltered from the worst environmental hazards, but they are still seen to be exposed to health risks. The Women's Environmental Network (WEN), based in the UK, asserts that "[b]reast cancer has almost doubled worldwide since 1980 and [this raises] . . . many questions about the role of hormone-disrupting chemicals in the environment" (WEN 2003b: 12). They go on to point out that "[a] UK woman's chances of getting breast cancer in her lifetime have increased from 1 in 12 to 1 in 9 in just five years" (WEN n.d.b). In addition, WEN (2003a) insists that the chemicals in cosmetics "can trigger allergic reactions or chemical sensitivity. Some are . . . hormone disrupters . . . ; others have been linked to birth defects." In light of this, WEN offers a critique of "the cosmetics industry . . . [as] BIG business. . . . We spend £5billion a year in the UK alone on cosmetics and toiletries. Women—and increasingly, men and children—are under huge pressure to use cosmetics to subscribe to a certain image" in ways that can ultimately damage their health (WEN 2003a).

Bodily Nautonomy

The fourth node of oppression hinges on what we call bodily nautonomy,[13] by which we mean processes that harm women's bodies or impinge on their capacity for bodily self-determination.

One essential dimension of this is the commodification and objectification of women. Subhashini Ali, for instance, proclaims that "practices which are antiwomen, which . . . lower and demean the status of women, are . . . used by the market to promote the sales of goods" (interview, Mumbai, January 20, 2004). Although the objectification of women's bodies may date back centuries, it is understood to be intensifying under conditions of capitalism and "escalating through the process of [neoliberal] globalization with women being projected as objects of sale and [with the] objectification of women to promote sale" (Mahila Jagruthi 2004: 2). Beauty contests are seen as a central part of this process in India, with Sushma of Mahila Jagruthi explaining that their purpose is "to commodify women, making them more and more consumerist" (interview, Mumbai, January 17, 2004), and Ali decrying the fact that they function to turn women "into consumption articles" (interview, Mumbai, January 20, 2004). Brazilian activists highlight rather the "the culture of the body" in their country, explaining that "[y]ou have to be young, and you have to look good, and your body has to look wonderful. . . . [I]f you don't look that way, you don't have a place" (Greice Cerqueira, interview, Amsterdam, December 22, 2004). In this context, Julia Di Giovanni of SOF remarks "how much medicine [women] take to control their bodies" and how "Brazilian women are big consumers of plastic surgery, in one of the most unequal countries in the world. And this is really terrible" (interview, Porto Alegre, January 27, 2005).

Another dimension of bodily nautonomy, one receiving particularly wide attention among all the groups in our study, is women's lack of control over their fertility. In India, the "two-child norm" mentioned earlier restricts women's bodily self-determination and is a contributory factor in the phenomenon of female feticide. As Amarjeet Kaur explains, "When you are not able to change the attitudes towards girls and you have a male preference and then impose a two-child norm, then there is more danger of girls being liquidated" (interview, Mumbai, January 20, 2004). Ali also links the problem of feticide to the growth in the institution of dowry payment upon marriage of daughters: "Because people are scared of what will happen to their daughter, how will they get her married? So they kill them after they are born or they abort them after they take the sex determination test" (interview, Mumbai, January 20, 2004). Both the two-child norm and increasing pressure around dowry payments are linked to the spread of neoliberalism. In the case of the former, many feminists have pointed out that overpopulation has been presented as an obstacle to economic development, environmental sustainability, and political stability in need of redress (e.g., Braidotti et al., 1997: 55; Hartman 1994), and, in the case of the latter, as we discuss more in detail in the next section, the growth of demands for dowry can be seen as a response to rising unemployment and worsening poverty.

In the UK and France, in contrast, activist concerns about women's lack of control over their fertility focus more on the restriction of abortion. Thus, although Anne Kane of Abortion Rights acknowledged in her interview that the issue has "died down" in the UK because of legislation since the 1960s, she and her organization insist that a campaign is still important because of continued efforts to repeal the legislation and because of the remaining obstacles and delays that discriminate against women. After all, "[a]bortion in the UK is not available at the request of the woman [but] only if two doctors certify that the risk to her physical or mental health is greater if she goes ahead with pregnancy than if she has an abortion" and the service is not fully funded in all parts of the country (Abortion Rights 2004). In

France, groups from Femmes Solidaires to the Collectif National pour les Droits des Femmes (CNDF) list protecting the right to abortion among their priorities. Anne Leclerc of CNDF and the World March explains how in the early 1990s, France saw not only the intensification of neoliberal policies but also, connectedly, "the rise of the extreme right . . . and with that the activities of Catholics . . . against abortion clinics." The organization Coordination Nationale d'Associations pour le Droit à l'Avertement et la Contraception (CADAC), the predecessor of CNDF, emerged as a direct response (interview, Paris, November 16, 2003).

Restrictions on abortion are also a controversial issue among feminist antiglobalization activists in Brazil. Virginia Feix points out that "abortion in Brazil is permitted when the woman is raped," but "none of the public hospitals will do the service" so the law is not implemented (interview, January 22, 2005). The situation is especially acute for poor, lower class, black Brazilian women given that middle-class women can pay for the service and are less likely to be imprisoned, as Greice Cerqueira of the Women's Global Network of Reproductive Rights (WGNRR) indicates. In contrast, "women living in this land below the poverty line, who don't have access . . . [t]hey're the women dying, they're the women suffering every day" (Greice Cerqueira, interview, Amsterdam, December 22, 2004). This claim is reinforced by estimates that across Latin America and the Caribbean 4,200,000 abortions are carried out every year, the majority in secret and terrible conditions, with 7,000 women dying annually of complications (Flora Tristán CMP n.d.d). In this context, the "global gag rule," instituted by the Bush administration—which cut off aid to organizations around the world seen to be offering advice that could lead to abortion—is singled out as highly damaging (Corrêa 2003). Thus, Nadia Van der Linde of WGNRR lambasts:

> the injustice, all the unfairness [of the] . . . American government . . . global gag rule which makes sure that organizations around the world have difficulties finding any funds to supply services to women and men around the world regarding their sexual and reproductive health. As a result, you know, women are dying from unsafe abortion, from not having information, from not having access to safe contraceptives. . . . [I]t goes on and on and on. (Interview, Amsterdam, October 19, 2004)

There is an additional concern in Brazil around sterilization policies. Despite the fact that sterilization was not legalized in Brazil until 1996, it was widely used without informed consent on women during prior decades. Indeed, a 1986 investigation concluded that 44 percent of Brazilian women between the ages of fifteen and fifty-four had undergone irreversible surgical sterilization, and by 1996 this had become the most common

method of contraception (Knight n.d.: 4; see also Diniz et al. 2001: 36).
This leads Cerqueira to assert that she is "very strongly against population
control which is disguised as . . . family planning policies, many are very
much about population control and controlling the poor" (interview, Amsterdam, December 22, 2004). Similarly, Thais Corral of Rede de Desenvolvimento Humano (REDEH) draws our attention to the problems posed by
"the new technologies of birth control" (interview, Rio de Janeiro, January
11, 2005). In fact, REDEH was founded by women striving to prevent the
approval of a contraceptive vaccination for distribution in Brazil (REDEH
n.d.b). Moreover, the racist dimensions of these policies are not lost on our
Brazilian interviewees. As CRIOLA puts it: "Black women in this context
live in an emblematic situation, where the consequences of inequalities are
deep and intense . . . [characterized by p]overty, mass sterilisation [and]
unsafe abortion" (CRIOLA n.d.).

The final dimension of bodily nautonomy brought to our attention
by our interviewees is sexual exploitation. In India, for instance, AIDWA
points to the fact that "'expanding tourism' means [an] increase in prostitution and [the] trafficking of women and children" (AIDWA Maharashtra
State Committee n.d.), while Amarjeet Kaur reminds us that certain groups
of women, such as underemployed agricultural laborers or the widows of
the many thousands of male farmers who have killed themselves, are particularly vulnerable to being forced into "the flesh trade" in order to survive
(interview, Mumbai, January 20, 2004). In France, sexual exploitation and,
more specifically, the links between sex work and violence have been a central issue for the feminist movement from the very start (Hagemann-White
2002: 241). The CNDF has a Commission on Prostitution that approaches
this issue in terms of its social, economic, and political dimensions and
that argues that any solution should focus on how best to safeguard human
rights, especially with respect to trafficked women (CNDF n.d.b). Relatedly,
members of the feminist caucus in ATTAC in France point to the alarming
growth in sex trafficking in Europe in the 1990s:

> In this decade, a new form of prostitution is appearing. Pervasive, cheap and
> constituted by young women coming principally from Eastern Europe, but
> also Asia and sub-saharan Africa . . . [t]his is [p]rostitution brought about by
> the rise of liberalism without limits . . . with prostitutes . . . becoming cross-
> border commodities. . . . The industry is extremely lucrative, with estimates
> that the money made from prostitution amounts annually to 60 billion euros
> worldwide and 10 billion euros in Europe. (Jeffers et al. 2003: 135–36, our
> translation)

Beyond our French groups, there is less of a consensus on this issue. Indeed,
prostitution and sex work, and its relation to trafficking, is a very divisive
issue for northern feminists (see, e.g., Foerster 2009). We saw in chapter 3,

for example, how NextGENDERation argued against the dominant French position on prostitution at the Paris European Social Forum, criticizing the conflation of prostitution with violence and characterizing it as a form of labor. Where there is some agreement, perhaps, is on the fact that women in the sex industry are particularly vulnerable to violence, the fifth and final node of oppression to which we now turn.

Violence

Of all the nodes of oppression, the one that features most prevalently in our interviews and documentation is violence against women. Widely understood by feminists to be a universal problem (Hagemann-White 2002: 250; Hanmer 2002: 269), albeit taking different forms in different places, violence is defined as a means of "controlling women" (Women in Black n.d.a), which involves overt, coercive, physical attacks on women's bodies. Summing up the range of forms that this can take in India, Mahila Jagruthi states that:

> Women are . . . prone to [suffer] much violence. Dowry murders, female foeticide, infanticide, sati, witch hunting, rampant prostitution, all speak of the degradation of women. Rape is also used as a weapon to weigh them down, by patriarchy and in the armed forces of the state. (Mahila Jagruthi 2001)

Two circumstances amplify the likelihood of violence, according to our interviewees. The first is when a society is in a situation of war or armed conflict. As WEDO and REDEH put it: "In war and armed conflict, women's experiences of displacement, violence and loss are disproportionate because of their unequal status. . . . [D]omestic violence and sexual exploitation rise steeply" (WEDO, REDEH, and Heinrich Boll Foundation 2002). In a similar vein, Women in Black declare (n.d.a): "Most women have a different experience of war from that of most men. All women in war fear rape. Women are the majority of refugees." While none of the countries in which we conducted our fieldwork were undergoing outright war, India was suffering (and continues to suffer) from a rising tide of communal violence, most notoriously in the form of the massacres of Muslims in Gujarat in 2002: "it was a horrendous thing, a state-sponsored genocide of a minority community" (Subhashini Ali, interview, Mumbai, January 20, 2004). In this context, women are often targeted (e.g., Karat 2005: 13). As Articulación Feminista Marcosur (AFM) reminds us, "fundamentalism . . . flourishes in societies which negate the full diversity of the human race and which legitimate the use of violence to subordinate one group to another, or one person to another" (AFM n.d.).

Economic deprivation is the second circumstance that can lead to an increase in violence against women, according to interviewees in all four national fieldwork sites. This is certainly a long-standing worry for British feminists, with Anne Kane bemoaning the fact that "the choices that women may have had . . . to leave abusive relationships or . . . to have children alone, or whatever, are limited by closing economic circumstances now" (interview, London, October 12, 2004). Kane's concerns converge with wider feminist arguments that the recent weakening of the welfare state has not only made women more dependent on their male partners and, therefore, less likely to leave home when they face abuse, but has also undermined feminist efforts to set up shelters to provide help when they do manage to escape (Lovenduski and Randall 1993: 15; Stienstra 2000: 220). In the South, escalating poverty in the context of neoliberalism is also blamed for a rise in violence against women, perhaps most vociferously by our Indian interviewees. For Subhashini Ali, the priority is "[t]he question of violence. . . . [G]lobalization is increasing this violence. When people become poorer and hungrier they are more vulnerable" (interview, Mumbai, January 20, 2004). Kalpana Kannabiran situates domestic violence as a response to the impact of SAPs on rural areas: "You just have to look for the connections. . . . [T]hey [men] are frustrated because there is no money; and there is no money because they are not being paid enough, the wages have dropped" (interview, Hyderabad, January 10, 2004). And, P. Pavana reminds us:

> dowry deaths are increasing. . . . Because of the privatization, they [men] . . . lost their jobs and because of that there is no food or money. . . . If they want to start a business or something they start beating their wives to get money [from her family] and that beating would go to such an extent of killing the wife. (interview, Mumbai, January 18, 2004)

Indeed, by 2000 the Indian Home Ministry reported more than 6,000 dowry deaths a year, and many more deaths go unrecorded (Crossette 2003: 143).

Taking us full circle, Sujatha Surepally of the Dalit Women's Federation declares that poverty is a form of violence. Highlighting its brutality in the context of caste discrimination, Surepally asserts: "the violence I see, the violence in poverty levels, the violence [of struggling] for survival, the violence of going [and] living in the road with no house, no shelter. That is violence" (interview, Mumbai, January 17, 2004). While Surepally focuses on the oppression faced by Dalit women, and it is clear that oppression varies in different contexts and for different constituencies of women, the overall picture that emerges from our data is one in which, as we quoted at the start of this chapter, "the vast majority of women" are maintained "in a situation of cultural inferiority, social devaluation, economic marginalization, 'invisibility' of their existence and labour, and the marketing and commercialization of their bodies" (World March of Women 1999a).

The World March of Women (2004b) speaks for all our activists when they declare: "We reject this world!"

CONCLUSION

In this chapter, we have explored what feminist antiglobalization activists are fighting against. Deploying the concept of oppression, we have tried to unpack the precise ways in which our interviewees depict its structural features and to systematize their claims about its impact on the daily lives of women around the world.

We have argued that feminist antiglobalization activists reserve their ire for what they describe as systems of oppression, namely patriarchy, racism, and neoliberalism. All three systems are seen as global in scope, socially pervasive, internalized and state-mediated, and as intertwined with each other in complex ways. Moving on to their impact, we distilled five main nodal points of oppression from activist accounts, ranging from economic inequality to violence. This grim picture of an omnipresent, manifold enemy is not the sum total of feminist political beliefs, however. As we shall see in the next chapter, our interviewees also develop visions of alternative worlds in which relations of oppression are transformed.

NOTES

1. E.g., Rowbotham 1977; Combahee River Collective 1977; Ramazanoğlu 1989; Valentine 2007.
2. It is important to note that Allen is actually defining domination rather than oppression. She and Iris Marion Young both separate out these two concepts (see also Allen 2008; Fraser 1997: 193–94), but we are not convinced that this is a helpful move. We see oppression as the broader term, of which domination is a subset. In any case, Allen's comments here apply equally to oppression.
3. Not all feminists agree with this structural move. We note, for example, that Ramazanoğlu (1989: ch. 4) works with an understanding of oppression as interpersonal and agentic, as does Patricia Hill Collins (2000: 4): "Oppression describes any unjust situation where, systematically and over a long period of time, one group denies another group access to the resources of society."
4. Iris Marion Young argues against the analytical device of identifying "separate systems of oppression," on the grounds that this assumes such systems are "unified and distinct" and attach themselves to different oppressed groups. Consequently, each group, defined by a single source of oppression, is likely to be represented as overly homogenous and as entirely different from any other group (1990: 63–64). In our view, however, this is not how systems of oppression are usually theorized in feminist circles, including among our interviewees. Rather, groups are typically seen as overlapping and shifting, and as constituted at specific intersections of multiple

systems of oppression, as we will explain in what follows (see also Crenshaw 1998; Collins 1998, 2000; Nash 2008).

5. For some, the problem with the concept of globalization lies in its inherent abstraction, which means that it "is used to represent more than what it really means—for example, imperialism, organizing new forms of work, a new international division of labor" (Nalu Faria, interview, São Paolo, January 17, 2005); that its meaning is only accessible to elites; and that it is seen as something that happens "out there," far away, rather than "something happening inside, at the national level, or as something people experience in their daily lives" (Lúcia Xavier, interview, Rio de Janeiro, January 12, 2005). As Xavier continues, there is also a problem with the fact that this reliance on a "new" term masks historical continuities with imperialism and slavery. Most often, interviewees were uneasy with the concept of globalization as a descriptor of what they oppose because not all aspects of globalization are harmful and some should even be welcomed, such as "more communication between countries than ever before" (Helena Kotkowska, interview, London, October 13, 2004) and "the globalization of alternatives" (Gabriela Rodriguez, interview, Rio de Janeiro, January 12, 2005). Most still use it, however, as a term to convey what they oppose.

6. A handful of interviewees describe gender inequality in nonstructural terms, relying rather on what could be seen as a liberal feminist framework in which inequality is perceived as anachronistic "discrimination" (Shantha Sinha, interview, Hyderabad, January 6, 2004), rooted in individual attitudes and feudal tradition. Thus Helena Kotkowska, for example, argues that in the UK, "we are in a stage of development where it's [feminism is] not needed anymore. . . . On the other hand, in countries like Afghanistan, I can see where feminism, once it takes hold, is going to be a full-time occupation, because there's so much to do" (interview, London, December 10, 2004).

7. As Iris Young affirms, taking a structural approach does not mean that "within a system of oppression individual persons do not intentionally harm others in oppressed groups," nor does it deny that "specific groups are beneficiaries of the oppression of other groups, and thus have an interest in their continued oppression" (1990: 42). But for Young, as for our interviewees, both dynamics take place within a context of structural oppression within which they are made possible and sustained.

8. See, e.g., Mackinnon 1987; Pringle and Watson 1998; Pateman 1998; Charles 2000; Kahn 2004; Kantola 2006.

9. See, e.g., Crenshaw 1998; Collins 1998; Valentine 2007; Nash 2008. Among our interviewees there is some disagreement over precisely how an intersectional analysis should be elaborated. Sarah Bracke, for example, argues that one key difference in approach between NextGENDERation and the World March at the Paris European Social Forum was that the latter did not fully integrate an account of racism and heterosexism into their analysis: "they made a distinction between what is shared by all women and what would be specific problems, specific to certain groups of women only. This totally runs counter to our intersectional point of departure" (interview, Dublin, July 10, 2004). Nonetheless, it is clear that the dominant orientation across our data is to strive for an intersectional understanding, even if the number of systems identified, the extent of their interplay, and the details of how this works may differ.

10. E.g., Moghadam 2000; Ong 1987; Mies 1982; Mohanty 2003; Chang and Ling 2000.

11. We were surprised that such claims were not more widespread given that French women did not gain the vote until the 1940s and that British feminists have long complained of the centralized and exclusionary character of the British political system (Randall 1992: 81; Gelb 1986: 105; Gelb 1990: 14; Lovenduski and Randall 1993: 363). Further, until recently, the UK had some of the lowest levels of representations of women in Parliament among established liberal democracies (Curtin 2006: 240; Beckwith 2003: 179; Studlar 2006: 89).

12. It is important to remember that, until the 1962 Civil Code reform, women in Brazil were seen as wards of the state along with minors and indigenous peoples (Aboim n.d.: 1). During the military dictatorship, women were expected to stay at home and were refused entry into state politics (Alvarez 1990: 6).

13. This term from political philosophy has been defined most influentially by David Held, as the "asymmetrical production and distribution of life-chances which limit and erode the possibilities of political participation" (1995: 171). We are using it rather more narrowly here, to imply simply systematic constraints on individual autonomy.

6

Imagining Other Worlds

The Utopian Dimension of
Feminist Antiglobalization Activism

> We dream of a future
> Where women
> Speak out their thoughts
> Act out their dreams
> Walk paths they choose
> Where girls grow up
> Brave sure gracious
> Honing their talents
> Carving an identity
> Moving towards a future
> That is peaceful, just and free. (Asmita n.d.)

Another world is not only possible, she is on her way. On a quiet day, I can hear her breathing. (Roy 2004)

Feminist antiglobalization activists have offered not only sophisticated critiques of oppression, but also proleptic visions of a fundamentally transformed world. In this chapter we seek to inquire into where their feminist imagination takes them, what ethical goals they uphold and strive toward, and what principles of action guide them in their struggle. In other words, having elaborated on what they are fighting against, we now turn and ask: what are feminist antiglobalization activists fighting for?

The first step in our answer to this question is to suggest the notion of "utopian imagination" as a way of framing our exploration of the aspirations of feminist antiglobalization activists. Our choice of this term is intended to highlight the highly ethical and creative nature of their endeavor as well as its radically transformative orientation. These features have long been recognized as widespread within feminist thinking,[1] even if the notion of utopia itself is more controversial (e.g., Ramazanoğlu 1989: 186). More particularly, drawing on the work of Seyla Benhabib (1992), Greg Johnson (2002), and Sasha Roseneil (1995), we pay attention in our study of the utopian imagination of feminist antiglobalization activists to its *situated*, *universal*, and *practical* character. While we accept that any specific instance of utopian thinking will manifest all three of these dimensions—Johnson, for example, insists that feminist utopian thinking "provides the point of convergence between our need to speak from our location and our ability to argue for the universally intended dimension of our claims" (2002: 30)—for our purposes it is helpful to separate out these different levels of analysis and consider them in their own terms.

The structure of this chapter maps onto these three avenues of analysis. In the first part, we consider a panoply of concrete proposals for social change, arguing that they reflect a situated, historically and socially specific elaboration of utopian imagination. In this context we find a remarkable range of suggestions—a diversity that is explicitly valued and defended by our feminist activists. In the second part, we draw out the universal dimension of feminist utopian imagination by identifying the shared ethical goals that, in our view, underpin these various proposals for change, namely economic equality, democracy, sustainability, bodily integrity, and peace. Taken together, we argue that these add up to a call for what we characterize as "gender justice." In the third part, we illuminate the practical moment of utopian thinking through an exploration of the ethos, or principles of action, that serves to guide how feminist antiglobalization activists should engage both with each other as part of a political community and with their various external interlocutors. In this regard, we identify "participatory," "dialogical," and "holistic" principles as underpinning their internal relationships while characterizing their engagement with external interlocutors as simultaneously "critical" and "multilateralist."

SITUATING UTOPIA: CONCRETE PROPOSALS FOR OTHER POSSIBLE WORLDS

We begin the chapter with an examination of the notion of situated utopian thinking, which we borrow from Greg Johnson (2002: 30). For Johnson, and indeed for Benhabib (1992), feminist visions of a better world respond to lived experiences of gender oppression and, in this context, reflect the desire to "fashion new openings for the lives and experiences of women" (Johnson 2002: 27). In other words, they emerge through a dialogue between "situated critics," that is, living subjects who come to know the world, themselves, and others through their experiences (Johnson 2002:

25). More specifically, these experiences, and thus the visions to which they give rise, are "embedded," on the one hand, and "embodied," on the other (2002: 26). For us, the embedded and embodied nature of the situated utopian thinking of feminist antiglobalization activists is best exemplified in their concrete proposals for change.

These proposals are elaborated in group websites and pamphlets, often in much detail, and are articulated in the form of demands and imperatives. Moreover, as we will demonstrate, they address specific interlocutors, most often states (or specific agencies of the state) and interstate organizations; are outcome oriented, in that they express a desire for changes in policies or prevailing practices; and reflect the micro-level, context-dependent experiences of specific groups of women. As such, these proposals cover a wide range of issues, as can be seen in the proposals excerpted in textboxes 6.1 through 6.4, one from each of the countries in which our fieldwork was conducted.

All of these proposals demand that states engage in some form of policy action, either at the national or international level, with respective national governments being called upon to provide "free and compulsory education" for "all girls/women" (textbox 6.1), to comply "with treaties and international conventions on human rights and the rights of women" (textbox 6.2), to offer "[p]ayment for all caring work" (textbox 6.3), or to set a "quota of social housing for female victims of violence" (textbox 6.4). Moreover, we find a concern with problems pertaining to women's everyday lives including the division of domestic labor, health policies, food security, pay equity, and violence in the home. In all cases, the recommendations of each proposal cut across the different nodes of oppression discussed in the previous chapter. Thus, Indian organization Mahila Jagruthi targets both economic inequality and the political exclusion of women with its call for 50 percent reservations in both the job market and political institutions, while the Global Women's Strike, based in the UK, seeks to counteract women's inequality in the labor market, violence, and environmental degradation. French network Femmes Solidaires touches on most of these as well as adding political exclusion to the agenda.

Interestingly, the concrete proposals of our transnational groups follow a similar template. The interlocutors remain states and interstate institutions and their recommendations are often equally grounded in the realities of women's lives. What is noticeably different, however, if not surprising, is that they tend to incorporate global-level solutions more prominently. Thus, the International Gender and Trade Network (IGTN) argues for the "immediate reduction of the scope of the WTO [World Trade Organization] to trade related issues only," "debt cancellation," "enforceable corporate accountability mechanisms at national, regional and global levels," and "democratic structures to ensure participation, access and accountability in

---

Textbox 6.1.   "Status of Women in the New Society," Mahila Jagruthi, Bangalore, India

[I]t is hard to imagine what a society bereft of inequality and injustice would be, of what it would be . . . to realise our full potential as women and as members of a non-exploitative socio-economic structure. A generalised portrayal of what this new society that we strive to usher in can possibly mean to women is enumerated below . . .

Economic and Political Sphere

In villages feudal property would be seized, and women will get an equal share with men in all lands distributed to the landless and poor peasantry. . . . [A]ll the private property of comprador capitalists and imperialist capital will be nationalised and full participation of women in social production ensured. There will be 50% job reservation for women in all sectors . . . and equal pay for equal work and adequate pay for all workers. The exploitative Sexual division of labour will be abolished. General and reproductive health care facilities, crèches and child care centres will be a must at all work places. 50% reservation for women in all political institutions. . . .

Socio Cultural Sphere

All girls/women will have free and compulsory education. Co-education will be promoted. Instead of building gender, class, caste and racial prejudices . . . [t]he realm of education will now seek to imbibe real democratic values of equality, mutual help, care, respect. . . . Prostitution will be abolished whilst making alternative work available to women engaged in the same. Pornography and the entire sex industry will be abolished. All Capitalist-Imperialist inspired sexist propaganda and all media distortions and derogatory references to women will be ended. . . . With drastic changes in the social conditions people will be relieved from the compulsion to consume liquor. Strict measures will be instituted against the practice of amniocentesis, female foeticide/infanticide and the use of anti-women contraception. . . . The system of dowry will be completely banned. . . . Women and men will have equal rights and obligations in family and social life. Domestic work will be gradually socialised. Sharing of domestic work by men will be promoted. . . .

(Mahila Jagruthi 2001: 52–53)

---

trade negotiations and policies" (IGTN n.d.b). To take another example, the World March of Women demands the implementation of the Tobin Tax, the investment of 0.7 percent of the GDP of rich countries in aid for developing countries, the financing and democratization of the United Nations programs that are essential for women and children's rights, an end to structural adjustment policies, and the rejection of the Multilateral Agreement on Investment (World March of Women 1999b). Despite addressing

Textbox 6.2.   Objectives of Coletivo Feminino Plural, Porto Alegre, Brazil

- The defense of the rights of women and girls from the perspective of gender and human rights.
- The combating of all forms of discrimination and prejudice of gender, race, ethnicity, age, or conditions that wear down women and girls, whether through norms, laws, positions, behaviors, or actions.
- The development of mechanisms, instruments and public policies to fight all forms of discrimination and violence, whether it is physical, sexual, psychological, or symbolic.
- The compliance with treaties and international conventions on human rights and the rights of women.
- The guarantee of the exercise of sexual and reproductive rights, free from prejudice and with the security of holistic health policies.
- For the grassroots and sustainable development of the planet, in ways that ensure work and a quality of life for all women and the end of the exploitation of young children, in particular of girls.
- The exercise of substantive citizenship, that is to say that which is effectively lived by women in all areas of their lives, whether in public or private, that will enable them to empower themselves.

(Coletivo Feminino Plural 2005, our translation)

Textbox 6.3.   Demands of the Global Women's Strike, Coordinated from London, UK

- Payment for all caring work—in wages, pensions, land & other resources. What is more valuable than raising children & caring for others? Invest in life & welfare, not military budgets or prisons.
- Pay equity for all, women & men, in the global market.
- Food security for breastfeeding mothers, paid maternity leave and maternity breaks. Stop penalizing us for being women.
- Don't pay "Third World debt." We owe nothing, they owe us.
- Accessible clean water, healthcare, housing, transport, literacy.
- Non-polluting energy & technology which shortens the hours we work. We all need cookers, fridges, washing machines, computers, & time off!
- Protection & asylum from all violence & persecution, including by family members & people in positions of authority.
- Freedom of movement. Capital travels freely, why not people?

(Global Women's Strike n.d.)

Textbox 6.4. Priorities of Femmes Solidaires, France

Femmes solidaires is a feminist organization for all the women who live in France, whether they are French or immigrants, an organization for all the women that want to uphold their rights and liberties. . . . Femmes solidaires acts [against] . . . sexism, racialism, violence, poverty and discriminations. . . .
[Priorities for campaigns include:]

For the right and access to work, women being on an equal footing with men at work

- Against imposed part-time work and flexitime
- Against wage differential and sexist discriminations
- For a big rise of the SMIC (minimum wage) and [in] low wages, 80% of which are female wages.

Against violence upon women

- Against all violence: conjugal violence, sexual harassing, rape and sexual assaults, genital mutilations, imposed marriages, prostitution
- For a quota of social housing for female victims of violence
- So that family allowances and national insurance benefits will be taken into account whenever flats are attributed [distributed].

For parity

- For a real parity [of women and men] in all elections . . .
- For a real social diversity of the people's representatives.

Against poverty and for a fairer distribution of wealth

- For the taxation of speculative flows of capital
- For a raising of family allowances up to €155 for each child, from the first to the last one
- For a beginning of term school allocation of at least €250 per child, whatever the family resources may be
- For the non deduction of family allowances from the RMI [minimum income allowance for adults] . . .

(Femmes Solidaires n.d.)

---

global institutions and their focus on global analysis and global solutions, our transnational groups remain committed to representing the actual, everyday concerns and aspirations of women at the local and national level. Expressing this aim explicitly, the Women's International Coalition for Economic Justice states that it seeks "to bring our local perspectives on gender and economic issues to the international arena, and, conversely, to bring our shared analysis from the international arena back to our regions" (WICEJ n.d.a).

Following Johnson, we argue that all the concrete proposals of our core groups are situated to the extent that they are embedded, in at least two ways. First, they are embedded in ideologies, most obviously feminism. We discuss what we mean by ideology, and the ways in which our interviewees deploy ideological identifications, in chapter 8. Here we want simply to point out that their proposals (like their critiques) reflect an often self-conscious adherence to feminist ideas and traditions. Ideological differences among feminists, such as whether a group also adheres to anarchist principles or to socialist ones, are less evident at the level of proposals. One exception is Mahila Jagruthi's report (textbox 6.1). Member Sushma told us that "we like to be called Marxist" (interview, Mumbai, January 17, 2004) and along with other groups we met at Mumbai Resistance, Mahila Jagruthi are also influenced by Maoist arguments for a "new democratic revolution" via the peasantry. The emphasis in their report on tackling feudalism and redistributing land can be understood in this context, as can the style, presenting detailed recommendations for total transformation (this is the only document in our data to provide a kind of blueprint of another world). As will become clear below, however, we do not think the contents of the report are entirely determined by this particular Marxist orientation. Moreover, our point remains that ideologies other than feminism are not strongly evident in the other concrete proposals considered here.

These proposals are quite clearly embedded in a second sense that has to do with national context. By this we mean that the documents excerpted above reflect interaction with a particular set of state institutions and historically specific national cultural traditions. With respect to India, we suggest that many of the aspirations listed in Mahila Jagruthi's document are strongly supported by other Indian activists who do not share a commitment to Maoist-inspired Marxism. Thus, demands for the abolition of dowry and specific religious laws, the end of sex-selective abortion, tackling the abuse of alcohol and caste exploitation, and the provision of education for girls can be found in most Indian proposals. This overlap is clearly evident in the visionary statement from the All India Democratic Women's Association (AIDWA), a group considered to be "revisionist" by Mahila Jagruthi:

> [We want a] world where women will enjoy equal economic, social, political rights, where minimum wages, maternity benefits, free education, health and social security will be rightfully ours, a world free of violence, caste discrimination and religious oppression, a world of peace, freedom and dignity. (AIDWA Maharashtra State Committee n.d.)

Similarly, the convergence of aims between Mahila Jagruthi and Phoenix, an NGO based in Hyderabad that lobbies the government on "issue-based concerns such as violence against women, dowry death, domestic violence and sexual harassment at work" (Mahe Jabeen, interview, January 7, 2004), is striking.

Turning to the Brazilian context, we find a shift in language and focus to questions of sexuality and reproductive health, racism, and the environment, among others. Sonia Corrêa of Development Alternatives with Women for a New Era (DAWN) states that "a strong emphasis on sexuality . . . is not surprising. It has to be understood as connected to Brazilian culture . . . how the culture perceives itself. . . . [T]his was a very strong agenda for us from the beginning" (interview, Rio de Janeiro, January 10, 2005). Indeed, calls for sexual and reproductive rights can be found in documentation from all but one of our Brazilian groups. Another priority for many of our Brazilian groups is tackling racism. This mandate is expressed by CRIOLA when it pushes for policies that "ameliorate" the living conditions of Afro-Brazilian women by providing them with the skills and confidence to enter into the labor market and earn "a living wage" (CRIOLA n.d.) and by Fala Preta!, which in turn sees one of its main tasks as contributing "to the construction of a critical knowledge about Black women and the Black population in areas of sexuality and reproductive health" (Fala Preta! n.d.b, our translation). Even groups with wider agendas include the abolition of racism as one central pillar. The Centro Feminista de Estudos e Assessoria (CFEMEA), for instance, seeks to:

- Defend and promote equality of rights and gender equality in legislation, as well as in the planning and implementation of public policy, taking on board the inequalities generated by the intersection of sexist and racist discrimination.
- Shine a light on the budgetary process with the view to its democratization and transparency, as well as incorporating a gender and race perspective into public expenditure. (CFEMEA n.d., our translation)

Among our British and French interviewees, we find yet another combination of issues, with gender stratification in the labor market, environmental hazards, sexual and domestic violence, and abortion featuring strongly in their reconstructive agendas. Thus, the recommendations of Femmes Solidaires include the right to work and a quota of social housing reserved for victims of domestic violence (see textbox 6.4). Notably, Femmes Solidaires, like other French groups, see prostitution as a form of violence. As the feminist caucus in the Association pour la Taxation des Transactions pour l'Aide aux Citoyens (ATTAC) makes clear, this leads to an "abolitionist" position that insists on the criminalization of clients, "like in Sweden," and coordinated state action "to protect prostitutes . . . to give them access to fundamental rights of the person. . . . It is also necessary to adopt a political program which will effectively combat in society and in schools the sexist representations which objectify and devalue women" (Jeffers et al. 2003: 141, our translation). In the British context, there appears to be less of a consensus on this issue, with groups such as the Global Strike adopting a pro–sex worker rights position, arguing for better economic conditions for sex workers and for an end to laws that criminalize those who work in the sex industry (see International Prostitutes Collective n.d.). Another theme that emerges strongly in the UK is that of the environment. The Women's Environmental Network, for instance, "links women, environment and health" (WEN 2002). Declaring that "everyone has the right to pollution free products, good food and less waste," WEN explains that it:

> is empowering people to take action on links between the environment and health—calling for a precautionary approach to harmful chemicals. . . . Locally-produced, organic food should be the norm, not a luxury. WEN fosters food growing and composting skills and campaigns for more local food. . . . Making less wasteful choices should be as easy as throwing things away. (WEN 2004)

Interestingly, ideological and national differences in proposals for change are not seen as a liability by our activists. On the contrary, the diversity of agendas is seen as a good in itself. Recall as mentioned in chapter 3 that banners at feminist sessions at the World Social Forum in Mumbai pluralized the slogan of the forum—"another world is possible"—to read "other worlds are possible."[2] And consider the assertion of the World March's "Charter for Humanity" (2004b) that "[w]e are building a world where diversity is considered an asset." One interviewee who makes this point explicitly says that her preferred future "allows for diversity and difference. . . . [I]t should be a society that allows different models to emerge" (Isabelle Fremeaux, interview, London, November 9, 2004). Feminist writer Angela Miles hints that this is not unique to our interviewees but typical of many feminist activists: "diversity is an essential characteristic not only of political dialogue and organization but of the society to be achieved" (1996: 139).

In addition to being socially embedded, feminist utopian visions, according to Johnson (2002: 26), also speak to and from the experiences, needs, and aspirations of specific, embodied subjects. The proposals of feminist antiglobalization activists are no exception to this. So Phoenix speaks for Hyderabadi "slum women" and fellow Indian NGO Akshara works with "young women and men" in the Mumbai area and beyond (Akshara n.d.). Femmes Solidaires acts for "all the women who live in France," and CRIOLA (n.d.) seeks to represent "Afro-Brazilian women, adolescents and girls primarily in Rio de Janeiro." Finally, the World March sets out to galvanize "grassroots women" around the world (Nadia De Mond, interview,

Paris, November 14, 2003). To this extent, the concrete proposals elaborated above do not evoke images of a "new" woman or man upon which some future society will be erected, but rather make demands on behalf of what Benhabib calls "situated selves" (1992): women with particular lives and experiences seeking to rebuild the societies of which they are members.

UNIVERSALIZING UTOPIA:
THE ETHICAL GOALS OF GENDER JUSTICE

As mentioned at the start, utopian imagination is not only situated but also universal. Johnson's understanding of universalism, however, is one that makes room for "the plurality of modes of being human . . . , without endorsing all these pluralities and differences as morally and politically valid," rather than one based on a "disembedded and disembodied subject situated beyond history and cultural contingency" (2002: 25). Elaborating further, Johnson suggests that the universalism underpinning a feminist utopian imagination has two inherent logics. The first has to do with its universal intent. As he puts it, "normative claims against the sex-gender system and for something other are claims that interactively emerge in a situation but are *intended* universally" (2002: 32, emphasis in original). By this he means that those engaged in utopian thinking seek to speak out against an oppression that is judged to be wrong in all circumstances and everywhere it appears, and, in this way, to achieve the betterment of all. It is in this sense that Miles characterizes feminist activism as an inclusive human struggle that is "universal but not universalizing" (1996: 141). The second has to do with the fact that utopian imagination is an interactive "process that seeks agreement" with others (Johnson 2002: 25) in which those putting forward the utopian vision must "'woo the consent' of everyone" (Benhabib, cited in Johnson 2002: 31). In order to achieve this consent, we suggest, proponents of utopian visions need to articulate them through a moral language that is understandable to others and, thus, which must draw on widely recognized traditions of thought.

For us, these two logics of universalism are most obviously manifested in what we call the ethical goals of feminist antiglobalization activists. Whereas the concrete proposals of these activists addressed a specific interlocutor, their ethical goals are generalizable and transferable in the sense that they address a wide audience. And whereas the concrete proposals are outcome oriented, ethical goals are aspirational, open ended, and processual; that is, they do not signify a predetermined end state. Finally, while concrete proposals reflect micro-level, context-specific experiences, ethical goals abstract from specific experiences, capturing and responding to perceived patterns in people's suffering worldwide. Despite these differences, however, concrete proposals and ethical goals are not entirely discrete normative moments; on the contrary, on our understanding, ethical goals provide the moral touchstones for the recommendations of our activists and the parameters within which they are formulated. Some statements that foreground ethical goals are shown in textbox 6.5.

These statements capture for us the main features of the ethical goals as explained above. They voice claims that are not directed to a specific interlocutor but that rather address "all human beings" and call for another "world." What this future world will look like is not specified in detail, with aspirations remaining at a level of generality—a "world where exploitation, oppression, intolerance and exclusion no longer exist," or "an

---

Textbox 6.5.   Ethical Goals: World March, AWID, DAWN

The World March of Women's "Charter for Humanity"

We are building a world where diversity is considered an asset and individuality a source of richness; where dialogue flourishes and where writing, song and dreams can flower. In this world human beings are considered one of the most precious sources of wealth. Equality, freedom, solidarity, justice and peace are its driving force. . . . [This is a] world where exploitation, oppression, intolerance and exclusion no longer exist, and where integrity, diversity and the rights and freedoms of all are respected. (World March of Women 2004b)

The Values of the Association for Women's Rights in Development (AWID)

AWID's members are dedicated to achieving gender equality, sustainable development and women's rights, around the world. . . . We work towards a world and an economic system based on social and economic justice, interdependence, solidarity and respect rather than competition and exploitation. We want a world without war and without the systems of oppression against which women and men have struggled in patriarchal societies for thousands of years. (AWID 2005)

DAWN's Vision

We want a world where inequality based on class, gender and race is absent from every country and from the relationships among countries, where basic needs become basic rights and where poverty and all forms of violence are eliminated. We want a world where the massive resources now used in the production of the means of destruction will be diverted to areas where they will help to relieve oppression both inside and outside the home, a world where all institutions are open to participatory democratic processes, where women share in determining priorities and making decisions. This political environment will provide enabling social conditions that respect women's and men's physical integrity and the security of these persons in every dimension of their lives. (DAWN n.d.)

economic system based on social and economic justice"—so that they may be pursued in a variety of ways. There is also a shift here from the concrete, embodied subject to the generalized subject, as captured by appeals to "women around the world" and "women and men." Finally, several ethical goals are name checked across these statements. Thus, the World March seeks "[e]quality, freedom, solidarity, justice and peace"; AWID calls for "gender equality . . . social and economic justice, interdependence, solidarity and respect"; and DAWN for participatory democratic processes and respect for physical integrity.

It is our argument that, taken together, these ethical goals amount to a vision of what we call "gender justice." This term is invoked explicitly by a handful of our interviewees, although without much elaboration. DAWN, for instance, makes a "conscious effort to make advocacy for gender justice a priority within progressive non-feminist organisations" such as the World Social Forum (Slatter 2002). Interviewee Virginia Vargas from Articulación Feminista Marcosur (AFM) also uses the concept when she characterizes contemporary feminist struggles as fighting for "an agenda that attempts to integrate gender justice with economic justice" (Vargas 2003: 912–13). The Women's Environment and Development Organization (WEDO n.d.a) "seeks to empower women as decision makers to achieve economic, social and gender justice" and both Amarjeet Kaur and Rukmini Rao in India referred to the salience of gender justice in their interviews. Moreover, some feminist scholars have also deployed the concept of gender justice in a very general way in their work (e.g., Hawkesworth 2006: 11). Here we seek to give content to this notion of gender justice by defining it in terms of five key ethical goals invoked across our data: economic equality, democracy, respect for the environment, bodily integrity, and peace.

Economic Equality

The first ethical goal is economic equality, which implicates at least two imperatives. The first relates to the need to extend equality to women, which entails eradicating gender-specific oppressions that disadvantage them relative to men. Thus the Andhra Pradesh Chaitanya Mahila Samakhya "works towards a culture where labour is respected, gender equality is accepted and oppression is opposed" (APCMS n.d.b: 9–10) and CFEMEA wants a "fair and egalitarian state and society; . . . we want equality between the genders" (Guacira Oliveira, interview, Porto Alegre, January 26, 2005). More specifically, we found that demands for equality were often contextualized in terms of the labor market, from the call by the Global Women's Strike for "pay equity for all" (textbox 6.3) to the Instituto Eqüit's claim that "lingering inequalities in work conditions and in remuneration" lead them to struggle for "equity between women and men as a matter of human rights and conditions for social justice" (Instituto Eqüit n.d.). In making this argument for pay equity, a number of our feminist activists highlight the need to find ways of revalorizing domestic and care work as well as redistributing its burdens. To this end, Mahila Jagruthi proclaims that in their new society "[d]omestic work will be gradually socialised" and that the "[s]haring of domestic work by men will be promoted" (textbox 6.1); the Collectif National pour les Droits des Femmes campaigns for free nurseries and for the sharing of parental responsibility (CNDF 2002); and the Global Women's Strike demands "payment for all caring work" (textbox 6.4).

Another salient dimension of the general call for economic equality is the desire for a redistribution of economic resources in order to tackle poverty and deprivation. More particularly, we found that this goal was articulated in the context of a discourse about "basic needs." As one of our interviewees from the Women's Global Network for Reproductive Rights (WGNRR) puts it, "it's not about money to buy [things], that's not what I'm talking about, I'm talking about health, housing . . . food, water, the basic things every human being should have" (Greice Cerquiera, interview, Amsterdam, December 22, 2004). The Women's International League for Peace and Freedom confirms this emphasis, calling for an "international economic order founded on the principles of meeting the needs of all people and not those of profit and privilege" (WILPF 2007). Thus, while they may differ slightly on the content covered by the notion of a basic need, with the Global Women's Strike including "leisure time" and WEN stressing that water "is not a commodity" but a "basic human right" (Sutton 2002), there is general agreement that "basic needs become basic rights" (DAWN n.d.a).

Democracy

The second ethical goal we find expounded by feminist antiglobalization activists is democracy, understood expansively to refer to the right to full participation in community life as well as in decision-making processes, wherever within the state or other political sites. As Sissy Vovou of the World March puts it, "Democracy in the last analysis is not a still [static] word, it is a living struggle for changing society under concrete conditions and structures" (e-mail interview, November 11, 2004). Jackie Lewis of the International Lesbian and Gay Association (ILGA) elaborates further when she says, "Democracy is far more . . . than going along to tick a box, or not, when there's an election. It's far more than that, isn't it? It's actually about being able to influence, to have input, to help shape the way things are being directed" (interview, London, November 10, 2004).

One way of gaining this influence for many of our interviewees is through the implementation of the principle of equal representation, or what French activists call parity, which involves integrating women in numbers equal to men into decision-making processes. In the context of state and interstate institutions, this demand finds expression in Mahila Jagruthi's promise to offer 50 percent representation to women in political bodies (textbox 6.1), Femmes Solidaires' request for "real parity in all elections" (textbox 6.4), and WEDO's efforts to "[a]dvance women's equality in decision-making by pushing for a gender-balance at local, national and global levels" (WEDO n.d.a). Echoing this sentiment, DAWN strives for "a world where all institutions are open to participatory democratic processes, where women share in determining priorities and making decisions" (textbox 6.5). There are also clear articulations of the need for parity within social movement processes and spaces, such as the World Social Forum, as evident from chapter 2. Speaking about the Forum, as well as her own organization, the National Association Against Racism (NAAR), Milena Buyum explains: "Our constitution is very . . . clear about the parity between men and women, and the issue of black leadership of the antiracist movement. . . . [W]e want to build a movement that is inclusive and completely open to everybody." She goes on to defend the feminist struggle for equal representation in the context of the European Social Forum in London, arguing that "you have to push for it, and you have to establish it as a principle" (interview, London, November 5, 2004).

We find that an expansive understanding of democracy is also expressed in demands for citizenship. This is particularly the case in Brazil, which is predictable given the recent transition to liberal democracy there and the analysis of activists that the "majority of the people in Brazil are excluded from all rights and . . . [d]on't know they are citizens" as discussed in chapter 5 (Virginia Feix, interview, Porto Alegre, January 22, 2005). Virginia Feix goes on to argue persuasively for the need "to build citizenship" in such a way as to foster the "power of belonging, the understanding that they belong to this group, as part of this society, that they can do things" (interview, Porto Alegre, January 22, 2005). Such a discourse on citizenship often intersects with one on rights. Thus, the organization CEPIA (Cidadania, Estudo, Pesquisa, Informação, Ação) is "dedicated to developing projects that promote human and citizenship rights especially among groups historically excluded from exercising their full citizenship in Brazil" (CEPIA n.d.a), while the Instituto Eqüit (n.d.) "seeks to build women's citizenship with regards to democracy and human rights and disregard to market logic." Furthermore, Coletivo Feminino Plural makes clear that citizenship must be "substantive," that is, "effectively lived by women in all areas of their lives, whether in public or private, [in ways] that will enable them to empower themselves" (see textbox 6.2, our translation).

Respect for the Environment

A third ethical goal that we identify among feminist antiglobalization activists is respect for the environment, although we note that this is less prevalent than the others. While a range of our core groups do recognize the need for a "healthy planet" and most acknowledge that environmental degradation, as outlined in the previous chapters, undermines women's life chances, few of them articulate a defense of the environment as a separate ethical goal in its own right. More common is a demand to respect the environment as a prerequisite for global socioeconomic development, in general, and for women's economic betterment and health, in particular. In Brazil, Coletivo Feminino Plural takes a stand "for . . . the sustainable development of the planet, in ways that assure work and a quality of life for all women" (see textbox 6.2, our translation). In India, the Deccan Development Society has "worked on the premise that improving the environment and improving women's livelihood and rights go together" (Rukmuini Rao, interview, Hyderabad, January 6, 2004) and the Andhra Pradesh Mahila Samatha Society (APMSS) teaches women working on the land to preserve the environment by reviving local agricultural practices (interview with A. Padma, Hyderabad, January 8, 2004).

One of the few groups to articulate a more strongly ecocentric perspective, in which respect for the environment is seen as something important in its own right, is WEN in the UK. Summarizing its 2002 survey of member's aspirations, WEN declares that we should:

> respect the earth and all forms of life, with participants imagining a world, so different from our own, where this is a reality. . . . Again and again women expressed the hope that we respect the earth, summed up in the following vision: "*En cha huna—it too has life. Recognize the value of life other than our own. Women must lead the way.*" (WEN 2002, emphasis in original)

Bodily Integrity

Bodily integrity is our fourth ethical goal, and a passionate aspiration for a large number of feminist antiglobalization activists and groups. For Joanna Hoare of NextGENDERation:

> that's my starting point . . . the body issue. Everybody should have the right to decide what happens with their body and with their life. And for as long as . . . certain sections of the population are being told that they don't have that

right, then I don't think we've got gender equality, and I will continue to be a
feminist. (Interview, London, November 8, 2004)

So what does bodily integrity actually mean? We suggest that there are
two dimensions to this concept. The first is an emphasis on sexual and
reproductive rights, which the WGNRR define as "a series of interrelated,
basic human rights which enable women to have safe, responsible and
fulfilling sex lives and to freely decide if, when and how often to have
children, free from coercion, discrimination and violence. This includes
the right of access to safe, legal abortion" (WGNRR n.d.a). Understood in
this way, such rights are fundamentally about women's self-determination
in all matters pertaining to their bodies and intimate relationships. Thus,
as Mariana Mozdzer points out, "reproductive rights or sexual rights are
a lot more than just abortion" (interview, Amsterdam, October 1, 2004).
Promoting these rights means working "democratically and jointly for a
woman's right to control her own body and for the full enjoyment of her
sexuality without discrimination based on class, race, ethnicity, creed, age
or sexual preference" (Catholics for the Right to Decide in Mexico n.d.). It
also means embracing the idea that all women should be free from sexual
control and exploitation. This argument is reflected clearly in the World
March of Women's "Charter for Humanity" (2004b), which states that "no
person may be held in slavery, forced to marry, subjected to forced labour,
trafficked, sexually exploited. . . . All individuals [should] enjoy collective
and individual freedoms that guarantee their dignity." As Milena Buyum
concludes, "you cannot think of . . . women's liberation without thinking
about reproductive rights. It would be unthinkable. The issue is completely
at the heart of the women's movement and has been so for decades" (interview, London, November 5, 2004).

A second dimension of bodily integrity involves reclaiming women's
bodies from corporate power and processes of objectification and revaluing
women's beauty. Anne Kristin Kowarsch of the International Free Women's
Federation in the Netherlands makes the need for this clear when she admits
that women "still have this feeling of being ashamed of our own bodies. . . .
We want to question that, especially with young girls . . . so that they really
feel comfortable, or that they know their body belongs to them" (interview,
London, October 16, 2004). Greice Cerqueira of the WGNRR agrees, saying,
"there's a need . . . [to] start seeing women in a different way. We still have
strong stereotypes about women and how you should look" (interview, Amsterdam, December 22, 2004). For the Brazilian branch of the World March,
this has inspired an "offensive against commodification. . . . We should try
to break through these traps" (Julia Di Giovanni, interview, Porto Alegre,
January 27, 2005). Simultaneously, Fala Preta! sees one of its central tasks
as having an "active presence in the media as a space for the production

of meaning, contributing [to] the elaboration of new images . . . [of] black women" (Fala Preta! n.d.a).

Peace

Fifth and finally, peace is an ethical goal for many feminist antiglobalization activists. So, for instance, Women in Black declares that it is "committed to peace with justice and actively opposed to injustice, war, militarism and other forms of violence" (Women in Black n.d.a); WILPF states that it is working "toward world peace; total and universal disarmament; the abolition of violence and coercion in the settlement of conflict and their substitution in every case by negotiation and conciliation" (WILPF n.d.c); and WEDO and REDEH strive for not only a healthy but also a "peaceful planet" (WEDO, REDEH, and the Heinrich Boll Foundation 2002). Once again, peace, like democracy, is defined in an expansive way that is not reducible to conventional understandings. Most obviously, peace involves for our interviewees not only the absence of war but also the transcendence of more general gendered patterns of violence within societies, including all forms of domestic and sexual violence. To this end, the Global Women's Strike demands that women should have "protection and asylum from all violence & persecution, including by family members and people in positions of authority" (see textbox 6.4), while in India, Women in Black have fought for an end to domestic violence (Women in Black UK n.d.a).

As indicated above, these five ethical goals taken together constitute a vision of what we call gender justice. To this end, they must be understood as interdependent and indivisible; none can be realized in isolation from the others. Moreover, in terms of their content, the link with our interviewees' analysis of oppression, outlined in chapter 5, is apparent in at least two ways. To begin with, each of the goals described above maps onto one of the nodes of oppression identified in that chapter. Thus, economic equality as an aspiration addresses exploitative and unequal gender relations in the labor market as well as the deprivation suffered by poor women. Similarly, arguments for democracy, whether in the form of claims for parity in institutions and movements or for more substantive and inclusive citizenship, are responding to the exclusion of women from decision making in state and interstate institutions as well as throughout social life. Perhaps more importantly, these goals, and the others explored here, speak not only to the impact of oppression on the ground in context-specific forms, but also to the underlying systems of oppression that feminist antiglobalization activists identify as causal, namely patriarchy, racism, and neoliberal globalization. In this way, although gender justice may start with an emphasis on gender, it does not end there. A desire for the structural transformation of multiple systems of oppressions is evident in DAWN's wish for "a world where inequality based on class, gender and race is absent from every country and from the relationships among countries" (see textbox 6.5). It can also be seen in Glaucia Matos's "dream of a world where it does not matter about class, or skin colour, religion, sexual orientation, gender or the body. . . . People have the right to be themselves" (interview, São Paulo, January 18, 2005). A final example is provided by WILPF's constitution:

> Believing that under systems of exploitation . . . a real and lasting peace and true freedom cannot exist, WILPF makes it its duty to further by non-violent means the social transformation that enables the inauguration of systems under which social and political equality and economic justice for all can be attained, without discrimination on the basis of sex, race, religion, or any other grounds whatsoever. (WILPF 2007)

Turning from the substantive content of gender justice to its universal dimensions, we can see both aspects of the universal moment in the utopian imagination indicated above. First, gender justice embodies universal intent to the extent that it targets patterns of oppression that are judged to be wrong wherever and to whomever they occur. Thus, while the concrete proposals of feminist antiglobalization activists may speak to specific addressees, their ethical goals are oriented to all women and men worldwide. Second, these ethical goals set out to "woo the consent" of others and build agreement across differences. This can be seen through their efforts to draw on widely recognized moral languages that have broad appeal including human rights discourses, particularly in reference to citizenship and to sexual and reproductive rights. In fact, as explored in chapter 4, transnational feminist organizing has focused much of its attention over the past thirty years on reframing the language of rights so that it speaks to women's oppression (see, e.g., Petchesky 1994; Corrêa and Petchesky 1994; Richter and Keysers 1994), an endeavor that, as we have seen, still shapes feminist antiglobalization activism today. In addition to liberal discourses around human rights, feminists have also sought to critically engage with left-wing normative frameworks that argue for social justice understood largely in terms of economic equality and material redistribution (e.g., Young 1990; Fraser 1997). These feminist engagements have directly influenced some of our interviewees. Virginia Vargas, for instance, draws on the work of Nancy Fraser when she defines gender justice in terms of claims for both recognition and redistribution (2003: 912–13). Indeed, we suggest that the vision of gender justice elaborated above can be understood as the latest feminist attempt to reframe and expand the agenda of the Left. In this context, it can be seen as more inclusive and potentially radical than the concept of social justice to the extent that it addresses multiple systems of power; recognizes, but also goes beyond a call for material redistribution; and reflects an aspiration that is universal in its intent while simultaneously speaking to and from concrete, situated proposals for change.

STRIVING FOR UTOPIA: PRINCIPLES FOR ACTION

As we stated at the start of this chapter, feminist utopian thinking is not only situated and universal but also practical in orientation. In making this claim, we are following Benhabib's argument that utopian thinking reflects a "practical-moral imperative" (1992: 229) to the extent that it has an action-oriented dimension, one which Erin McKenna describes as "seek[ing] to create and sustain people willing to take on responsibility and participate in directing their present toward a . . . more desirable future" (2001: 3).

One way of capturing this practical dimension is through the exploration of what Sasha Roseneil indentifies as principles of action or an "ethos," by which she means a "powerful moral discourse about the practising of feminism"—one no less powerful for not being systematically codified by activists themselves (1995: 61). Rejecting the concept of "strategy" as overly instrumentalist and rationalist, Roseneil proposes that the practices and activities of the women's peace camp at Greenham Common in the UK can be better understood in terms of its ethos. We read this as comprised of two sets of principles. The first underpins the "internal mode of action" or "the way individuals act together to constitute a collectivity," while the second informs the "external mode of action" or "the way [social movements] confront the outside world and their political opponents" (Offe, cited in Roseneil 1995: 71). We explore both below with regard to feminist antiglobalization activism.

Principles Guiding the Internal Mode of Action

When building solidarity among themselves and among women more generally, feminist antiglobalization activists seek to be *dialogical*, that is, they put a strong emphasis on dialogue as a method of acknowledging and navigating differences between women. See, for example, AWID's portrayal of its role as "advanc[ing] work on gender and development and women's human rights by facilitating ongoing, inclusive debates on fundamental and provocative issues" (AWID 2005). In parallel, AWID's president has insisted "that the women's movement should not waste energy arguing about the 'correct view' but rather commit to hearing from a range of viewpoints and work to understand the points of convergence and action" (Kerr 2002). This propensity to talk through differences is corroborated by Roseneil's study of Greenham, which found that "there was commitment to talking through problems and decisions, often exhaustively. The attempt was made to air all sides of a debate, to allow everyone to speak" (1995: 65).

In addition, we found that this commitment to dialogue involved encouraging women to speak up, speak out, and also speak for themselves. As Pennie Quinton of Indymedia in the UK put it, "I want my own voice, and I don't want other people to speak for me" (interview, London, November 10, 2004). We can see this written into the names of some of our core groups and their actions: Women Speak Out in the UK is, after all, a space for "opinionated exchange" (Women Speak Out 2001b); Fala Preta! means "Black Women Speak!" (Glaucia Matos, interview, São Paulo, January 18, 2005); and the first and major role of Communicação, Educação e Informação em Gênero (CEMINA) in Rio has been to create a radio program *Fala Mulher* or *Women Speak Up* (CEMINA n.d.a: 1). In terms of what our core groups do, the All African Women's Group (n.d.) supports members in "speaking out about our experiences" and the Women in Black groups build their agendas by "encourag[ing] every woman in speaking for her[self] and then discussing with others. . . . That's our way of acting" (Giselle Donnard, interview, Mumbai, January 17, 2004). For Sara of the Global Women's Strike, it is very important that particular groups of women speak for themselves:

> Real democracy is when grassroots people speak in our own voice about our own situations. That is what autonomy is, when we are able to speak for our sector—if we are women with disabilities, if we are sex workers, if we are lesbians, etc.—we make a space to speak about what are the core issues for us and how we want it presented. (Interview, London, October 12, 2004)

Sarah Bracke takes this one step further and refuses to speak for others within her group: "I always say that I cannot speak for the network [NextGENDERation] but from my experience of being involved in it" (interview, Dublin, July 10, 2004). Similarly, Cassandra Balchin of Women Living under Muslim Laws (WLUML) declares, "I can't speak for the individual organizations who are linked through us" (interview, London, November 9, 2004). Nancy Burrows of the World March sums up the point when she says, "one of the unique aspects of feminism, and for me, one of the richnesses . . . is that there aren't many spokespeople. . . . Because one of the things that characterizes us as feminists is the collective process" (interview, Paris, January 14, 2003).

The second, closely related, principle guiding internal action is that of *participation*. Again, this is not unique to our data but is a continuing theme in feminist arguments about self-organization, emphasized particularly in small-group, second-wave feminist organizing (see Eschle 2001: ch. 4). More specifically, the participatory principle calls for and values active involvement in movement politics, as made particularly clear in the documentation of the World March of Women. When signing up, groups are asked to:

- make a commitment to this irreversible movement . . . adopting its actions as your own;
- encourage other groups in your country to participate in activities concerning the Charter (and other future actions), . . . working in tandem with them;
- help to organize national and international actions;
- participate in actions near you;
- pass on information about the March to members of your group, inviting them to have discussions and mobilizing them to act. (World March of Women n.d.c)

As Nadia De Mond of the World March confirms, "it is very grassroots orientated . . . organizing women, mobilizing them and bringing them to be active in participation" (interview, Paris, November 14, 2004). Furthermore, this commitment to participation brings with it an inclusive emphasis on the involvement of as wide a range of people as possible. Thus, Anne Kane argues that the feminist underpinnings of her organization Abortion Rights necessitate "making sure everyone [in the staff and on the board] participates and that what is actually happening in the campaign is properly discussed, [that] everyone has a chance to comment on that and so on" (interview, London, October 12, 2004). AIDWA claims that its structure, "with elected committees of women from the village or urban locality level to the national, . . . enables the widest participation in struggles and in decision-making processes" (Karat 2002: 3). Or take the fact that "WLUML's open structure has been designed to maximize participation of diverse and autonomous groups and individuals as well as collective decision-making" (WLUML 2005).

Participation in this context also entails an imperative to foster self-determination, in the sense of enabling women to make their own decisions and pursue their own agendas. In line with this, the self-description of WGNRR (n.d.b) states, "We work on the basis of equal relationships and input from our members rather than as a disciplined, ideologically homogenous, centrally controlled organization. We believe that each group or individual is the best judge of their own situation." Perhaps the most explicit statement can be seen in the World March's description of the "values underlying the action" that it undertakes:

- The leadership of the organization is in the hands of women;
- All regions in the world are responsible for organizing the actions;

- Active participating groups must subscribe to the purpose and values, objectives and overall plan of action for the March but are independent in organizing actions in their respective countries. (World March of Women n.d.a)

The third and final element of the internal ethos of feminist antiglobalization activism is what we characterize as a *holistic* approach to feminist activists and to women more generally that involves seeing them as thinking, feeling, embodied beings. This is found, for example, in Monica Maher's claim that the methodology of groups involved in the international Grail network of Catholic women rejects the "dualism of mind/body," instead "incorporating the whole body, the spirit and the mind" (interview, Porto Alegre, January 29, 2005). Speaking bluntly, Nadia Van der Linde of the WGNRR declares of activism, "I don't know how you can do it without emotion" (interview, Amsterdam, October 19, 2004), while London-based activist Sian Sullivan suggests that "one of the most radical things that we can do is to make spaces where people can reveal the way they are feeling to each other without feeling threatened or without feeling that they are compromising themselves" (interview, London, November 4, 2004). In addition, a holistic approach entails an effort to learn from women's experiences and self-understandings and to acknowledge and value their feelings about these experiences as a source of knowledge and agency. As Nalu Faria puts it with regard to her group Sempreviva Organização Feminista (SOF), "starting from the experience that the women have and from what they know, we go forward" (interview, São Paulo, January 17, 2005). In this way, the holistic approach to the individual underpins the insistence on dialogical and participatory organizing: it is because women are valued as producers of knowledge and potential agents for change that their full and equal involvement is sought in feminist struggle.

Principles Guiding the External Mode of Action

The external mode of action of feminist antiglobalization activism is guided, in our view, by two main principles that shape the relations of our interviewees with interlocutors outside their political community. The first involves what we define as a *critical sensibility*, by which we mean a wariness of power holders and an awareness that they can and do function as sources of oppression. We see this critical orientation most explicitly expressed with respect to the state, albeit to different degrees. An overtly "antistatist" rhetoric is drawn on by Lydia of the Wombles, the London-based direct action network, who says, "In an ideal world you wouldn't have states. What is produced and what is done to satisfy social needs [would be] collectively done for social benefit, and in a nonauthoritarian way" (interview, London, June 11, 2005). An antistatist sentiment is also articulated by the mass Marxist organizations and the Mumbai Resistance groups in India. In this context, P. Pavana of APCMS explains:

> we don't go to courts or police stations to solve the problems of women. . . . Police stations and legal bodies are very corrupt. Most of the time the verdicts are delivered with [a] patriarchal mind-set. And so we practice such tactics, i.e., making a small group of people from that slum itself and [we] sit together and try to solve the problems at slum level. . . . In each of the cases we try to expose the attitude of the state. . . . We don't think you can change the state from inside the state . . . [but rather] believe in . . . throwing down the present state and bringing in a new state . . . a people's government. (Interview, Mumbai, January 18, 2004)

Although the majority of our interviewees do not express such overtly anti-statist views, there is still a widespread assumption that the state plays a role in reproducing oppression; there are no naive pluralists here. For Giselle Donnard of Women in Black, as mentioned in chapter 5, "globalization is ruled by . . . states or international institutions" and it is these that activists should be challenging (interview, Mumbai, January 17, 2004). In a very different context, FEMNET, the pan-African NGO network, stresses that it sees itself as playing "vanguard and catalytic roles in the treatment of feminist issues that cannot be handled by government gender mechanisms due to the threat that such issues pose to patriarchal states" (FEMNET 2009).

This critical stance is not reserved solely for the state, but is also found with regard to other external interlocutors. As we have already argued in chapter 4, feminist antiglobalization activists have criticized several social movements for perpetuating some forms of oppression even as they attempt to overturn others. Some strands of feminism are accused of reproducing racist and imperialist hierarchies; the Left is often charged with neglecting gender issues; and many of our black feminist interviewees point to the "chauvinism inside the Black movement that we face as women" (Noelci Homero, interview, Porto Alegre, January 22, 2005).

Whether oriented to the state or other social movements, this critical sensibility is seen to require, at times, a confrontational stance. Justifying this impulse, Virginia Vargas argues that there are forces "on the Left" that:

> are very difficult to negotiate with. . . . There is a tendency to perceive main, principal struggles and others that are less important, or secondary struggles. . . . [T]hose people I confront in a way that tries to change their mind. We have some very good relations with some of the women and men in the unions, but when we have to confront them, we have to confront them. (Interview, Hyderabad, January 18, 2004)

We also found an expectation of, and readiness to confront, "state aggression" (Rebecca, interview, London, June 11, 2005). Capturing this view, Pennie Quinton tells us about "the violence in Genoa [during protests against the G8 in 2001, which] made me realize that the state could be as frightening as it wanted and . . . get away with that, and therefore it was very important to challenge the state at every opportunity" (interview, London, November 10, 2004), and Lydia highlights the importance of "the use of padding and shields [when] working as a group to confront the cops" in the Wombles (interview, London, June 11, 2005). Confrontation is also seen as necessary in a more general sense, with Nadia De Mond of the World March pointing out: "it is not enough to be in the UN conferences in Beijing and elsewhere and have nice declarations; you need to have women on the streets to have the relationship of power, the force, to implement it" (interview, Paris, November 14, 2004).

In addition to this critical, sometimes confrontational, stance, we detected a second principle at work in the external mode of action, in the form of a *multilateralist* approach. This hinges on the assumption that change on any given issue requires the participation of multiple actors across society and the effort to build bridges and make connections between them.[3] Such an imperative to be outward facing and open to others explains the priority afforded by feminist antiglobalization activists to networking with other social movement actors, a process that is discussed in chapter 8 in more detail. Indeed, our findings on this resonate with feminist claims about the increasing centrality in contemporary movement organizing of a coalitional model of politics,[4] involving an effort to sustain multiple linkages with forces for change around shared goals and convergent identities (e.g., Moraga and Anzaldúa 1983; Reagon 1998).

In this way, a critical stance toward state and interstate institutions is tempered by a belief in the necessity of engagement. As Sonia Corrêa of DAWN puts it: "it is important that we say institutions are a problem, but the challenges we face in the world cannot be faced without institutions, no way" (interview, Rio de Janeiro, January 10, 2005). Similarly, Jacqueline Pitanguy of CEPIA declares that it is "important . . . to have a strong, vocal, organized civil society, able to have an interlocution with the government, and to make criticisms but also proposals and positive demands" (interview, Rio de Janeiro, January 12, 2005). While particularly strong in Brazil, this multilateralist discourse with respect to the state can also be found elsewhere. Joanna Hoare of NextGENDERation in London, for instance, reflects that "if you don't engage with the powers that be, and you just put yourself in this place where you refuse to have anything to do with the larger political economy and with the state, then how are you ever going to be heard?" (interview, London, November 18, 2004). Of course, any such interaction with state institutions is likely to be undertaken in a highly strategic manner.

Thus Nadia De Mond draws our attention to the World March's differentiated approach to the United Nations and to the World Bank in 2000: "it was not a dialogue—well, it was a dialogue with the United Nations, and with the World Bank it was a denunciation of their policies" (interview, Paris, November 14, 2004). In all, we are left with the picture of an approach to the external mode of action that combines both a critical stance and a multilateralist impulse in context-specific and careful ways.

CONCLUSION

Asking what feminist antiglobalization activists are fighting for, this chapter has argued that we should think about activist visions of the future in terms of a utopian imagination. We followed feminist theorists in suggesting that this imagination must be treated as situated (in the sense of being both embedded and embodied), universal (in intent and in its effort to seek agreement), and practical in orientation (providing principles for action or an ethos).

What does this utopian imagination look like with respect to feminist antiglobalization activists? In the first part of the chapter, we pointed to their diverse concrete proposals, which are embedded in feminist and Left ideologies and national contexts and which speak to and from the lives of particular groups of women. Such diversity is valued in itself by activists, as an essential aspect of an alternative world order. These proposals, however, are nonetheless bounded, gaining their coherence from a commitment to shared ethical goals. These ethical goals were discussed in the second part of the chapter. Taken together, we suggested that they amount to what we called gender justice, an ethical vision that seeks the structural transformation of underlying systems of oppression in the form of patriarchy, neoliberalism, and racism. In the third and final part of the chapter, we outlined the ethos of feminist antiglobalization activists, demonstrating that how they behave is as normatively driven as why they mobilize in the first place. In the next chapter, on movement practices, we will explore the ways in which this ethos underpins the range of activities that feminist antiglobalization activists undertake.

NOTES

1. See, e.g., McKenna 2001; Sandoval 1995: 220; Bartky 1995: 190; Miles 1996: 142; Hierro 1994: 174; Bouchier 1979.
2. We cannot be certain that feminist groups originated this change of slogan. Interviewee Sian Sullivan claims she first saw the phrase "at a squat party in London,

after the Paris European Social Forum, called 'Reclaim the Future' partly . . . on the theme of the Reclaim the Streets events," i.e., not an overtly feminist event (interview, London, November 4, 2004).

3. In addition to the postures of confrontation and multilateralism, our activists reserve the right of withdrawal. In other words, they may seek, if temporarily, to turn their backs on external interlocutors and organize autonomously, building their own, alternative institutions. This can be seen vividly in more anarchist-influenced groups, in what Sarah Bracke describes as the "autonomous spirit" of NextGENDERation (interview, Dublin, July 10, 2004), for example, and in Women Speak Out events that, "in a true spirit of DIY autonomy . . . take place in [a] squatted building. . . . The result is a free, independent event, creatively and collectively controlled, shaped and shared" (Women Speak Out n.d.).

4. See, e.g., Albrecht and Brewer 1990; Sandoval 1995; Sudbury 1998: ch. 6; Bystydzienski and Schacht 2001; Fowlkes 1997; Lyschaug 2006.

7

Collective Action

The Political Practices of Feminist Antiglobalization Activists

There is a little phrase I like very much that says: "together we can do what alone we can only dream of." (Greice Cerqueira, interview, Amsterdam, December 22, 2004)

Having examined in the previous chapter what feminist antiglobalization activists are fighting for, we now turn our attention to the different ways that they are struggling to bring about this social transformation. This chapter asks, then, what it is that feminist antiglobalization activists do?

Feminist scholarship has shown that women's and feminist activism takes multiple forms, occurs in various sites, and addresses a range of interlocutors. So Cheryl Hercus tells us that an analysis of feminist "doing" needs to look at "more than the usual activities associated with being an activist, that is, organizing and/or attending protests or rallies, signing petitions and so on," and examine in addition "a myriad of actions taken in daily life" (2005: 11–12). Julia Sudbury agrees, pointing to the "invisible activism" of black women's organizations within the community and the family, as well as to their interaction with "power brokers" at the local, national, and global levels (1998: ch. 3). The "unobtrusive" mobilization of feminists within institutions like the church and the military is highlighted by Mary Fainsod Katzenstein (1990, 2003) while Lee Ann Banaszack, Karen Beckwith, and Dieter Rucht (2003) show how feminists in several countries have adapted their activities in the context of neoliberal restructuring, institutionalizing in order to make more effective demands upon the state. What we take overall from these diverse accounts is that a feminist approach to movement action must be open-minded about what such action looks like and where to find it. For this reason, in what follows we deploy the concept of "political practice," by which we simply mean the "act of doing something repeatedly" (Keck and Sikkink 1998: 35) in order to achieve political goals. In contrast to the notion of strategy, which, as we mentioned in chapter 6, has been critiqued as overly instrumental and rationalist, political practice is agnostic and does not prejudge what counts as political activity.

Our ensuing analysis of what feminist antiglobalization activists do identifies six different kinds of political practices, namely protest, advocacy, knowledge production, service provision, popular education, and movement building. Although there are context-specific variations in the ways these practices are pursued and in their prevalence, it is our argument that they all share the ethos outlined in the previous chapter. In what follows, we discuss each of these practices in turn, situating them along a spectrum from externally to internally oriented modes of action. Thus, we start with protest, which is directed primarily toward the state, and end with interviewee efforts to build organizations and network with each other.

PROTEST

Feminist antiglobalization activists participate in a range of what social movement scholar Sidney Tarrow calls "conventional" protest actions, which he defines as relatively institutionalized forms of protest that fall within the law (1998: ch. 6). Such actions may target the state or the wider public and deploy a variety of methods, although Tarrow emphasizes the "organized public demonstration" (1998: 93). One group that has coordinated creative demonstrations on a global scale is the World March of Women. This group launched itself as an international actor with a yearlong campaign of demonstrations against poverty and violence across 100 countries, culminating in a mass mobilization on October 17, 2000, in New York that was accompanied by meetings with high-ranking officials from the World Bank and the IMF and in which a petition of over 5 million signatures was presented (see World March of Women n.d.b). In order to promote their new "Charter for Humanity," four years later, the World March organized a world relay of the document, along with a "global solidarity quilt." The relay ended at noon on October 17, 2004, when "women in every time zone . . . unite[d] in one hour of collective action as part of the 24 hours of global feminist solidarity" (World March of Women 2004a).

More localized efforts at mass street protest are widespread in our data and include the procession opposing sexual violence organized by the World March of Women in the Youth Camp at the World Social Forums in 2003 and 2005, as described in chapter 2; the regular contribution of the Global Women's Strike (2003: 1–2) to a picket at Parliament Square in London against the Iraq war; and Code Pink's colorful antiwar interventions in the United States. Remembering one such demonstration, a Code Pink participant described the following:

> There was one march where they found out the route . . . , got a room in a building that was along the . . . way, on one of the upper floors, and hung a huge pink slip, a piece of clothing, but it symbolizes . . . "you are fired." And it said some anti-Bush, anti-Rumsfeld thing on it. [T]here are 500,000 people on the march and they turn the corner and they see this pink slip, which is Code Pink. And it is a way to get the message to a broader public. Absolute creativity. They think about every situation and how they can have the most visibility and the most fun. (Anonymous interviewee, Porto Alegre, January 26, 2005)

Another type of conventional protest action, albeit one not explored by Tarrow, is the vigil. To protest against the war in Iraq, which was then pending, Code Pink held vigils in front of the White House every day from November 2002 until Women's Day, March 2003, when thousands of people encircled the house dressed in pink slips and ball gowns (anonymous interviewee, Porto Alegre, January 27, 2005). Women in Black in London continue at the time of writing to hold silent vigils against the war and other conflicts every week, a practice repeated around the world by other Women in Black groups (Women in Black n.d.b; Women in Black UK n.d.b).

Finally, feminist antiglobalization protesters also engage in a range of what Tarrow calls "disruptive" tactics, aimed at obstructing the routines of both opponents and bystanders and including innovative acts of civil disobedience that deliberately break the law (della Porta and Diani 2006: 181; Tarrow 1998: ch. 6).[1] In this vein, Mahila Jagruthi's opposition to the hosting of the Miss World pageant in India inspired them to "beautify . . . with cow dung and black paint" the offices of the multinational company sponsoring the event, an act for which sixteen activists were imprisoned (Sushma, interview, Mumbai, January 17, 2004). Another example is the action organized by Women Speak Out on International Women's Day in 2002 outside Holloway women's prison in London. Armed with drums, whistles, spoons, plates, and shakers of dried lentils, about twenty activists made a fearsome din to express both their opposition to the "growing numbers of working class women being imprisoned for crimes of poverty" and their solidarity with the female prisoners inside, also blocking a van containing women prisoners from entering the prison gates (Women Speak Out 2002; see also Schnews 2002). Or take Code Pink's commitment to "nonviolent civil disobedience" (Starhawk 2002a) as "a way of being a very squeaky wheel" in a tightly controlled media machine (Kricorian n.d.). Deploying only a few activists, dressed all in pink, this organization made itself heard at the U.S. National Republican Convention in 2004 three nights in a row, with one woman standing on her chair, waving a banner and screaming at President Bush to end the occupation of Iraq. Arrest and media coverage followed (Kricorian n.d.).

Although we found protest deployed as a political practice by groups across national sites, we were particularly struck by the distinctive ways it was enacted in the Indian context. Demonstrations and marches in India are often on a huge scale, with the All-India Democratic Women's Association (AIDWA) galvanizing as many as 50,000 protestors against the privatization of electricity and consequent price rises in the summer of 2000 (AIDWA n.d.a). Moreover, we note that some of the associated tactics are particularly confrontational. One form of protest that we found to be unique to our Indian activists is *geraoing*, which involves laying siege to the offices of public officials in order to demand a hearing. As Subhashini Ali of AIDWA explains, "we surround the particular office and we won't let the officials leave until they have heard us" (interview, Mumbai, January 10, 2004). In addition, AIDWA also organizes collective actions to retrieve dowries and stop coerced reconciliations between wives and husbands (Karat and Sangwan, n.d.).

The protest actions that we have described here are all oriented to external actors and predominantly to agencies of the state. In fact, even when protest actions are performed for the public, they are often intended to call the state to account and to force it to respond. Ali expresses this view when she insists on "pressurizing the central government to change its policies by . . . big mobilizations and making this an issue among the people. See if something becomes an electoral issue with a strong backing, then it might get heard" (interview, Mumbai, January 10, 2004). In terms of the ethos discussed in the last chapter, it is our view that feminist efforts to take the state to task, whether through conventional protest or more disruptive actions, reflect their awareness of its complicity in the perpetuation of oppression. This critical sensibility can be seen in the efforts of the Global Women's Strike to get the British government to pull out of the Iraq war and in the intention behind the Women Speak Out protest at Holloway to highlight state incarceration of women. Indeed, of all the practices on the spectrum discussed in this chapter, protest is the most confrontational toward the state. After all, the *geraoing* of elected representatives in India and the interventions of Code Pink in the United States put women's bodies in the way of state authorities and involve overt defiance of the law as well as of the norms of polite conduct. As we shall see below, however, activities targeting the state are not always confrontational in orientation.

ADVOCACY

Turning to a second way in which feminist antiglobalization activists interact with the state, we found that a large number of them in all four of the national contexts in which we conducted our fieldwork pursue advocacy as a central practice. In its conventional sense, advocacy simply means efforts to "persuade, pressure and gain leverage over much more powerful organizations and governments" (Keck and Sikkink 1998: 2). The methods deployed to gain this leverage can include lobbying and litigation as well as participation in the formulation and monitoring of state policies.

One group that engages in all these aspects of advocacy is the Centro Feminista de Estudos e Assessoria (CFEMEA) in Brazil. Based in the capital, Brasilia, this feminist NGO tracks government legislation and in particular the budgetary process, with a view to incorporating gender and race into its calculations and to making it more democratic and accountable (CFEMEA n.d.). More concretely, CFEMEA works on an ongoing basis with representatives of the Brazilian Congress, especially those of the Women's Group and the Budget Commission, and testimony to its influence is the parliamentary commission on maternal mortality set up in response to the group's campaign in 2000 on this issue (International Women's Health Coalition 2008). In addition to lobbying government on legislative issues to do with gender, CFEMEA spends much of its time researching the impact of government legislation. In 2005 it carried out a comprehensive review of the annual budget law, compiled the results, and published them in its journal, which was then distributed widely to policymakers. As a result, a series of discussions with the Ministry of Health took place and affirmative action measures were introduced (UNIFEM Gender Responsive Budgeting 2005).

CFEMEA is not alone in its advocacy efforts, as a majority of the Brazilian core groups listed in textbox 1.1, chapter 1, undertake this practice. Thus, CRIOLA in Rio de Janeiro "organized a seminar . . . with the [Federal] Health Ministry on the black population's health. . . . One of the outcomes . . . was the drawing up of public policy in relation to that and also the Health Ministry organized a committee of which CRIOLA is a part" (Lúcia Xavier, interview, Rio de Janeiro, January 12, 2005). "Together with the mayor, the town hall and the human rights department" in Porto Alegre, Coletivo Feminino Plural has "developed a public policy" on child trafficking (Nelia Tegrão, interview, Porto Alegre, January 22, 2005). Sempreviva Organização Feminista (SOF), based in São Paulo, does "articulation [networking] with the government and talking to deputies to change legislation, national and local" including "consulting for the ministry that develops work in the countryside" (Nalu Faria, interview, São Paulo, January 17, 2005). The prevalence of advocacy in Brazil is unsurprising given the democratization process of the 1980s. Indeed, a number of the Brazilian groups in textbox 1.1 became involved in the constitutional review process at the end of the decade with the express purpose of ensuring that women's rights were written into the new constitution, and many have retained a focus on changing legislation ever since.

This level of engagement with advocacy contrasts with what we found in India, where, as we discussed in chapter 6, more overtly antistatist attitudes are evident. Here a number of core groups share the views of the Forum against the Oppression of Women, which is "adamantly opposed to working with the state" (Ray 1999: 135). Nonetheless, despite being less likely overall than their Brazilian colleagues to collaborate extensively with state organs and representatives, we do find some exceptions. The National Federation of Indian Women (NFIW), for example, pushes for legislative change on issues of rape, family law, and economic policy, in part through the activities of affiliated parliamentarians (Amarjeet Kaur, interview, Mumbai, January 20, 2004). Some NGOs, both in and beyond our core group sample, have worked as consultants, as in the participation of the Deccan Development Society in a World Bank feedback session (interview, Rukmini Rao, Hyderabad, January 6, 2004). In fact, the Andhra Pradesh Mahila Samatha Society (APMSS) has its roots in a government program to enhance women's education, although it is now constitutionally independent (Mahila Samakhya Uttar Pradesh n.d.).

We also found advocacy to be an important part of feminist antiglobalization activism at the transnational level. As discussed in chapter 4, WEDO (Women's Environment and Development Organization) played a crucial role in the UN Conference on Environment and Development in 1992, organizing the World Women's Congress for a Healthy Planet and subsequently drafting Women's Action Agenda 21. This was to become the benchmark for feminist lobbying efforts in the official negotiations of the Rio Declaration (WEDO n.d.b). Similarly, DAWN (Development Alternatives with Women for a New Era) became a central protagonist, alongside WEDO, in feminist advocacy at the UN Conference on Population and Development two years later (see Stienstra 2000: 214–17). The outcome of this conference has been seen by many feminists as a success because of its emphasis on women's rights rather than population control (e.g., Smyth 1998; Petchesky 2003: 35–50).

With regard to the ethos described in the previous chapter, advocacy, by definition, involves a multilateralist stance toward the state. Whether in the form of the collaboration of Coletivo Feminino Plural with the government of Porto Alegre with regard to child trafficking or of the parliamentary representatives affiliated to the NFIW pushing for policy changes on rape, there is an assumption that engagement with state institutions and actors in specific instances, on specific issues, should be actively pursued.

Nonetheless, a critical analysis of the state as a site and source of oppression also remains evident in the advocacy practices of our interviewees. Rukmini Rao, for instance, tells us that the Deccan Development Society may work with the Indian government and the World Bank, but that it also recognizes that the two institutions are closely intertwined, that they are incompetent, and that their interests are not aligned with those of her organization: "The Bank is interested not because of the poor but because they are under pressure to put their money out into rural development, that's my analysis . . . they will try anything. But we are opposed to the way the government does things always, we are forced to because they do things so badly" (interview, Hyderabad, January 6, 2004). Even core groups in Brazil that prioritize advocacy recognize their interlocutor to be embedded within and reproducing wider structures of oppression and thus in need of structural reform. So while the Instituto Eqüit argues for the need to "reassert the sovereign right and responsibility of nation states to determine their own development agenda," it also seeks "systems of governance, at the global, regional and national levels that are democratic, transparent, accountable and respectful of human rights" (Instituto Eqüit n.d.). CFEMEA also adopts this critical stance, as can be seen by the fact that it not only lobbies the state, but also monitors its policies, and participates in large-scale campaigns to apply pressure from below: "We always keep an eye on the budget . . . [and] we are involved with the movement. . . . We participate in many networks . . . [and] national campaigns" (Guacira Oliveira, Porto Alegre, January 26, 2005). This skeptical approach explains Nadia De Mond's refusal to describe the interactions of the World March with international institutions as lobbying, with its overtones of pleading for the attention of a savior. "And that is not what we want. We want to say, 'Hey, here we are!'" (interview, Paris, November 14, 2003)—to demand action from states and interstate institutions and to force them to change.

Shifting to their relations with their internal constituency, feminist antiglobalization activists adhere to both dialogical and participatory principles in their advocacy practices. Evidence of this can be found in the efforts of our interviewees to enable women to speak *for themselves* in the public sphere, as opposed to speaking on their behalf. Examples of this trend abound, particularly in India. The Deccan Development Society, for instance, took rural women to London in 2002, where they presented a damning report on the agricultural policies of Andhra Pradesh to the British Parliament. Explaining the thinking behind this strategy, Rukmini Rao states, "if we can provide an opportunity, very poor women can articulate and can voice their views for themselves . . . in the global arena" (interview, Hyderabad, January 6, 2004). Pursuing a similar strategy at the local level, Rao has also pushed for the establishment of women's committees tasked with settling family and marriage disputes. As she elaborates,

I have trained these women, a committee of women. They go to the husband's village, they sit with the elders, they sit with the husband, they settle the disputes there. If they want to sort it out and go back home, or if the women don't want to go back because the man is often an alcoholic and may beat them, then we get a settlement. If the man has land, then he has to give the wife or children land or he gives cash compensation. The matter is settled on the ground, by the village women and villagers. (Interview, Hyderabad, January 6, 2004)

In this way, rural women are encouraged and trained to negotiate directly with the power brokers in their own communities.

A similar example is provided by APMSS, also in India, which organizes women and teenagers into collective pressure groups, or *sanghams*, to push for specific changes. After receiving training on a range of issues pertaining to health, discrimination at work, food supplies, women's rights, children's rights, and the local political system, women in these *sanghams* are encouraged to vocalize their needs and to take them up with local elites in their own ways (APMSS n.d.; A. Padma, interview, Hyderabad, January 8, 2004). This practice thus exemplifies the aspiration to enable women to speak in their own voices; it also illustrates the principle of fostering participation, in the sense of enabling them to devise and pursue their own agendas. After all, APMSS claims that the women participating in the *sanghams* should "determine the form, nature, content and timing of all activities in their village. Planning decision-making, and evaluative process are accountable to the collective. . . . Project functionaries . . . are facilitative and not directive" (APMSS n.d.).

KNOWLEDGE PRODUCTION

Knowledge production is not only an important practice among feminist antiglobalization activists in its own right, it also plays an essential role in sustaining other practices, including advocacy. We define knowledge production as involving three processes: (a) developing critical studies of existing data as well as undertaking original research; (b) gathering, classifying, and housing primary and secondary sources in the form of documentation centers and libraries; and (c) disseminating this knowledge through the publication of regular newsletters and journals and through public awareness campaigns.

The production and analysis of research is prevalent across all national contexts, although its intended audience may vary in different places. Thus, while in Brazil we found that our core groups direct their research primarily to state officials and servants of the state (e.g., police, social workers, teachers), in India the main aim appears to be to educate the wider public and social movements. One interesting example of the latter is provided by Akshara. Describing itself as "a women's resource centre . . . which believes in the power of the word, in the right to information and in its use as a tool for the transformation of individuals and society" (Akshara n.d.), Akshara produces low-cost pamphlets that seek to inform a wide array of external movements about the key issues, debates, and campaigns shaping women's activism (Akshara n.d.; Naari Today 2001; Indianchild n.d.). Transnational networks also engage in research, with DAWN particularly notable in this regard. In her interview, member Peggy Antrobus explained to us how, through a series of regional workshops, they gather statements from a range of women about their experiences. These perspectives are then discussed by other women who offer critiques "in terms of their own experience, their own region," prior to the holding of an interregional workshop from which "the final analysis comes" (interview, Dublin, July 10, 2004). As discussed in chapter 4, DAWN's research statements (e.g., Sen and Grown 1987) have been highly influential in shifting the transnational feminist agenda toward one that is more critical of economic orthodoxy and more inclusive of southern concerns, and they continue to use their research as the basis of lobbying external interlocutors at interstate conferences and at social movement events like the World Social Forum (e.g., Corrêa 2003).

Gathering, classifying, and housing primary and secondary sources in the form of documentation centers and libraries is another important aspect of knowledge production. To this end, Akshara has run a women's movement library in Mumbai since 1995 (Indianchild n.d.), while Flora Tristán: Centro de la Mujer Peruana (n.d.c) has established a resource center in Lima. Connected to this effort to bring together already published material on subjects of relevance and interest, a few of our core groups are engaged in a fascinating mission to retrieve the past voices of women and feminists that would otherwise be lost to the historical record. Two examples of such a search and rescue mission are the project of Rede de Desenvolvimento Humano titled Women—500 Years Hiding behind the Scenes, which aims to document the history of Brazilian women over the centuries (REDEH n.d.d), and the work of Hyderabadi NGO Asmita to uncover the forgotten poetry and stories of long-dead women writers who challenged gender hierarchies (Kalpana Kannabiran, interview, Hyderabad, January 10, 2004).

Turning to the dissemination of information, this is a principal aim for many feminist antiglobalization groups and, indeed, the main raison d'être of transnational networks like Women Living Under Muslim Laws (WLUML) and the Women's Global Network for Reproductive Rights (WGNRR). There are at least two ways in which dissemination is undertaken.[2] The first is through the publication of newsletters. The triannual newsletter distributed by the WGNRR systematizes, distills, and makes available information received from its members so that it can be of wider political use. In so doing, the WGNRR seeks to "ensure that different regions and organizations are represented. . . . We especially encourage grassroots organizations to contribute to the platform and increase its visibility and attract potential allies and partners" (WGNRR n.d.c). The central office does not enforce a strict editorial line on contributions, instead allowing groups to represent their own agendas, as is illustrated by their handling of the prostitution versus sex work debate:

> we have a disclaimer, so anyone can say what they want and take any position they want. . . . [W]e as a network have to help them get connected and get them to discuss why they are using the term prostitute [for example] and not sex worker. . . . [W]e have to take a very global view because there are many differences and very many approaches to the same problem. (Mariana Mozdzer, interview, Amsterdam, October 19, 2004)

A second way in which information is distributed is through public awareness campaigns. Consider, for example, the Campaign against Fundamentalism, one of the major contributions of Articulación Feminista Marcosur (AFM) to the World Social Forum, as described in chapters 2 and 3. Immensely creative and high in impact, this campaign has involved screenings of short films, a hot air balloon launch, and the distribution of distinctive red-lipped mouth masks with the slogan "Your mouth: fundamental against fundamentalism" (see AFM n.d.). Another example is provided by the WGNRR's Women's Access to Health Campaign, which was launched on May 28, 2003, together with the People's Health Movement and which has issued a call for action focused on

> access to proper health care, reproductive and sexual rights and reproductive options, and freedom from sexual violence. The Call for Action is intended to promote mobilizations on May 28th, which has been named the International Day of Action for Women's Health, and to educate and spark action and organizing until women worldwide have access to adequate health care and reproductive self-determination. (WGNRR 2007)

In terms of the ethos underpinning the diverse ways in which knowledge is produced and disseminated, we can see a number of the principles outlined in chapter 6 at play. When information is produced for and used to lobby external interlocutors, whether states or other movements, it is clearly informed by a multilateralist impulse to engage with others in order to effect change. Campaigns like that of AFM at the World Social Forum, or DAWN's activities aimed at persuading UN negotiators to take on board a critical analysis of the impact of neoliberalism on women in the South, are born out of a belief that feminist antiglobalization activism must seek to engage with and persuade others in order to build support for social transformation. Conversely, when information is produced among and for the internal constituency of feminist antiglobalization activists and women, the principle of fostering participation is evoked. As we have shown, the process by which DAWN produces its reports entails the active involvement of women from around the global South, while the WGNRR newsletters are mouthpieces for the views of network members rather than of the editor with members allowed to pursue their own agendas without central direction.

SERVICE PROVISION

Although not a particularly prevalent practice among feminist antiglobalization activists, we were told of several initiatives to provide services that aimed at improving women's life chances and quality of life. These can be grouped, broadly, into material provision and psychological counseling, both of which can take a variety of forms. With regard to the former, we found on offer economic aid, medical help, and advice and support for women facing violence. Thus, Phoenix in Hyderabad provides the resources and training for a chutney-making cooperative of poor women (interview with Mahe Jabeen, Hyderabad, January 7, 2004), while the Deccan Development Society has set up "seed banks" in villages that enable subsistence farmers to have an alternative source of seed from those supplied by multinational corporations (Rukmini Rao, interview, Hyderabad, January 6, 2004). In Brazil, CRIOLA has for several years supported an annual festival celebrating Afro-Brazilian health and culture by "organis[ing] professionals in different areas who make themselves available for public consultations about women's health and preventative self-care" (CRIOLA n.d.) It is perhaps not surprising, given the relative economic deprivation of these countries, that the provision of material services in terms of economic and medical aid is more prevalent in Brazil and India than in France or the UK.

Services in response to violence against women, however, are provided in all four fieldwork contexts. Talking about what drove her to set up a self-governing women's shelter during the early years of her feminist activism, Rukmini Rao told us:

> after two or three years, we thought, what are we doing? Every time a woman dies we jump up and down and want the police to investigate but the woman is already dead. So our group of friends, we wanted to make a place where women can actually come and have an option to survive. . . . We set up an office, and decided to take people home. . . . [But] it was not very practical, so to help them survive we set up a shelter . . . in the slum . . . managed by . . . women who were very poor. (Interview, Hyderabad, January 6, 2004)

Rao has continued this work within the Deccan Development Society, which has "set up a shelter for women in distress" (interview, Hyderabad, January 6, 2004). To take another example, the Black Women's Rape Action Project (part of the Global Women's Strike and based in London) offers "support and advice to Black women and other women of colour, immigrant and refugee women, who have suffered rape, sexual assault or other violence" (Women against Rape n.d.). Maria Mulher, working with black women in Porto Alegre, gives "legal assistance [for victims of violence] . . . and then we sometimes forward them, direct them, to other places that we know can shelter them" (Noelci Homero, interview, Porto Alegre, January 22, 2005). Another group in Porto Alegre, Themis, runs a hotline that informs women facing violence of their rights and refers them to appropriate services (Themis n.d.a), as well as training women from local communities to give legal advice in situ. Known as *promotores legais popularis* (popular legal promoters, or PLPs), these women set up weekly "offices" in public spaces to dispense help and support to women facing violence or other problems and to liaise with the police and other authorities (Themis n.d.b).

In addition to services aimed at improving the material conditions of women—whether economic aid or the provision of shelters and helplines—several of our core groups offer psychological assistance. So Maria Mulher mobilizes a team of social workers, psychologists, educators, and nurses to give counseling to women who have suffered violence (Noelci Homero, interview, Porto Alegre, January 22, 2005). Also in Brazil, Umas e Outras has sought to build self-esteem among lesbian women: "This is our principal action because this is very difficult. The parties and other people don't care about this sort of thing, it is secondary. But it is not. We believe that when we are strong we can fight against anything" (Fernanda Elias, interview, São Paulo, January 19, 2005). To this end, the organization has invited psychologists and counselors to its meetings as well as facilitated self-help groups and participated in Gay Pride events (Umas e Outras 2003, n.d.). Women Speak Out in the UK has held a range of workshops on subjects as varied as racism, herbalism, and self-defense at events intended to offer a safe space for women to meet and share their feelings. As one participant writes, "I leave Women Speak Out gatherings feeling energized, relaxed, powerful and magical, and not alone in [my] thoughts" (Women Speak Out 2001a).

All of the examples above, in our view, point to the holistic, dialogical, and participatory principles underpinning service provision. The combination of material and psychological services in itself demonstrates a holistic sensibility by targeting the effects of and interconnections between material inequality, bodily damage, and emotional suffering. And far from expecting women to be passive recipients of services, the groups involved aim rather to enable women to articulate their own concerns and devise their own solutions. The shelters that Rukmini Rao has had a hand in establishing, for example, are intended to become self-governing, controlled by the women of the community. And the Themis program of establishing PLPs aims not only to provide legal assistance to women in the community but also to facilitate their independent action and capacity to speak for themselves:

> through this program . . . they [the PLPs] will be much more powerful and empowered to negotiate their own relationship at home and to be able to go to the policeman and say, "Yes, you have to fill in this application of this woman who is being battered by her husband," and they won't be quiet when the man in the police station says it does not matter. (Virginia Feix, interview, Porto Alegre, January 22, 2005)

POPULAR EDUCATION

Although popular education, as a concept, draws on the language of the Brazilian educationalist Paolo Freire and is most frequently invoked in his home country, the practice itself is pervasive across our fieldwork sites. Defined by the Indian group APMSS as "[c]onscientisation, the process of becoming aware of one's own self and reality and building on this awareness to grow and change" (Bhaiya and Menon-Sen 1996: 9), popular education can be understood as a form of educational outreach that seeks to target "ordinary" or "grassroots" women in the community.

So what do our interviewees teach in their popular education programs? From our research, it seem that their curricula revolve around social critique, practical skills, and self-esteem. In terms of the first, the main aim is to encourage women to explore the ways in which patriarchy, racism, and neoliberal globalization intersect to shape their life chances. This mandate is summarized by interviewee Monica Maher in her description of a workshop organized by the Brazilian wing of the Grail movement of Catholic women at the World Social Forum:

> The point was to look at the forces of globalization at the grassroots level on women's lives . . . that is, where gender fits in. So women spoke about these forces . . . war, poverty . . . militarism . . . rape as a weapon of war. . . . [I]t was like an analysis and then what do we do in response? (Interview, Porto Alegre, January 29, 2005)

One striking example from India of popular education oriented to social critique can be seen in the mass *jatras* (fairs) organized by Asmita in rural Andhra Pradesh. Bringing together thousands of poor, illiterate, rural women under tents for a day long teach-in, these events provide such women with a chance to discuss a range of issues, from violence to ill health, that affect their lives and to learn about their legal rights in the Indian context (Kalpana Kannabiran, interview, Hyderabad, January 10, 2004). On a much smaller scale, in Brazil, Fala Preta! offers workshops to black women addressing issues around gender and human rights. The approach taken to these training sessions is to "respect the culture and the comprehension that these people have about life and about themselves" but also to "introduc[e] the content that they don't have," namely research that demonstrates that "the people that suffer most are black women" (Glaucia Matos, interview, São Paulo, January 18, 2005). In France, interviewee Christiane Marty of the feminist caucus in ATTAC, told us that her group had begun to work with WIDE (Women in Development Europe) to develop strategies for encouraging "economic literacy." In addition:

> we really want to develop our popular education, so we [have] contacted this group called Ni Putes Ni Soumises [Neither Whores Nor Victims], it's a network of young women from the suburbs, girls from immigrant groups and child[ren] of immigrants, they are very active and we would like to work together. . . . We haven't begun yet but we want to go into the suburbs and organize meetings . . . to discuss economic education, the impact of [neo]liberal politics on the situation of unemployment, on [job] precariousness for them, to make clear the links with globalization. (Christiane Marty, interview, Paris, November 15, 2003)

Popular education initiatives seek, second, to impart practical skills to women. APMSS, for instance, helps women gain social and economic independence and lessens their workload by teaching them to read, fix water pumps, and build their own homes (Bhaiya and Menon-Sen 1996: 48–49); CRIOLA (n.d.) organizes classes in needlework and silk screening in order to provide women with self-employment opportunities; CEMINA (Communicação, Educação e Informação em Gênero) trains women in radio broadcasting to enable them to make and disseminate programs about women's issues (CEMINA n.d.a, n.d.b); and Coletivo Feminino Plural runs a "smart girls" project that helps young girls from the most violent areas of Porto Alegre to create their own webpages on subjects of their choice (Telia Negrão, interview, Porto Alegre, January 22, 2005). Moreover, several groups listed in textbox 1.1, particularly (although not exclusively) transnational networks, also run practical training workshops oriented toward the development of leadership skills. The Association for Women's Rights in Development, under the auspices of its Young Feminist Activism Program, gives intensive classes to a small group of young women on a range of subjects, from the workings of the UN to effective lobbying techniques (AWID 2008). The Centre for Women's Global Leadership delivers a similar program on advocacy at the UN to twenty-five students a year in a two-week residential course (CWGL n.d.b) and, in 2005, DAWN followed suit by running its first leadership training institute in Africa (Peggy Antrobus, interview, Dublin, July 10, 2004; DAWN n.d.b).[3]

Third, popular education interventions address issues of self-awareness and self-esteem, in ways that chime with the arguments about service provision made above. As Vera Viera of the Brazilian group Rede Mulher states, "If you don't work on self-esteem in women you cannot do anything more. . . . This is the first thing you need to work on" (interview, São Paulo, January 18, 2005). Concrete examples in our data include the summer camps run by the Dutch-based International Free Women's Federation, which seek to give migrant women and their children "the opportunity to experience their strengths and abilities . . . to gain experiences that they can't gain within their ordinary lives" (Ann-Kristin Kowarsch, interview, London, October 16, 2004). To this end, participants are encouraged to identify topics for seminar discussions and to participate in both cultural and sporting events. In addition, the International Free Women's Federation organizes workshops that challenge what they see as an entrenched connection between women's lack of self-confidence and prevailing representations of beauty. Similarly CRIOLA holds sessions titled Obinrin Odara ("beautiful woman" in Yoruba), which celebrate "an afro-Brazilian aesthetic" and provide training in hair and body care techniques that "aim[s] to strengthen the identity and raise the self esteem of black women, adolescents and girls" (CRIOLA n.d.).

Having discussed the content of the popular education initiatives of feminist antiglobalization activists, we now want to consider the pedagogical techniques that they deploy. The use of testimonials that provide ordinary women with the opportunity to share their experiences is one such technique, particularly evident at the World Social Forum in Mumbai, as described in chapter 3. We also found a range of other creative, aesthetic methods that are used to generate and impart knowledge. So Nalu Faria of SOF, for instance, described to us how in their self-esteem and sexuality workshops they "use collages a lot, [and] bring lots of magazines so women can cut them up." They also use clay: "Each person models her own body with her eyes closed" (interview, São Paulo, January 17, 2005). To take examples from India, Kalpana Kannabiran told us how the *jatras* run by Asmita, described above, make extensive use of songs, hand-painted posters, and storytelling in their outreach work with rural women (interview, Hyderabad, January 10, 2004), while A. Padma of APMSS confirms that "posters, banners, audiovisual materials, as well as games" are central to their educational practice (interview, Hyderabad, January 8, 2004). Indeed, games are widely used as a teaching tool. Nandita Shah of Akshara shared with us a number of games devised by her group to teach young people about gender relations and women's rights. As she explains of one:

It's snakes and ladders, you know, the game we play as children? We made it into a ladder of a woman's life and you actually play it as a game. . . . There are things that take you up and things that bring you down—marriage and caste and what kind of support [you have] and whether you can make decisions about what you want to do, whether you work or not, [the] sexual division of labor, all is there. And then you actually have a dialogue and it's amazing. It's really fantastic. . . . Every game is followed by discussion. (Interview, Paris, September 14, 2003)

Or as A. Padma of APMSS describes:

Another game is making them hold their hands and we ask them to come out without . . . breaking the chain. . . . When a person wants to come out there is lot of resistance, lot of turbulence because they have to break these hand[holds]s, which are very strong, they have to see somewhere the gap and then they come out of there. So this is how we try to make the group think and analyze difficult issues of patriarchy, societal practices and power relations. (Interview, Hyderabad, January 8, 2004)

Moving from the content and methods of popular education to the ethos that underpins it, what comes through most strongly is a holistic approach to women. The implicit model of the learner here is one that foregrounds her emotions and body, thereby challenging the idea that knowledge is entirely rational and cognitive. When we asked Nalu Faria if the use of art in SOF workshops was a response to illiteracy among the women they were teaching, she explained to us that this was only part of the story: "We don't want to use only verbal language. Many times, people draw something that they would not speak. We don't want to repeat dichotomies like rational/emotional, objective/subjective. We want to break with . . . traditional education" (interview, São Paulo, January 17, 2005). Furthermore, there is an emphasis here on seeing women's daily lives as a source of knowledge, reinforced by a Freirian pedagogy that draws on "people's lived experiences . . . [as a] basis from which to question their positions in society" (Trapese Collective 2005: 121). The sharing of experiences necessitates an empathetic stance on the part of the listener, a nonjudgmental openness to the feelings of others, as Nancy Burrows of the World March of Women elaborates:

there is something about the pedagogy of feminism . . . that becomes so much more human. . . . When you start from your experiences there is no right or wrong. I can't tell you your experience is wrong. I can't tell you, you didn't feel what you were telling me you were feeling. You have to listen in order to get into the debate. (Interview, Paris, September 14, 2003)

Participatory and dialogical principles also inform popular education practices. In terms of the former, we can see an active and inclusive approach to knowledge generation in which women share their diverse experiences and try to develop a broader framework to make sense of them. Burrows puts it this way: "one of the strengths . . . of feminism is going from . . . personal reality and then . . . building shared analysis as well" (interview, Paris, November 14, 2003). In terms of the latter, whether feminist popular education sessions take the form of game playing or emotional testimonials, they are predicated on women talking about their experiences, listening to each other, and being open to debate. In this context, the role of the teacher is, in general, conceived as that of a moderator of dialogue and as a participant in a learning community. As APMSS claims:

> The facilitator and the learners engage as equal partners in the process of learning, which affects and changes them both. The facilitator is not seen as an expert who knows all the answers, and the learners are not "empty vessels" who know nothing. (Bhaiya and Menon-Sen 1996: 10)

MOVEMENT BUILDING

A final practice in which feminist antiglobalization activists engage on a continuous basis is what we call movement building. This involves, first, establishing and running feminist antiglobalization groups and, second, creating alliances between these groups.

In terms of the first, a large proportion of the sixty groups listed in textbox 1.1 have pursued a strategy of institutionalization.[4] In fact, we would estimate two-thirds have medium to high levels of institutionalization. By this we mean they have developed some organizational apparatus and continuity in the form of constitutions, offices, and the like; they have professional, paid staff; and there is a clear division of labor between those staff. Approximately nineteen of the sixty take the form of highly formalized, specialized organizations constituted solely by paid staff and volunteers. These groups, such as REDEH and Phoenix, have no wider membership structures and are thus entirely reliant on external funding, which is an additional driver of institutionalization.[5]

Institutionalization inevitably brings bureaucracy and hierarchy in its train, as legal statutes and funding bodies require a clear, routinized, vertical allocation of decision-making responsibilities. This is tempered, however, by the ethos of feminist antiglobalization activism with regard to the internal mode of action, in the form of a commitment to fostering participation. Thus, it was widely claimed in interviews that formal structures—"for the English," as our Brazilian interviewees put it—are combined with or supplanted by ongoing processes through which volunteers and interns are brought on board, and enabled, along with staff or board members, to actively engage in decision making. For example, at least two Brazilian groups, SOF and Themis, have very large boards of several dozen volunteer members, who periodically come together to make the most important decisions about the policies to be pursued by the paid staff (interviews with Nalu Faria and Vera Viera, São Paulo, January 2009). There is a resonance here with Kathleen Ianello's argument about the emergence of a "modified consensus model" in contemporary feminist institutions, in which "routine decisions" are delegated "to those in the organization with particular skill and knowledge. . . . But critical decisions, those that determine the overall path and goals, are retained for the entire membership and are arrived at consensually" (Ianello 1992: xii).

Of the one-third of groups in textbox 1.1 that have relatively low levels of institutionalization and more horizontal organizational forms, around thirteen, including Women Speak Out and NextGENDERation, consist of little more than active, committed people getting together in a room or online on a regular basis with little division of labor between them and no permanent organizational home. In such groups we find an explicit commitment to fully participatory democratic structures and processes in which all affected can involve themselves in decision making, on the most mundane issues as well as the most critical. Thus, Umas e Outras (2003) claims to be characterized by a "total lack of hierarchy" with decisions made in large meetings to which all members are invited. When there is significant disagreement, "we have more meetings" (Fernanda Elias interview, São Paulo, January 19, 2005). A modified consensus model is evident here too, in the sense that the typical second-wave feminist insistence on total consensus for every decision has been relaxed to allow for dissent and for individual and collective autonomy (a development that is noticeable in other movements; see Polletta 2002: chs. 7, 8). Sarah Bracke of NextGENDERation gives a vivid example of how this works in her discussion of the establishment of an internal caucus within NextGENDERation to coordinate activities for the European Social Forum:

> We had discussions about how to relate to the broader network, how to speak for NextGENDERation . . . and basically we can't because of the diffuse, nonstructure of the network. There is no structure of representativity. So we called ourselves a working group, we said, "OK, as a working group we can do this, we are not pretending to do this in the name of NextGENDERation," and we announced it on the list. . . . "There are four of us, we are going to do this, if anyone wants to join you are welcome." (Interview, Dublin, July 10, 2004)

Apart from setting up and managing their own groups, feminist antiglobalization activists also work hard at the construction of alliances with each other, as part of a much wider strategy that our Brazilian interviewees call *articulacão* (articulation) or networking. It is through networking that our interviewees are able to expand their activities horizontally, outward into society, and also vertically, in terms of making links both upward to transnational organizing and downward to the local level. Thus, Vera Viera of Rede Mulher characterizes her group's approach to networking as one in which they try to link "the local, the national, the regional, the international and we come back from there, back to the local" (interview, São Paulo, January 18, 2005). In a very similar vein, Cassandra of WLUML explains that "the idea is that these linkages are two-way, so that if there is a national group, it interacts with local, grassroots community groups" and then its analysis is "fed back up to the wider network, and the network analysis . . . is relayed back to that national organization and then hopefully made available . . . to any grassroots groups" (interview, London, November 9, 2004).

There are some notable variations in the degree and extent of networking pursued within this movement sector, however, as became evident through our mapping of the linkages between the groups listed in textbox 1.1.[6] Transnational organizations—which, importantly, are themselves usually networks composed of many groups—are the most well-connected, accounting for almost half the total number of these intergroup linkages. Further, the four transnational networks with the most connections of all, namely the World March, DAWN, AFM, and the International Gender and Trade Network (IGTN), are all prominent participants in the World Social Forum, including having an organizing role in the International Council, making their centrality in our core group sample eminently predictable. What is more surprising to us is not only that these networks collaborate extensively with each other, but also that a large proportion of all the groups listed in textbox 1.1 participate in and network with *both* the World March and the AFM, notwithstanding the differences in approach between these organizations highlighted in chapter 3. In addition, we note that groups based in Brazil are very well-connected. As well as the Brazilian emphasis on *articulacão*, the long history of regional-level feminist organizing through the Latin American *Encuentros* is key here, ensuring many of the Brazilian groups are part of regional and international networks, even if they are not particularly large or wealthy.

The least well-connected groups of our sample are from India. Although a handful, including Phoenix and AIDWA, are participants in the World March, and although the National Network of Autonomous Women's Groups was set up in India in 2004 "in response to the need to take feminist political and networking efforts beyond national organizing" (Feminist Dialogues 2006), organizations such as the Dalit Feminist Group, Mahila Jagruthi, and APMSS have few if any connections with the rest of the groups listed in chapter 1. While such groups have an ideological orientation that may discourage networking with feminists perceived as bourgeois, as is discussed more in the next chapter, it is our view that this is a less significant factor than the obvious economic and geopolitical obstacles they and other

Indian groups face in integrating into transnational networks. After all, as the president of AIDWA remarked:

> for traveling abroad and all that we don't have that kind of money at all so we are not able to go to all these international conferences and make a big splash. . . . We don't have many women that are fluent in English. We don't have many women who are computer literate, so how much work can a few people do? (Subhashini Ali, interview, Mumbai, January 20, 2004)

While there may be some hierarchies and gaps in intergroup networking, we suggest that it is still possible to detect the effect of the participatory principle here, particularly in the attempts by transnational networks to de-centralize their internal governance structures and to foster self-determina-tion among members.[7] Cassandra Balchin of the WLUML elaborates thus:

> we have a very strong principle of not dominating and controlling . . . net-working. So I will give somebody's . . . email to another friend and say, right, you get on with it . . . but don't do it through me, so that we're not here at the international office controlling people's communication because that's privileging knowledge . . . , that's controlling power. (Interview, London, No-vember 9, 2004)

Nadia Van der Linde of the WGNRR confirms this view:

> we as a network don't particularly favor one strategy or tell people to lobby their government or . . . to organize a demonstration because it is up to them. They should see what works for them and what works in their context and what works for their type of organization. . . . And we as the Coordinating Of-fice support that by providing information, by providing a platform for them to share their experiences and analyses, by providing an analysis, by having a campaign which is a way of joining people together, of mobilizing people in different forms, by creating solidarity, by showing our own solidarity, an-swering information requests, linking people together, that is what we as an office do to support them in their different strategies. (Interview, Amsterdam, October 19, 2004)

CONCLUSION

This chapter set out to investigate what it is that feminist antiglobalization activists do. Framing our discussion in terms of political practice, we have mapped six different types of activities along an external to internal spec-trum, namely protest, advocacy, knowledge production, service provision, popular education, and movement building. In our examination of these practices, we have sought to highlight the context-specific variations in their

deployment and to illustrate the ways in which all the practices are underpinned in some shape or form by the ethos described in chapter 6.

Ultimately, however, our discussion of this array of political practices
undermines any sharp dichotomy between those oriented toward internal
audiences and those directed externally. It is apparent that most of the
activities of our interviewees are in effect *dual-facing*, engaging simultaneously with interlocutors within the movement and with those outside.
Take the example of knowledge production, which can involve research
undertaken to support lobbying of the state, campaigns targeting the general public, and the production of regular newsletters bringing movement
activists into dialogue with each other. Moreover, individual groups further
blur the internal-external division by *multitasking*, that is, by engaging in
practices from across the range we have delineated here. Thus, participants
in Women Speak Out British group protest the incarceration of women
in state prisons and organize workshops for women activists on a range
of topics and skills. To take another example, Phoenix in India provides
economic and educational services for poor women as well as participating in movement building through membership in the World March of
Women. In this way, feminist antiglobalization activists seek not only to
call the state and other external actors to account, but also to better the lives
of women and to build an activist community. It is to this last dimension
of practices that we turn in the final mapping chapter, exploring in more
detail the ways in which feminist antiglobalization activists forge solidarity
among themselves and with others in a broader movement struggle.

NOTES

1. Della Porta and Diani consider disruptive tactics to be the "staple of protesters
all over the world." As they go on to make clear, "for the most part social movements use forms of action which can be described as disruptive, seeking to influence
elites through a demonstration of both force of numbers and activists' determination to succeed" (2006: 181).

2. Dissemination can take place through the formal education system as well as
through popular education, which we discuss later in the chapter. We have written
elsewhere on how our own university teaching is or could be influenced by the
views of feminist antiglobalization activists (Eschle and Maiguashca 2006). Further,
several of the interviewees are themselves academics and school teachers. Lakshmi
Lingam, who teaches at the Tata Institute in India, explicitly aims to train would-be
activists. As she explains, "I am part of a network of women activists who come from
various organizations and I link with them continuously and we do many things
together. Like we have designed a course on gender, health, and development and
taught it outside the university framework through an NGO, and many of us went
and taught there" (interview, Mumbai, January 20, 2004). When she is teaching

gender analysis to her own students, she encourages them to take women's experiences seriously as sites of knowledge. As she says, "When I do a gender analysis I don't have an abstract case but actually have a case that comes from my friends' organization." By paying attention to the perspective of poor women, her students learn that you "cannot have homogenized concepts. You cannot have a concept which is homogenizing everybody's experience so the fact that every standpoint is important comes up" (interview, Mumbai, January 20, 2004).

3. In addition we are struck by what appears to be a distinctive practice in Brazil of training service providers employed by the state, including health professionals, police, firemen, educators, and lawyers. This seems to involve imparting a mixture of practical skills and social critique. CEPIA (Cidadania, Estudo, Pesquisa, Informação em Genero), for instance, puts together courses on gender, human rights, and health for medical students and on domestic and sexual violence for the police (CEPIA n.d.b). Coletivo Feminino Plural trains civil society leaders involved in health services to help them enforce existing laws as well as police, firemen, social workers, and teachers who work with young girls (Telia Negrão, interview, Porto Alegre, January 22, 2005), while REDEH trains 400 schoolteachers a year on human rights, racial, and gender issues (REDEH n.d.c).

4. We examined each of the groups listed in textbox 1.1, chapter 1, to consider whether it has formal NGO status or not; whether it has a constitution or written rules and how extensive these are; whether it has its own office or hierarchy of offices; whether it has a paid staff, recruited on the basis of technical expertise; and if there is a functional division of labor between the staff and between staff and members (see Kriesi 1996). This allows us to place groups on an institutionalization spectrum, with highly formalized, professionalized, and internally differentiated organizations at one end, and informal groups without a constitution, office, paid staff, or division of labor at the other. Our information here is partial and incomplete, so our conclusions should be seen as tentative.

5. The issue of whether or not to accept external funding is highly controversial among interviewees, particularly in India. Mass Indian women's organizations oppose external funding on ideological grounds derived from Marxism as encouraging dependency and co-optation in the context of imperialist globalization. Thus, Sushma from Mahila Jagruthi told us, "We don't believe in collecting funds from other agencies either from the government or the imperialist agencies. Our basic thing is that we survive on people's money" (interview, Mumbai, January 17, 2004). Yet other groups apparently influenced by Marxist perspectives, or whose members told us they personally identified with Marxism, actively pursue external funding, such as SOF and Fala Preta! in Brazil. Interestingly, the World March of Women, to which several of the more Marxist-influenced Indian and Brazilian groups are affiliated, is also externally funded: it refuses to charge membership fees because of its desire to foster active participation. More anarchist-influenced groups also appear divided on the issue: Women Speak Out in the UK "relies on mostly participant generated voluntary donations" (Women Speak Out n.d.); in contrast, NextGENDERation has accepted funds from the Dutch-based feminist organization Mama Cash to subsidize participation in the Paris and London European Social Forums. It should be noted that several interviewees from groups who rely on external funding insist they have not changed their agendas to conform with the priorities of funding bodies.

More pertinently here, they also draw attention to financial instability and associated job insecurity, and to the amount of time spent on trying to gain or replace funds. For example, Virginia Feix of Themis discussed how her organization was responding to the withdrawal of major funding from the Ford Foundation: "We are in a very difficult moment of our institutional life. . . . We have to go to the private sector" (interview, Porto Alegre, January 22, 2005). So external funding may foster institutionalization, but it can also bring instability in its wake.

6. Here we draw on recent innovations in social movement theory to help map what has been called "network density." Following Mario Diani, we have counted the numbers of interactions between a closed population of nodes in a sample (the groups listed in textbox 1.1) to help us calculate the relative level of density of the movement sector we have called feminist antiglobalization activism, as well as the relative centrality or prominence of groups within it (Diani 2002, 2003a, 2003b).

7. There is a need to be careful here to avoid a widespread propensity to romanticize the network form, a tendency from which feminist scholars are not immune (e.g., Moghadam 2001: 134). As Peter Waterman points out (2000: 144), networks have "different architectures . . . implying differential influence and control"; they can include vertical as well as horizontal relationships. With regard to our sixty core groups, at least five different types of network structure can be discerned. *Globalized think tanks*, such as DAWN and the International Feminists for a Gift Economy, are wide and light, having only a few participants from around the world. *Umbrella organizations* are more structured networks with a strong central hub and lots of connecting spokes between that and peripheral groups, such as WGNRR, WLUML, and AWID. *Cuckoo organizations* have a much lighter central hub that shifts around between member organizations, such as AFM and the Women's International Coalition for Economic Justice (WICEJ). Tangled *webs* like the Women in Black and Code Pink have connections running between groups in multiple directions and hubs are virtual and very light or even nonexistent. Last, there are *hybrid networks or federations* such as the Women's Environmental Network in the UK (WEN), which has autonomous groups affiliated to it and which also gives some coordination to local groups that identify as WEN branches but still have a lot of autonomy of action. The World March could also fit here. This has group members dispersed worldwide, clustering around national coordinations, which cluster around a small central hub in the form of the international secretariat (at the time of writing this is SOF in São Paulo).

8

Forging Solidarity

Mobilizing Identities in Feminist Antiglobalization Activism

> [F]eminism is a space to stay in the world. . . . When you say that you are a feminist . . . it is to advise the people to look, pay attention, because . . . I am in this field in a very particular way. (Magaly Pazello, interview, Porto Alegre, January 23, 2005)

We closed the previous chapter with a discussion of movement building among feminist antiglobalization activist groups. Here we look at how political affinity is built in, across, and beyond these groups, that is, at the ways in which our interviewees forge a sense of togetherness and develop a shared commitment to others in political struggle. In other words, we ask in this chapter: how do feminist antiglobalization activists create a sense of solidarity?

We suggest that one fruitful feminist approach to solidarity involves bringing the concept of "identity" into the frame. Feminist scholars have strongly underlined the salience of identity-based categories and identification processes in the context of movement organizing, although there is much debate among them about how this actually works. In the discussion that follows, we draw on Paula Moya (1997, 2001), Linda Martín Alcoff (2000, 2006), and Alison Weir (2008a, 2008b) in seeing identities as socially constructed to the extent that they are processual and continually negotiated; relational, in that they gain their meaning through interaction with other identities; and as having some density and stability, helping to shape who we think we are and how we act. Moreover, like Moya, Alcoff, and Weir, we are particularly interested in those identities that are constructed in explicitly political terms—those that are mobilized in order to confront systems of oppression and in pursuit of a better world.[1] In our view, this conception of identity yields at least three lines of inquiry for a study of solidarity within feminist antiglobalization activism. First, it brings with it an emphasis on both the oppositional and affirmative dynamics of identity. Second, it pushes us to investigate the complex forms that identity takes. Finally, it implies a need to examine the relationship between identity and movement action.

Structuring our chapter accordingly, in what follows we first show how the identity categories of "woman" and "feminist" are mobilized by the feminist antiglobalization activist to oppose male domination and gendered oppression, on the one hand, and to affirm a sense of community and a shared vision of change, on the other. Second, we argue that these categories are highly complex, articulated either in conjunction with or in parallel to other identities and expressed in different ways in different national contexts. Finally, we explore how their deployment can serve to forge extensive connections with others. Before we begin, however, a few words of explanation are needed about the identity categories on which we focus here.

WE ARE WOMEN, WE ARE FEMINISTS

In this chapter, we focus our attention primarily on "woman" or "women" and "feminist" or "feminists" because these are the dominant identity categories at play within feminist antiglobalization activism.[2] We think of "woman" as a kind of *social identity*, a term used widely in sociology to indicate an identity "grounded typically in established social roles such as 'teacher' and 'mother' or in broader and more inclusive social categories such as gender categories or ethnic and national categories" (Snow 2001: 2; see also Gleason 1983). Of eighty-five interviewees, we identify empirically seventy-nine as women—as Alcoff reminds us, "Social identities are often carried on the body, materially inscribed, perceived at a glance by well disciplined perceptual practices" (Alcoff 2000). More relevant for our purposes, however, is the granting of political importance to the categories of "woman" or "women" by most interviewees themselves.

This can be seen by the fact that many have organized within women-only groups. As feminist social movement theorists Verta Taylor and Nancy Whittier point out, the development of separate institutions around a particular identity is one way of creating "boundaries that insulate and differentiate a category of persons from the dominant society" (1992: 122, see also 111–14; and Whittier 2003: 107–8).[3] Most of the women-only groups we identify from our sample (see textbox 8.1)[4] have "women" in their title, thus making the political mobilization of this identity explicit.

At the same time, most of these same interviewees declared to us a feminist identity for themselves or their group—84 percent in total, making this

---

Textbox 8.1. Women-Only Groups

1. AfricaWoman
2. All African Women's Group
3. All India Democratic Women's Association (AIDWA)
4. Andhra Pradesh Chaitanya Mahila Samakhya (APCMS) (Mahila means *woman*)
5. Andhra Pradesh Mahila Samatha Society (APMSS)
6. Articulação de Mulheres Brasilieras (AMB) (Mulheres means *women*)
7. Articulação de Mulheres Negras Brasilieras (AMNB)
8. Femmes [Women], Genre et Mondialisation (ATTAC caucus, France)
9. Center for Women's Global Leadership
10. Coletivo Feminino Plural
11. CRIOLA (a play on words, meaning *black woman*)
12. Dalit Women's Federation
13. Development Alternatives with Women for a New Era (DAWN)
14. Fala Preta! (Black Woman Speak Out!)
15. Femmes Solidaires
16. FEMNET
17. Flora Tristán—Centro de la Mujer Peruana (Centre for Peruvian Women)
18. Forum against the Oppression of Women
19. Furcaza Feminista
20. Global Women's Strike
21. Grail Movement (Women of Spirit Working for Change)
22. Indymedia Women
23. International Feminists for a Gift Economy
24. International Free Women's Foundation
25. Mahila Jagruthi
26. Maria Mulher
27. National Federation of Indian Women (NFIW)
28. National Network of Autonomous Women's Groups (NNAWG)
29. Phoenix: Organisation for Woman and Child
30. Rede Mulher de Educação
31. Umas e Outras
32. Women in Black
33. Women Living Under Muslim Laws (WLUML)
34. Women Speak Out
35. Women's Environment and Development Organization (WEDO)
36. Women's Environmental Network (WEN)
37. Women's Global Network for Reproductive Rights (WGNRR)
38. Women's International Coalition for Economic Justice (WICEJ)
39. Women's International League for Peace and Freedom (WILPF)
40. World March of Women

---

the most widespread *ideological identity* by some distance. We understand ideology here in a very loose and nonpejorative way as "a ready-made set of meanings and interpretations" often in textual form "that can help us to make sense of our world and tell us how to act in relation to our world" (Weber 2005: 4). As Steven Beuchler puts it, ideology can function as a "cultural system of meaning" for movement activists "that defines political opportunity, fosters collective culture and promotes collective identity and solidarity" (2000: 201).[5] To think about feminist identity in this way is to see it as analytically separable from the social identity of "woman" or "women," thus allowing for the possibility of men identifying as feminists and women choosing not to. Overall, we are suggesting that feminism is the most important ideological source of identity and solidarity for what we have called feminist antiglobalization activists, the majority of whom are simultaneously mobilized on the basis of the social identity category of "woman."

We want to acknowledge at this point that there was some contestation over the usage of the "feminist" label among our interviewees, particularly in India, where only just over half subscribed to it. A number expressed anxiety about the widespread stereotyping of feminists as "antiman" (Sarat-babu Vasireddy, interview, Hyderabad, January 8, 2004) and "antifamily" (A. Padma, interview, Hyderabad, January 8, 2004), and as referring to westernized women who smoke and drink alcohol. Furthermore, several of the Mumbai Resistance interviewees were critical of what they called "bourgeois feminism" (P. Pavana, Mumbai, January 18, 2004), seen as separating gender oppression from class, or as Sushma of Mahila Jagruthi explains, "the 'feminist' term as we know it in India is antimen without class perspective . . . so we wouldn't want to be called feminist, but . . . more like women's activists or women's rights activists" (interview, Mumbai, January 17, 2004). Here a pro-woman identity is juxtaposed or articulated in opposition to a feminist identity.

A handful of interviewees outside of India also rejected or pointed to problems with identifying as "feminist." A critique of the feminist neglect of class was echoed in a different kind of language in London by interviewees of the Global Women's Strike: "Our main complaint has always been about the careerism: climbing up the ladder and leaving everybody else behind" (Anna, interview, London, October 12, 2004). Both Anna of the Global Women's Strike and the black Brazilian activists we interviewed pointed to the racial and class privilege of many self-labeled feminists. Thus, Anna talked of meeting "outspoken black and working-class women . . . who didn't want to say they were feminists. They didn't want to be identified with it, because clearly already it had the taint of . . . not representing them" (interview, London, October 12, 2004). Finally, neither of the two interviewees from ILGA saw feminism as defining of their politics, as Rosanna Flamer-Caldera put it: "I don't use the word 'feminist' . . . my identity is as a lesbian activist" (interview, Amsterdam, December 22, 2004).

These reservations about the feminist label are important and need to be taken seriously. Nonetheless, they are not shared by the majority of our interviewees, and we think some of the underlying assumptions here need to be questioned. We will leave aside here the stereotyping of feminists, which interestingly was often recognized to be unjust by those who articulated an anxiety around it, and rebut only the criticism that feminism, as an ideology, has a reductive understanding of oppression. Although this may well be the case with specific variants of feminism in particular contexts, it is certainly not true of feminism in toto. As we argue in chapters 5 and 6, the critique and vision of change proposed by feminist antiglobalization activists when taken as a whole gives equal weight to the contestation and transformation of at least three systems of oppression—patriarchy, racial supremacism, and neoliberalism. Furthermore, chapter 4 shows that feminists have long had links, as well as disputes, with other movements, including those on the Left. As we go on to demonstrate later in this chapter, self-declared feminists continue to interpret their relationship to feminism in ways that require them to join with others in a larger political project of social transformation. Before doing so, however, we discuss the dynamics involved in the mobilization of both "woman" and "feminism" as identities and their complex composition

OPPOSITIONAL AND AFFIRMATIVE IDENTITY DYNAMICS

Moya, Alcoff, and Weir point to two dynamics in the deployment of identity that deserve our attention. The first is an oppositional logic, whereby some identity claims are mobilized in and against systems of oppression. In this light, Moya defends the use of the identity label "Chicana" by women in the United States of Mexican and indigenous heritage:

> What distinguishes a Chicana . . . is her political awareness; her recognition of her disadvantaged position in a hierarchically organized society arranged according to categories of class, race, gender and sexuality; and her propensity to engage in political struggle aimed at subverting and changing those structures. (Moya 1997: 139)

But while they see identity as produced within and responding to relations of oppression, both Alcoff and Moya—*pace* poststructuralist and psychoanalytic perspectives that, in their view, reduce identity to "wounded attachments" (Brown 1993) that generate political damage (see, especially, Alcoff 2000; also Moya 2001: 5)—argue that some identities also have a second, more affirmative dynamic. In this sense, identities can also be "enabling, enlightening, and joyful structures of attachment and feeling" (Moya 2001: 5) and "produce strength, perseverance, and empathy . . . culture and community" (Alcoff 2006: 5). Weir agrees, seeing the construction of identities as involving "recognition and identification" with others (2008b: 122) in ways that give emotional sustenance.

Turning to the first dynamic, we can certainly see an oppositional deployment of identity categories among feminist antiglobalization activists. As Julia di Giovanni of the Brazilian group Sempreviva Organização Feminista

(SOF) and the World March reminds us, "sometimes you need an identity just to confront something" (interview, Porto Alegre, January 26, 2005), or as Fernanda Elias of lesbian network Umas e Outras indicates, "at the very moment of political fights, if you don't use them [identity labels], how do you make yourself understood and how do you claim your rights?" (interview [in translation], São Paulo, January 10, 2005).

More specifically, with regard to "women" as an identity, organizing in women-only groups involves a claim not only of difference from men, but also of opposition to male domination. It is important to note here that difference from men is usually asserted in social rather than biological terms. Thus, the transnational antiwar network Women in Black declares, "Women-only peace activism does not suggest that women, any more than men, are 'natural born peace-makers.' But women often inhabit different cultures from men, and are disproportionately involved in caring work" (Women in Black n.d.a). Code Pink, a women-led peace organization based in the United States that encourages male involvement, similarly argues that "women have been the guardians of life [but] not because we are better or purer or more innately nurturing than men. . . . We who cherish children will not consent to their murder" (Starhawk 2002a). Connectedly, "women" is not mobilized in opposition to men per se—as we argued in chapter 5, "men in general are not the enemy" (Moema Toscano, interview, Rio de Janeiro, January 13, 2005), but rather systems of oppression. There is still space for a critique of male privilege within these systems, however, and the ways in which some men may consciously or unconsciously act to uphold it. This is particularly evident in those instances where women-only groups have emerged from problematic experiences in mixed-gender organizations. Thus, for example, the Indymedia international women's list was set up in response to the overwhelmingly male-dominated character of the mixed organization for alternative reportage, a reflection of "the under-representation of women in Information Technology related fields" and also of the fact that many "tech" and "non-tech" men acted in ways which reinforced that dominance: women were "being silenced in meetings, . . . experience[ing] open[ly] sexist behaviour" and there was "a general atmosphere that made it hard for women to work" (IMC Women 2003). Nonetheless, the Indymedia women's list asserts, "we don't perceive our struggle as female versus males but as a general cause" (IMC Women 2003).

This oppositional dynamic finds an echo in justifications of black women–only organizing. Here we find an assertion of difference from men and from white women. With regard to the latter, Glaucia Matos of Fala Preta!, based in São Paulo, Brazil, points out that in the Brazilian feminist movement, "the majority are white women" (interview, São Paulo, January 18, 2005). Her compatriot Noelci Homero of Maria Mulher in Porto Alegre elaborates that "one of the banners that the feminist movement carries is 'We want to work!' But black women have always worked, since we got here we have worked, so that is not our struggle" (interview, Porto Alegre, January 22, 2005). In such ways, the numerical dominance of white women in the feminist movement is translated into the universalization of their concerns in feminist ideology and the marginalization of those of black women. It is this process of domination, rather than white women per se, that black women's groups seek to oppose. As Homero puts it, Maria Mulher was founded in response to "chauvinism inside the black movement . . . and inside the feminist movement" (interview, Porto Alegre, January 22, 2005).

In general, we would argue that the articulation of "women" as an identity in opposition to male and/or white domination needs to be understood within the broader context of a structural analysis of systems and nodes of oppression, of the kind discussed in chapter 5. See, for example, Women in Black's assertion that "we know what injustice and oppression mean, because we experience them as women. . . . All women in war fear rape. Women are the majority of refugees" (Women in Black n.d.a). Or take Ann-Kristin Kowarsch's claim about her organization, the International Free Women's Federation, that "as a women's group we tried to mobilize against both the racism on the streets as well as in the institutions" (interview, London, October 16, 2004). This structural analysis is even clearer with regard to the articulation of "feminist" as an identity, which for several of our interviewees is defined squarely in terms of a critique of patriarchy.[6] Of our interviewees in the UK, Sian Sullivan, for one, identifies "as a feminist because I think that patriarchal social organization is at the root, at the heart, of the problems that concern me, that depress me, that I think are tragic" (interview, London, November 4, 2004), while Isabelle Fremeaux claims, "it is the politics associated with the very, very profound power inequalities based in gender, it's the politics relating to the fact that we do still live in a patriarchal society" (interview, London, November 9, 2004). An alternative approach, but one still linked to a structural analysis of oppression, is that of Brazilian Greice Cerqueira of the Women's Global Network for Reproductive Rights (WGNRR), who defines her feminist identity in more concrete terms in opposition to the nodes of oppression of economic inequality, violence, and bodily nautonomy:

> Feminism means to me not being treated differently from a man just because I am a woman . . . not to live in poverty . . . 70 percent of the poor population are women, and this to me is unacceptable. That's what feminism is . . . and to live free of violence. Why should I be violated, why should I be raped, why should my body be disrespected and why should I be used? (Interview, Amsterdam, October 22, 2004)

Having emphasized the oppositional dimension of identities within our data, we now want to turn to their affirmative orientation. With regard to feminist identity, we suggest that the affirmative moment can be seen in terms of a commitment to the utopian vision of change described in chapter 6. We do not mean by this to imply that those in our sample who refuse the label "feminist" do not share that vision, as certainly some of them do. Rather, we are suggesting that self-identification as "feminist" or "feminists" must, necessarily, have this future-oriented dimension, and it is this which distinguishes it from self-identification as "woman" or "women." As another of our interviewees from WGNRR put it, identifying as feminist involves "believing in a better world where women have equal opportunities . . . where people and groups are all respected . . . [and] encouraged to be active and participate [in the creation of a] different social structure" (Nadia Van der Linde, interview, Amsterdam, October 19, 2004). For Joanna Hoare of the European network of students and researchers, NextGENDERation, feminism "means gender equality . . . every person in the world having the right to control their own lives and their bodies" (interview, London, November 8, 2004). A final example is provided by Sara Longwe of FEMNET, an African coalition of development NGOs: "a feminist to me is a person who recognizes that there is sex discrimination against women and she totally believes it is unfair and she is . . . *committed and passionate about changing it*" (interview, Porto Alegre, January 25, 2005, emphasis added).

Turning to "women" as an identity category, an affirmative moment can be seen in the fact that women-only organizations function as "structures of attachment and feeling" (Moya 2001: 5). An advocate of British group Women Speak Out puts it this way: "Women only space is not anti-male . . . it is simply a way of creating an alternative—offering women an opportunity to interact, connect and network" (Schnews 2002). Similarly, the Indian NGO Asmita was set up to "create a space for women to come together . . . [to] facilitate feminist analysis and action on critical issues . . . [and] provide resources to women in need" (Asmita n.d.). Lúcia Xavier echoes this in her discussion of how black women's NGO CRIOLA, based in Rio de Janeiro, aims "to be a comfortable space for black women to think about their condition, to discuss black identity . . . a space where being a black woman is not a problem" (interview, Rio de Janeiro, January 12, 2005). Finally, Umas e Outras, referred to earlier,

> sprang from the idea that women did not participate in events for homosexuals because in general these were arranged by and for men. We wanted to arrange something for women. . . . [W]e have created . . . an atmosphere where lesbian issues can be discussed naturally and where women who arrive can reach their own conclusions. (Umas e Outras 2003, our translation)

These and other examples imply that women-only, or black women-only, or lesbian women-only groups facilitate the (re)construction of shared identity in ways that are not possible or are threatened in mixed environments. In the next part we go on to explore the complex forms that identity can take.

COMPLEX IDENTITIES

The approach to identity articulated by Alcoff, Moya, and Weir has been greatly influenced by the reflections of women belonging to racial or sexual minorities in the United States, whose identities and associated experiences are multifaceted and complex.[7] In this light, Moya talks about how Chicana identity is forged at the intersection of "class, race, gender and sexuality" (1997: 139) and Alcoff rejects the view that "identities are always perfectly homogeneous or that identity groups are unproblematic" (2000: 2). Weir (2008b: 123–27) draws on Maria Lugones's theory of subjectivity as "world-travelling" to insist that an interest in and acceptance of differences among individuals may actually be part of what encourages them to come together. Taken together, these feminist theorists put forward the case that identity is not unitary but internally heterogeneous and not singular, but plural in form.[8]

Approaching our data in this light, we want to put forward two main arguments. First, the identity categories "woman" and "feminist" are mobilized by feminist antiglobalization activists not in isolation, but rather alongside many other identities. With regard to social identity, claims about what it means to be "women" are frequently made in conjunction with categories hinging on race, ethnicity, sexuality, and the like (see, e.g., Valentine 2007). What we shall call the *conjunctural* identities of "black women" and "lesbian women" are certainly mobilized among feminist antiglobalization activists, as we have seen above.[9] Other conjunctural identities are also evident, such as those of "Dalit women" and "Muslim women." In India, Nandita Shah of Akshara and the Forum Against the Oppression of Women has written of how "for each one of us there are multiple, layered, often contradictory identities" and of how this has manifested itself in one of her organizations: "we saw the emergence of a Muslim women's group and later a lesbian group from within it. If there was fragmentation, there was also an extremely useful visibilisation" (Shah 2004). Also in India, Sujatha Surepally of the Dalit Women's Federation told us: "Dalit women's situation is different, you know? . . . Dalit women are thrice oppressed, comparatively." The intersection of "caste, class and gender" for her means that Dalit women need to mobilize as such: "like women only can understand the women's problem, . . . Dalits only will understand the Dalit question. . . . I always think of Dalits and women simultaneously" (interview, Mumbai, January 17, 2004).

In addition, our activists have multiple ideological identifications. Thus, some of the feminist antiglobalization activists we interviewed are clearly influenced by ecological thinking as well as feminism. But by far the most common additional identification among our interviewees is with the Left. Just over half explicitly associate themselves with one of a range of left-wing ideologies, from Maoism, defended by women we met at Mumbai Resistance who called for a "'new democratic revolution' . . . [as] proposed by Mao Tse Tung" (P. Pavana, interview, Mumbai, January 18, 2004), to anarchism of a rather eclectic variety: "I'm not that much interested in this very traditional, Bakhunin, Kropotkin, whatever it is. . . . [M]y influences come from more autonomous politics and situationism and that sort of thing" (Lydia, interview, London, June 11, 2005). A much larger majority draw on the broader labels of Marxist or socialist, sometimes also expressing an affiliation with associated political parties (notably the Partido dos Trabalhadores [PT] in Brazil and the communist parties in India) or trade unions.

Interestingly, however, ideological identities tend to be held *in parallel* rather than fused together in a conjunctural way. Notably, our interviewees are generally very reticent to invoke specific conjunctures of feminism and left-wing affiliations, with only 9 percent accepting the composite label "socialist feminist," and most of those reluctantly. This is despite the fact that half of them self-describe as both "Marxist" or "socialist," and as "feminist." In this we can see a shift away from second-wave feminist articulations of identity, which commonly invoked conjunctural ideological categories. As Virgina Vargas puts it,

> We began by calling ourselves socialist feminists . . . but . . . we decided that we didn't want the label. . . . [W]e wanted a much more critical feminism with socialism and with political parties and with the traditional Left. So we decided that, for us . . . we said in that moment, "feminism without labels." That was our slogan. (Interview, Mumbai, January 18, 2004)

Or as Jacqueline Pitanguy insists, "I am too flexible to be a particular type" (interview, Rio de Janeiro, January 12, 2005).

The second main argument we want to make with regard to the complex forms in which identities are mobilized is that they are expressed in diverse ways in differing national contexts. Previous chapters have provided evidence for the fact that geopolitical location grants distinctive content to the category "woman" and the ways in which this identity is or can be politicized. Note, for example, the discourse touched upon in previous chapters around women as rights-holders, which was particularly prevalent in India, or the discourse in Brazil around women as citizens and as sexual beings deserving of freedom from the constraints of objectification. The conjunctural identity of "black woman," we suggest, is also mobilized in Brazil in very specific ways, drawing inspiration from the heritage of the *quilombo* communities of escaped slaves. Thus, the Articulação de Mulheres Negras Brasilieras (AMNB), a Brazilian-wide federation of black women's groups, is involved with the coordination of remaining *quilombo* communities and more than one interviewee talked of their involvement in a *quilombo* tent at the World Social Forum: "we also want to build a reference for the black community" in Brazil (Glaucia Matos, interview, São Paulo, January 18, 2005).

In a similar vein, parallel ideological identifications are also articulated differently in specific contexts. In terms of left-wing identities, for example, interviewee Sarah Bracke of NextGENDERation points to the "specific national traditions" of anarchism or "autonomy" (interview, Dublin, July 10, 2005). Other left-wing identifiers may indicate party memberships that shift from country to country. Thus while interviewee Sophie Zafari of the World March asserts that "personally, socialism is an emancipatory ideal," she doesn't call herself "socialist" because among French feminists, the "only ones who use the name in the title are the parties. . . . It refers to the social democrats [the Parti Socialiste]" (interview, London, October 13, 2004). In the UK, "socialist" does not necessarily indicate party membership and arguably is no longer widely used to refer to the social democratic Labour Party but to those much further on the Left. In India, the meaning of Left identifiers shifts again. There are relatively mainstream political parties labeled "communist," while those outside of the mainstream political system that we encountered at Mumbai Resistance identify with a Maoist interpretation of Marx, not mobilized in any of our other fieldwork sites.

Context-specific changes in feminist identity are not quite as obvious, as "feminist" rarely attaches to specific political parties. There are nonetheless contextual differences in associated critiques and aspirations, as we have argued in previous chapters, which feed into how this category is mobilized. So, in Brazil there is an emphasis among self-declared feminists on confronting dominant prisms of sexuality, while in India, struggles against violence, forced marriage, caste, and poverty are central and the feminist label may not be used. In France, as we have seen, there is a distinctive preoccupation with sexual exploitation and prostitution. As Jacqueline Pitanguy insists, "Feminism is a . . . way of acting, it is a political thinking, that . . . might take one shape in India . . . another shape in Brazil" (interview, Rio de Janeiro, January 12, 2005). Kalpana Kannabiran has a similar formulation: "I think feminism must engage with inequality in very fundamental ways. . . . But once it has done that I think each region, each culture finds its own way of articulating that resistance" (interview, Hyderabad, January 10, 2004).

This takes us to the fact that we found among our interviewees a wide-spread emphasis on the internal diversity of the categories "woman" and "feminist" and the need to value that diversity. Documentation from the Association for Women's Rights in Development puts it thus: "women come from all backgrounds, beliefs, abilities and experiences. As such, openness to diversity must be an integral aspect of advancing women's rights" (AWID 2005). Women Living Under Muslim Laws (2005), to take another example, "actively endorses plurality and autonomy, and consciously reflects, recognises and values a diversity of opinions" (WLUML 2005). Or as Peggy Antrobus of the think tank DAWN (Development Alternatives with Women for a New Era) asserts, "Solidarity means, first of all, acknowledging our differences, that we are not the same" (interview, Dublin, July 10, 2004). Such an attitude clearly informs the organization of women-only and feminist institutions among our activists. We can see it in the argument that the Planeta Fêmea women's tent at the first two World Social Forums in Porto Alegre was intended to "create a unity but also to be a space of diversity" (Telia Negrão, interview, Porto Alegre, January 22, 2005). Recall also the Diversity Boat organized at the World Social Forum in 2005. As one of the coordinating groups, Articulacíon Feminista Marcosur (AFM), asserts:

> In this new millennium, humanity should be capable of constructing collectives [and] spaces in which the whole range of diverse identities can participate in the construction of an "us" that is inclusive, plural, shifting and not entirely without conflict. This is the fundamental challenge facing an alternative political project. (Oliveira n.d.; also available at AFM n.d.)

IDENTITY AND MOVEMENT ACTION

Having discussed the complexity of identity categories among feminist antiglobalization activists, we turn finally to the relationship of identity to movement action. How does the work of Alcoff, Moya, or Weir help us here? We must acknowledge at this point that Alcoff and Moya are primarily concerned with the relationship between identity and knowledge, rather than action. More specifically, they are defending a version of standpoint epistemology that sees identity as "a location in social space, a hermeneutic horizon that is both grounded in a location and . . . [a] site from which we attempt to know the world" (Alcoff 2000: 22). Yet this view seems to us to imply a close connection between identity, knowledge, and action. As Moya indicates, identity "gives us a way of knowing *and acting* from within our own social location or 'flesh'" (1997: 150, emphasis added). By conceptualizing identity as "a site from which one . . . is open to the world" (Alcoff 2006: 30) or, to deploy another metaphor, a "horizon, an opening out"

(Alcoff 2006: 34), these thinkers present identity as a portal through which we interact with the social world. They imply, then, that we should focus less on the boundaries separating off one identity from another and more on the extent to which an identity facilitates engagement with others.

To this end, we examine, first, the role of identity in the relations *among* feminists or women (what we have described, following Roseneil (1995: 71) as the "internal mode of action"). In this regard, we wish to remind the reader of the extensive practice of networking, or articulation, among our interviewees, as discussed in chapter 7. Evidently, this practice involves forging connections among feminist antiglobalization activists through and across conjunctural and parallel identities. Thus, for instance, the merger of CRIOLA, Fala Preta!, and Maria Mulher in the AMNB exemplifies the impulse among black Brazilian feminist NGOs to connect with each other— "we always work through the AMNB" (Lúcia Xavier, interview, Rio de Janeiro, January 12, 2005). Furthermore, the AMNB is the conduit through which member groups participate not only in transnational organizing around race issues, but also in mixed-race feminist mobilizing in an effort to redefine what feminism means. This leads one participant to characterize the AMNB as "an important political actor in rethinking feminism in Brazil. . . . [I]t is through this organization that we have started to become more active in breaking through our isolation" (Lúcia Xavier, interview, Rio de Janeiro, January 12, 2005).

This propensity to engage and forge links with others can also be seen in the endeavors of relatively privileged feminists to reach out to so-called grassroots women who may not identify as feminists. Thus, for example, Centro Flora Tristán in Peru has since 1988 fostered a Network of Rural Women that works with 120 grassroots organizations to help build the capacity of poorer rural women (Flora Tristán CMP n.d.b). The Brazilian organization SOF, which defines itself as feminist, also has strong links with grassroots women. As interviewee Nalu Faria told us, "we work with local people by going to the community and talking to all the women and this is what we call base [grassroots] education, leadership education. . . . [W]e call a national conference and meet women from different places" (interview, São Paulo, January 17, 2005). In particular, SOF works with women from rural unions, "autonomous movements of *camponesas* [peasants] from the land" and women within Movimento Sim Terra (MST), the land squatters movement (interview, São Paulo, January 17, 2005).

If networking is widespread among feminist antiglobalization activists of differing parallel and conjunctural identifications, it is also a defining characteristic of the relations between these activists and those beyond their movement sector (what we have described, following Roseneil (1995: 71), as the "external mode of action"). We interpret this less as an effort to connect with a range of identities for its own sake and more as an attempt to reach out from an identity position to those who share similar analyses of oppression and utopian aspirations, in order to develop a shared political project.

Alliances forged on this basis are impossible to count definitively, but of those of which we are aware, the largest proportion are with groups working against economic oppression and for economic equality, including antipoverty, fair trade and solidarity economy organizations, and trade unions. DAWN, for example, has focused its alliance building on groups that have "a critical approach to the dominant paradigm in terms of development" (Peggy Antrobus, interview, Dublin, July 10, 2004), such as Social Watch in Latin America and Focus on the Global South in Asia. To take a very different example, most of the women's groups from which our French interviewees were drawn, as we saw in chapter 4, have very close links with trade unions. In this context, French interviewee Sophie Zafari argued that "one needs simultaneously to have an autonomous movement of women and, at the same time, women working inside ATTAC [the Association for the Taxation of Financial Transactions for the Aid of Citizens] and the unions to link the issues of women to the broader movement" (interview, London, October 13, 2004).

While economic inequality is the node around which most external alliances are formed, other nodes of oppression also feature. Thus, links to racial or caste justice groups are also high in number, albeit in very particular contexts. Several Brazilian groups, particularly but not exclusively those made up of black women, have links with antiracist networks, while some of our Indian groups are similarly linked to campaigns for Dalit rights or against communalist violence. A couple of groups from Europe are involved in campaigns against the xenophobic treatment of migrants. Coalitions have also formed around ecological degradation, understood as including a broad concern with land ownership and its management. So, for example, the Confederation de Paysannes (peasant farmers) in France has a women's group that has worked with the feminist caucus within ATTAC in that country, and several of our Brazilian groups have links with Via Campesina, the radical peasant union. Less numerous, but still present, are alliances with groups organized around lesbian and gay rights and against violence and war.

Many feminist antiglobalization organizations strive to sustain relations simultaneously with a veritable panoply of external groups. Thus, SOF works not only with women from MST, as mentioned above, but also with women from the PT and, in its capacity as regional office for the World March, is part of the Social Movements International Network, which nests within the office of a Brazil trade union and whose participants include ATTAC and Dalit rights groups (Social Movements International Network n.d.). Or recall the intermovement dialogue session at the World Social Forum discussed in chapter 3, where Virginia Vargas from AFM debated with representatives from a Filipino trade union, a Dalit rights group, and lesbian and gay networks, demonstrating the fraught, but productive nature of their interrelationships.

Such extensive interconnectivity means in effect that individuals and groups mobilized as "women" and/or as "feminists" work closely not only with nonfeminists, but also with men, or groups dominated by men.[10] This finds explicit justification in our interviews, with Mariana Mozdzer of WGNRR stating that "there should be some spaces that should be for women only sometimes. . . . But it is also important to cooperate with other people who are not feminists but have a lot to contribute, including men" (interview, Amsterdam, October 19, 2004). Greice Cerqueira from the same organization agrees: "men have a lot of power, so if we . . . talked to the ones that need to be converted, then our possibility to gain space . . . [and] to gain power is bigger" (interview, Amsterdam, December 22, 2004). Certainly the outreach work of DAWN, mentioned above, means that it "has stepped out of its comfort zone . . . to begin to build partnerships with male-led NGOs and networks" (Slatter 2002). All this underscores the point made earlier that the deployment of the identity labels "women" or "feminists" involves a claim of opposition to male domination and wider structures of oppression, but does not involve standing against men per se.[11] More precisely, it suggests that mobilizing as "women" or as "feminists" is the ground from which engagement as equals with men is made possible.

It is in the light of this sustained effort at networking with others in order to develop a shared political project that we should understand the marked tendency among our interviewees to argue for flexibility in the mobilization of ideological identities and, more specifically, for the need to be careful about the context in which one declares oneself feminist. One interviewee, for example, says she would "elaborate" on the category of feminist in different ways "depending on whom I was talking to" (Jackie Lewis, interview, London, November 10, 2004), while another acknowledges that she identifies as feminist only "in very particular moments" (Fernanda Elias, interview, São Paulo, January 19, 2005). The need for this flexible deployment of feminist identity is justified in two ways. On the one hand, there is a fear that terminology can misrepresent political goals. As Charlotte Bunch of the Center for Women's Global Leadership in the United States puts it: "I am a feminist who supports a very broad agenda. I don't like the labels because all the labels seem to imply some kind of limitation on your agenda" (interview, Porto Alegre, January 26, 2005). Similarly, Isabelle Fremeaux of the Laboratory of Insurrectionary Imagination in the UK argues that "the difficulty of labels in general is that one doesn't necessarily identify with what others might identify that label as meaning. . . . [P]eople are cautions about using labels for that reason" (interview, London, November 9, 2004). On the other hand, declaring an identity can be taken as an exclusionary move. Thus, one Indian interviewee told us that "this term 'feminist' is not commonly known by the people" and that, although it might be used in forging connections with those in middle-class circles, beyond this her organization preferred to draw on the concept of "women's rights," which has more popular resonance (Amarjeet Kaur, interview, Mumbai, January 20, 2004). A parallel argument was made by Anne-Kristin Kowarch when describing the work of the International Free Women's Foundation with migrant and refugee women in the Netherlands:

> we also don't really use the expression "feminism" when we are talking about ourselves, because it's one of our aims to connect different struggles of women . . . to enable exchanges and cooperation and we don't want to categorize it really. So, in introducing ourselves we wouldn't use the term feminism, but we don't exclude it. (Interview, London, October 16, 2004)

We indicated above that the feminist label is useful and often insisted upon when staking out a position against political opponents. But our point here is that it may also be suspended or waived in the effort to build bridges with others in a larger, more inclusive, more effective political struggle.

CONCLUSION

In this chapter, our exploration of how solidarity is forged among feminist antiglobalization activists has been framed in terms of the concept of "identity." Following feminist scholars, we have treated identity as constructed and political, seeking to inquire into the affirmative as well as oppositional dimensions of the ways in which it is mobilized, its complex forms, and its connection to collective agency.

More substantively, we began by pointing to two main identity categories mobilized within feminist antiglobalization activism: "woman" and "feminist." We argued that the mobilization of these identities involves not only an oppositional dynamic, but also a positive desire to affirm shared community and alternative political possibilities. After showing how these identities are deployed in complex and diverse ways, we went on to assert that, rather than separating off our interviewees from others, they propel connection across difference. In sum, identities are mobilized in ways that forge solidarity among feminist antiglobalization activists, and between them and the broader global justice movement of which they are a part.[12]

NOTES

1. In this regard, our approach chimes with a trend in social movement scholarship in recent decades to focus on questions of what is widely referred to as

collective identity. Given the potential for confusion here between the categories of "social" (discussed later) and "collective" identity, we prefer to use the terminology of *mobilizing identity* instead to capture what it is that social movement scholars are referring to, namely identities actively deployed for political purposes within a social movement. Identity, in this sense, is understood as "the process by which social actors recognise themselves—and are recognised by other actors—as part of broader groupings, and develop emotional attachments to them" (Della Porta and Diani 2006: 91). Or to put this another way, the concept of collective or mobilizing identity combines a "sense of 'we-ness'" with a "corresponding sense of 'collective agency'" (Snow 2001: 2).

2. In this chapter, when we write "woman" or "women" and "feminist" or "feminists" with quotation marks, we mean to invoke a mobilized identity category rather than an actual person or set of people bearing that identity.

3. Another strategy for establishing boundaries identified by Taylor and Whittier involves developing separate value systems. In contrast to Taylor and Whittier's study of lesbian community, however, it is much less clear from our data that "women's values" as such are invoked by our activists; the ethical goals discussed in chapter 6 are value laden, but there were only a couple of interviewees who explicitly identified these as specific to women in any innate way (as in Thais Corral of REDEH's argument about bringing in "feminine values . . . to do with caring, sharing, with being connected. . . . These are qualities critical for our survival" (interview, Rio de Janeiro, January 11, 2005). We prefer to see the values invoked by our activists more in terms of an ethos linked to *feminist* identity, as discussed in previous chapters.

4. We are being conservative here. There are doubtless more of the groups in textbox 1.1 that have women-only membership, but we do not have access to membership or staff lists so we are erring on the side of caution.

5. We would acknowledge that ideology is a notoriously slippery and contested concept, frequently given pejorative overtones (see Gerring 1997). For the last few decades, it has been seen as outdated in much social and political analysis (e.g., Fukuyama 1989; Bell 1960; Dalton 2005)—including in feminist thought (see Hennessy 1995) and social movement theory (Buechler 2000: 200). Nonetheless, we agree with social movement theorists Oliver and Johnston (2000: 7) that "ideology is of central importance in understanding social movements and other political formations" (see also Platt and Williams 2002; Beuchler 2000: 200–3).

6. As Oliver and Johnston point out, ideology can be understood as composed of three key moments: diagnostic or critical, involving a critique of what is wrong with the world, focusing primarily on power relations; reconstructive or prognostic, involving a view of "what should be done and what the consequences will be"; and prescriptive or strategic, involving a view of how to bring that alternative world into being (Oliver and Johnston 2000: 8). In this section of the chapter, we focus on the critical and reconstructive elements of feminism as an ideology, mapping these onto what we have termed oppositional and affirmative identity dynamics.

7. See, e.g., Combahee River Collective 1977; hooks 1981; Pratt 1988; Parmar 1989; Phelan 1989: 161–66; Anzaldúa 1987; Lugones 1990.

8. These assertions find an echo in theories of collective identity in social movement scholarship. Thus, della Porta and Diani, for example, influenced by Melucci's

claim that movements should not be seen as having "a homogenous and integrated identity," insist on the need for more attention to "the multiplicity of identities and allegiances amongst militants and movement groups" (2006: 98).

9. We have not mentioned class-based identities here. In fact, we think class can also be conceived as a form of social identity, despite the fact it is more often treated by analysts as a category based on interest rather than identity (for critiques, see Alcoff 2006 on Fraser 1997), and despite the fact it is "never . . . tightly guarded" as a form of identity, in part because it cannot be treated as having a physical, "authentic" core, like race, gender, and sexuality (batTzedek 1999). Having said that, our interviewees do not appear to mobilize identities at the intersection of gender and class. This does not mean that class is absent. In fact, we argued in chapter 4 that our interviewees are in part able to mobilize because they are relatively class privileged. But they do not claim an affinity on that basis.

10. On this point, it should not be forgotten that our interviewees participate directly in at least twenty-three organizations (not including political parties) that are male dominated or not explicitly feminist, from various branches of ATTAC and trade unions to Indymedia and the Wombles. In other words, we are not talking here about women's and feminist groups making alliances with mixed groups, but about those individuals identified as "women" or "feminists" integrating into such groups. In addition, it should be noted that some interviewees are members of *both* women's or feminist groups *and* mixed groups.

11. In this our argument chimes with Nancy Whittier's account of the changes in radical feminism in the United States, which asserts that "the boundaries between feminists and non-feminists . . . [and] between women and men" are becoming "more permeable" (2003: 108–9).

12. There is some convergence between our claims about feminist antiglobalization activism in this chapter and feminist philosopher Seyla Benhabib's (1994) argument in favor of a "social feminism" based on shared ethical principles, rather than the "politics of identity/difference." Yet, implicit in Benhabib's argument is the assumption that any feminist endeavor to build bridges requires the transcendence of identity. This is not what our analysis has shown. Instead, it is clear to us that identity still plays a very important role as the ground from which feminist antiglobalization activists act. Moreover, our analysis suggests that identity can be mobilized not only to establish differences and mark boundaries, but also to express what activists have in common: "what matters, what is meaningful for us—our desires, relationships, commitments, ideals" (Weir 2008: 111).

9

Conclusion

Rethinking the Global Justice Movement

In writing this book we have sought to challenge the neglect of feminism in studies of the global justice movement. As part of our quest to make feminist antiglobalization activism visible and audible, we have uncovered its presence at the World Social Forum and offered a feminist mapping of its main historical trajectories and characteristic features. More specifically, we have traced collective and individual sources of agency and explored the complex critiques of oppression elaborated by our interviewees. We have also highlighted the breadth of their utopian imagination and the range of their political practices, and examined the diverse and open-ended identities that they mobilize when building relationships with each other and on the wider terrain of the global justice movement. In sum, we have shown that feminist antiglobalization activism is a distinctive and significant form of collective action that needs to be acknowledged, analyzed, and taken seriously as a salient political force.

In this final chapter, we draw out the implications of our study for thinking about the global justice movement more generally. In other words, we seek to go beyond the empiricist strategy of "adding in" feminists and explore the ways in which our feminist reading of feminist antiglobalization activism confirms or disrupts narratives about the broader movement. To this end, we return here to the academic and activist-oriented literature we introduced in chapter 1. Expanding exponentially since the late 1990s, this literature is enormous, constantly shifting and impossible to summarize definitively. Rather than attempt a systematic review of it here, therefore, we pursue a strategy of selective engagement, underlining important areas of agreement as well as pointing to the ways in which our story may serve as a corrective to some key assumptions. We structure this undertaking in terms of the five themes that formed the basis of our mapping chapters, asking what the literature says about the origins of the global justice movement, what activists are fighting against and for, what they do, and how they forge solidarity. Our overall argument here is that our study of feminist antiglobalization activism opens up a number of empirical and conceptual lines of inquiry in relation to these themes which, if pursued, would strengthen our understanding of the global justice movement.

UNCOVERING ORIGINS

What are the origins of the global justice movement? The literature offers at least two answers to this question. The first locates the emergence of the movement in the shifting tectonic plates of global political and economic arrangements. The Gramscian-influenced account by Mark Rupert of mobilization in the United States, for example, emphasizes the "historical structural context" of the gradual collapse of the postwar Fordist compact between workers and capital (2000: 41), while Adam Morton (2002) similarly explains the emergence of the Zapatistas in terms of the changing relations of production in Chiapas and wider capitalist restructuring. Focusing more specifically on political realignments, other scholars have drawn attention to the impact of the end of the Cold War and the consequent proliferation of international forums for nonstate actors around the UN and international financial institutions (e.g., della Porta and Tarrow 2005a: 7–8; Pianta and Marchetti 2007: 33–39). Our account of the origins of feminist antiglobalization activism in chapter 4 gestures to similar factors, in particular with respect to its emphasis on feminist responses to neoliberal policies and on the role of the UN in enabling transnational networking.

Having said this, our analysis chimes more with a second approach to origins found in the literature, one centering on past traditions of collective action that have flowed into and inspired the development of the global justice movement. In this connection, centuries-old indigenous opposition to cultural genocide and peasant struggles against enclosure of land are often noted as important precursors (e.g., Starr 2005: 19; Notes from Nowhere 2003: 21–22, 27–28). More recent influences have been traced to movements in the 1970s and '80s, particularly protests against dominant development models and lending practices in the South,[1] and radical environmentalism and forms of direct action in the North (Rootes and Saunders 2007: 130; Plows 2004). Among these "movement families" (della Porta 2007b: 26; see also Kubrin 2004), left-wing mobilizations emerge as key progenitors of the global justice movement, in forms ranging from anticolonial struggles to nineteenth-century socialist internationals (Broad and Heckscher 2003: 714–17) and anarchist traditions (Day 2005: ch. 4; Juris 2008: 42–44). As Valentine Moghadam sums up:

> The global justice movement of today can be linked back to transnational movements of workers, socialists, communists, progressives and anarchists. Many of the older activists in the contemporary global justice movement were once affiliated with left-wing organizations or solidarity movements; many of the younger activists are involved in labor and economic justice causes; and the writings of Karl Marx are well known. (Moghadam 2009: 6–7)

Our story of feminist antiglobalization activism confirms, at least in part, this rendition of the origins of the global justice movement. As we argued in chapter 4, many of those we interviewed cut their political teeth in left-wing movements of the 1960s and '70s, and continue to seek a relationship with the Left today. Our research into their forebears, however, shows that there is another collective antecedent to which attention needs to be paid, namely second-wave feminism. This was, after all, the movement we identified as the most important for our interviewees, in terms of providing both inspiration and organizational infrastructure. Yet it is largely missing from analyses of the origins of the global justice movement, mentioned only very briefly in a handful of texts (Brecher, Costello, and Smith 2000: 13; Juris 2008: 37). A more complete history of the collective roots of this movement, then, clearly needs to acknowledge feminism as a central protagonist.

In addition to encompassing a greater range of past mobilizations, accounts of the forebears of the global justice movement should recognize, more than they currently do, the role played by internal movement hierarchies in triggering new waves of activism. As we argued in chapter 4, it was in response to what they saw as deeply entrenched sexism among their comrades that feminists began to organize autonomously. In a very similar dynamic, these feminist groups then reproduced the subordinated status of southern women, black women, Dalit women, Muslim women, lesbians, and others, who subsequently felt compelled to set up their own groups and to pursue their own agendas. It was this tendency to organize autonomously, we suggested, that served as a springboard for the realignment of feminists and the Left and it was in the context of such reconfigurations that feminist antiglobalization activism emerged. A less romanticized story of the collective roots of the global justice movement, therefore, requires that its movement forebears be seen not just as important positive influences, but also as sites of oppression and struggle.

Shifting our analysis from collective to individual agency, in the second half of chapter 4 we contended that a robust account of the origins of the global justice movement should address those factors that enable and motivate individuals to participate in activism. On this point, analysis in the global justice movement literature is relatively scant,[2] although we acknowledge that there is some work in the more academically oriented commentary on the social relationships and economic resources facilitating political engagement. In line with resource mobilization theory, this work underlines the fact that activists in the movement tend to be highly educated professionals and students (albeit often in unstable employment) and extremely well connected in activist networks at the national and transnational levels.[3] All this resonates with our analysis of the backgrounds of feminist antiglobalization activists in chapter 4, which highlighted their relative class privilege and their extensive social linkages. One additional insight hinted at in that chapter, however, is that such linkages should not be reduced to resources drawn on by individuals in instrumental ways, but rather understood in more expansive terms as also providing emotional triggers and sustenance for activism. Families and friends, after all, can be role models, shape our worldviews and ethical outlooks, and inspire us to act.

In addition to rethinking the mobilizing role of resources and networks, our research also points to the salience of exploring the reasons why people become involved in political action in the first place. On this point, we underlined in chapter 4 the claims about injustice made by our interviewees and their emotional responses. More specifically, in terms of the latter we pointed to the importance of anger and also empathy with and affection for other women as triggers for involvement. We acknowledge that the literature on the global justice movement does recognize that emotions underpin activism, albeit in a rather uneven and underdeveloped way. Anger, rage, and fury are by far the most frequently mentioned, although usually fleetingly.[4] The motivating role of empathy has only recently received analytical scrutiny (Reitan 2007: 20–21) and that of love and affection appears not to have registered. We would therefore like to see a more systematic analysis of the function that all three emotions serve in bringing individuals to the movement. Moreover, for us, the interplay of emotions with cognitive processes is an important and fascinating line of inquiry that could shed light on the origins of the global justice movement more generally.[5] Indeed, as Kolonel Klepto and Major Up Evil of the Clandestine Insurgent Clown Rebel Army conclude:

> Most of us became politically active because we felt something profoundly, such as injustice or ecological devastation. It is this emotion that triggers a change in our behaviour and gets us politicised. It's our ability to transform our feelings about the world into action that propels us to radical struggle. (Klepto and Up Evil 2005: 246)

Concerning the ways in which knowledge of injustice precipitates mobilization, in chapter 4 we distinguished between feminist antiglobalization activist articulations of their own negative personal experiences, on the one hand, and their awareness of the oppression suffered by others, on the other. In both cases, we have in effect assumed a sequential relationship between knowledge and agency, and in the former case, between experience and knowledge. While it is certainly possible that action follows from experience and knowledge in this way, here we want to propose that the politicization process may not always unfold in this order. Feminist scholars Cheryl Hercus and Chandra Mohanty provide us with alternative ways of thinking about this relationship. Hercus (2005: 12), arguing that it is "in the doing" that one may become a feminist, implies that knowledge claims do not always precede involvement in activism and may in fact develop out of it. Mohanty (1998), challenging the assumption that experience functions as the unmediated foundation of politics, implies that knowledge claims about experience are articulated in terms of injustice only when politicization has already taken place (see also Harding 1992: 186–87). Either way, further unpacking of the connections between experience, knowledge, and agency would undoubtedly enrich understandings of what brings people to act in the global justice movement—or, indeed, in any social movement.

NAMING THE ENEMY

Moving to the question of what activists in the global justice movement are fighting against, there is a clear consensus in the literature around the perception of a shared singular foe, or as Paul Kingsnorth puts it, around the clarion call of "one no" (2003). Most writers characterize the enemy as what William Ponniah and Thomas Fisher call "corporate capitalism" or "neoliberal globalization":[6]

> The perception is that corporate dominion has been organized across global space by the most powerful Northern states in the world, in collaboration with Southern economic and political elites. . . . Neoliberal globalization is not simply economic dominion of the world but also the imposition of a monolithic thought (*pensamiento unico*)[7]. . . . [T]he key instruments of contemporary globalization are the free trade agreements and policies propelled by the WTO, the North American Free Trade Agreement . . . and other regional trade agreements, and the privatisation policies of corporations, the G8 countries, the World Bank and the IMF. (2003: 10–11)[8]

In this context, neoliberal globalization is understood not simply in terms of the intentions and actions of specific individuals and groups, but rather as a system that is socially pervasive and global in scope and which has a wide range of detrimental impacts.[9] Examples of such impacts range from "dictatorship, monoculture, concentration of ownership, dependence, enclosure" (Kingsnorth 2003: 320) to "increasing privatization, commercialisation and depoliticisation of social life" (Smith et al. 2008: 13). Others add "war, social inequality, environmental problems, lack of democratic accountability, human rights, gender inequality and racism" to the mix (della Porta et al. 2006: 72). Of all the impacts identified, those that receive the most attention are economic inequality,[10] exclusion from decision making,[11] ecological degradation,[12] and violence.[13]

All in all, this description of "the enemy" of the global justice movement matches the critiques put forward by feminist antiglobalization activists outlined in chapter 5. Having said this, however, our work indicates that there is need for a more comprehensive analysis of what it is the global justice movement is fighting against. As we saw in chapter 5, feminist antiglobalization activists critically interrogate not only neoliberalism but also two other systems of oppression: patriarchy and racism. In other words, our interviewees issue an injunction of "many noes," rather than the "one no" portrayed in the global justice movement literature. In our view, there are several implications of this position. First and foremost, writings on the global justice movement must recognize these two additional systems of oppression if they want to offer a more complete narrative of what the movement is fighting against, that is, one that acknowledges and reflects the critiques of feminists within its ranks. At present, we find only a few scattered references in the literature to gender inequality, patriarchy, and racism (della Porta et al. 2006: 72; Yuen 2004: xvi; Ponniah and Fisher 2003: 10) and hardly any discussion of how they operate as distinct systems of oppression (for exceptions see Rupert 2000; Day 2005). Furthermore, as part of this inclusionary move, other systems of oppression may need to be brought into the frame. For example, as we noted in chapter 5, a handful of our interviewees emphasized the oppressive role of heterosexism. It would be interesting to investigate whether this view is shared by feminist antiglobalization activists beyond the sample of individuals to whom we talked or by other kinds of activists in the movement.

Another implication of the "many noes" injunction is the need to conceptualize multiple systems of oppression as multivalent and mutually constitutive. Thus, rather than simply adding racism, patriarchy, and other systems of oppression to the list of evils combated by the movement, analysts need to see them as intertwined. In chapter 5 we showed that these systems of oppression are experienced as mutually reinforcing at the level of impact. Here we want to propose that more conceptual work is necessary in order to explain how these oppressions constitute each other at the system level. Anne Sisson Runyan and Marianne Marchand agree, arguing that a feminist perspective on globalization pushes the researcher to look beyond the differential impacts of neoliberalism on men and women and to examine the interrelationship between systems of oppression or, as they put it, to explore "the *effects of gender on global restructuring* and the *effects of global restructuring on gender*" (2000: 228, emphasis added). But how, precisely, do we go about theorizing the relation between different systems of oppression? In what sense do they retain a distinct logic of their own, on the one hand, and yet constitute each other, on the other? A deeper reading of feminist work around the "intersectionality" of oppression could provide further resources for such an inquiry (Collins 1998; Crenshaw 1998; Nash 2008).

If we move from system-level analysis to the level of impact, we find no equivalent in the literature on the global justice movement to what we have characterized in chapter 5 as "bodily nautonomy." In effect, at present, the harm caused to women by the objectification and commodification of their bodies, the lack of control over their fertility, and sexual exploitation has not been thematized or explored in this literature. Acknowledging bodily nautonomy, however, is about more than just adding women into the picture. It is about recognizing a corporeal dimension to all suffering, including that of men, and giving it far more scholarly attention than it currently receives.

In chapter 5 we conceptualized the impact of oppression on women's lives in terms of "nodes of oppression." Here we want to reflect briefly on how this concept may be developed further in two main ways. In the first place, our analysis of the nodes of oppression identified by feminist antiglobalization activists suggests several *sites* in which oppression plays out, namely, the body, family, social movements, society, economy, state, and environment. These sites require more investigation in terms of both their specificity and their relationship to each other. In the second place, our analysis in chapter 5 pointed to a range of *logics* of oppression, inherent in the language of nautonomy, degradation, inequality, exploitation, exclusion, marginalization, and violence. Greater critical reflection on these logics of oppression would strengthen the narrative we have told here (for one effort to do this, see Maiguashca 2006a). What is at stake, for instance, when analysts choose to define a harm or node of oppression in terms of exploitation rather than inequality, or, say, marginalization rather than exclusion? Moreover, how do logics and sites relate to each other? It is possible to imagine that some logics of oppression cut across a range of sites. In chapter 5 we conceptualized violence as a distinct node of oppression, but here we propose that it would be helpful to see it as a type of harm that is experienced on many terrains—on the body, in the family, and in the economy, among others. After all, the more detailed and accurate maps we devise of the operations of oppression, the better our chances of creating a less oppressive and more just world.

IMAGINING OTHER WORLDS

Students of the global justice movement have vigorously rebutted the media charge that activists have multiple criticisms of the operations of power, but no solutions (see Chesters and Welsh 2006: 107–8). They point out that the World Social Forum, with its slogan "Another world is possible," embodies an open-ended aspiration to develop alternatives (Chesters and Welsh 2006: 120–25; Fisher and Ponniah 2003). Indeed, in a similar vein to our analysis in chapter 6, some authors see the Forum, and the broader movement, as embodying a "utopian" dimension (cf. Brecher, Costello, and Smith 2000: 62), which they define as ethical and imaginative, on the one hand, and radically transformative, on the other. Thus, Boaventura de Sousa Santos describes the Forum as a "critical utopia," emphasizing "the use of imagination to confront the apparent inevitability of whatever exists with something radically better" (2006: 10; see also Coté, Day, and de Peuter 2007; Juris 2008: 269).

In addition to this convergence between the characterization of activist visions in our work and that in other writings on the global justice movement, we find further overlaps when those visions are elaborated in more substantive terms. To begin with, the literature on the movement, like our account in chapter 6, tends to emphasize the diversity of what we called "concrete proposals," and mounts a normative defense of this feature. Consequently, it frequently presents a range of specific projects, stressing their differences, rather than one unified global program for change (*pace* Brecher, Costello, and Smith 2000: ch. 6). Take, for example, Amory Starr's survey of the aspirations of the movement (2005: part II), which includes the end of national debt, common ownership of the genetic building blocks of life, migrant rights, and the abolition of national borders (see also Smith et al. 2008: 91–104; Fisher and Ponniah 2003; Mertes 2004). Differences of ideological inclination and national context are often particularly highlighted (e.g., Polet 2007; Kingsnorth 2003; Smith et al. 2008: 91–104). Moreover, these differences are lauded as posing a challenge to the *pensamiento unico* of neoliberalism as well as to the more teleological and authoritarian versions of the Left. Thus, while Kingsnorth insists on the "one no" of the movement, he simultaneously celebrates its "many yeses," indicating the importance of striving for "many different worlds, cultures, economic and political models, within a shared humanity . . . diversity versus monoculture" (2003: 44–45). This is echoed by Naomi Klein, who, drawing on the writings of Subcomandante Marcos of the Zapatistas, states:

> Neoliberal economics is biased at every level towards centralization, consolidation and homogenisation. It is a war waged on diversity. Against it we need a movement of radical change committed to a single world with many worlds in it, that stands for the "one no and the many yeses." (Klein 2004: 209)

But diversity is not without boundaries, as the quotes above indicate. And it is on this point that we find yet another parallel between our work and the literature on the global justice movement. For as the reader will remember, in chapter 6 we argued that the concrete proposals of feminist antiglobalization activists are developed within the parameters of shared ethical goals. Kingsnorth, similarly, ends his book with a list of "principles and values" that antiglobalization activists have in common:

> This is a movement which stands for redistribution—redistribution of both wealth and power. It stands for equity—a world in which everyone gets their share, of material wealth, of representation, of influence. It stands for autonomy and for genuine democracy, both participatory and representative. It stands for a model of organising which rejects, in many though not all cases, traditional hierarchies and similarly rejects the old left-wing model of leader and followers, vanguard and masses. It stands for DIY politics—a willingness and a desire to take action yourself, to take to the streets, to act rather than to ask. It stands for economic independence, anti-consumerism and a redefinition of the very concepts of "growth" and "development." (Kingsnorth 2003: 317)

Other commentators provide alternative lists of ethical goals,[14] and although these may differ in their detail, they fundamentally coincide with most of the core values of feminist antiglobalization activists including economic equality, democracy, respect for the environment, and peace.[15]

Notwithstanding these affinities between our study and the global justice movement literature, there is a distinctive content to the concrete proposals for change of feminist antiglobalization activists that requires more consideration. As we showed in chapter 6, these proposals are situated not only in feminist ideology and national contexts, but also in the experiences and aspirations of specific embodied subjects, in this case, of particular groups of women, such as poor women in rural India, black women facing violence in Porto Alegre, Brazil, or women on welfare in the UK and France. Because of this, the demands of feminist antiglobalization activists have a unique focus on transforming the lives of these women, a focus that we think ought to be reflected in the surveys of goals of the wider movement. Moreover, in our view, any effort to be sensitive to diversity should acknowledge, in a more explicit way than we have seen thus far, the fact that all activist proposals necessarily speak to and from different constituencies. In this context, research is needed to explore whether there are other concrete proposals reflecting the aspirations of other, particular, embodied subjects, which are being missed or downplayed in accounts of the global justice movement.

With respect to ethical goals, our study yields at least two notable insights of wider relevance. First, it points to the importance of the goal of bodily integrity as articulated by feminist antiglobalization activists. In chapter 6, we discussed the content of this normative commitment in terms of sexual and reproductive rights, and the reclaiming of women's bodies from corporate power and processes of objectification. Without including such aspirations in agendas for change, our interviewees tell us, women's lives will not be transformed. Indeed, the desire to protect and care for the body and foster bodily self-determination can be seen as a universal goal, a good for all. Lists of the ethical goals of the global justice movement, then, are lacking in important ways without it.[16]

Second, our interviewees indicate that the ethical goals enumerated in the global justice movement literature should be formulated in a more expansive way. After all, if the nodes of oppression to which they are a response are conceptualized as multivalent (seen as constituted by the interplay of, at minimum, patriarchy, racism, and neoliberalism), then, for example, economic equality, as an ethical goal, has to incorporate demands not only for redistribution of resources, but also for the transformation of the division of labor in the home. Similarly, peace should be taken as implying both an end to war and also an end to domestic violence.

We argued in chapter 6 that the ethical goals of our interviewees, taken together, amount to a vision of "gender justice." Our discussion of this was only preliminary, but, in our view, the idea merits further elaboration. Any effort to do so could start by exploring parallel arguments within the global justice movement literature about the importance of "justice" as a metadiscourse binding the ethical goals of the movement together. Thus, della Porta and Tarrow (2005a: 12) claim that "'global social justice' has become a master-frame of new mobilizations" (see also della Porta et al. 2006: 67–79; della Porta 2007b: 74) and, in a more normative than explanatory register, Barry K. Gills makes a similar point: "let Global Justice become an eternal idea in the mind of humanity, and let it be our highest value and common ideal" (2008: 4). These authors suggest that global justice claims, as mobilized within the movement, are "multifaceted" (Rootes and Saunders 2007: 149). On our reading, there seem to be three main ways in which we can think about this. First, the notion of global justice encompasses a variety of grievances (or nodes of oppression) and a range of ethical goals (e.g., Rootes and Saunders 2007: 149). Second, it incorporates responses to different sites of oppression, in the sense that we find distinctions drawn between social, environmental, and economic justice (e.g., Reiter et al. 2007: 68; Caney 2008). Third, conceptions of global justice may rest on a range of underlying paradigms, from procedural to rights-based theories, and from equality of opportunity to equality of outcome (Patomäki 2008: 12).

Drawing on these analytical arguments, it is possible to formulate the following questions that may help to further elucidate the notion of gender justice. What is the relationship between gender justice and social justice? Does gender justice have its own logic, equivalent to environmental justice, reflecting the concerns of a distinct movement sector? What does our notion of gender justice have to offer to these emerging accounts of global justice more generally? As Gills suggests, "It is . . . necessary to open a serious discussion on the definition(s) and practice(s) of global justice, a discussion that is global, multi-civilizational and dialogic in nature and scope" (2008: 4; see also Patomäki 2008: 21–23). In our view, feminist arguments about gender justice should be an important part of this discussion. In fact, as already broached in chapter 6, feminist renditions of gender justice may well point to a more expansive and inclusive understanding of justice to the extent that it addresses multiple systems of power, recognizes but goes beyond material distribution, and reflects a universal aspiration while at the same time speaking to and from embodied subjects and situated proposals for change.

We turn finally to the concept of "ethos," which we fleshed out in terms of two sets of "principles of action" (1995: 61) and which we deployed to capture an essential component of the utopian vision of feminist antiglobalization activists. We argued in chapter 6 that this ethos prescribes holistic, participatory, and dialogical principles with regard to the "internal mode of action" and a more critical and multilateralist sensibility with respect to the "external." To what extent are these principles acknowledged in the global justice movement literature? We note some discussion with respect to internal interlocutors. For instance, there is certainly an emphasis on a holistic approach to other activists among those who engage in what Marieke de Goede refers to as "carnivalesque dissent" (2005: 382). This can be seen in the activities of the clown army whose humorous and ironic performances at protest sites involve "working with the body . . . [to] reveal the soft skin again, to find the human being . . . transforming and sustaining the inner life of the activists" (Klepto and Up Evil 2005: 244–47; see also Notes from Nowhere 2003: 173–83). Furthermore, there is a recognition among commentators that participatory and dialogical principles are a defining feature of so-called horizontal organizing. As argued at several points in the book, such organizing, influenced by anarchism (Graeber 2002; Epstein 2001), seeks to flatten hierarchies within groups in contradistinction to what are perceived as more vertical structures (see, e.g., De Angelis 2004). To this end, "everyone's needs and concerns are listened and taken into account" and "there is an attitude of openness, of respect for each person's position" (Starhawk 2002b: 172; see also Toft 2007). It would be fruitful to explore the extent to which these principles are found beyond the confines of carnivalesque and anarchist strands in the movement. After all, as pointed out in chapter 7, feminists strive to work in participatory and dialogical ways whether they are organized in horizontal or vertical structures, so it is at least possible that these principles are more widespread.

Turning to external interlocutors, we have less to work with. Arguments in the literature about how the global justice movement relates to the state, for example, tend to frame activities in terms of strategy rather than ethical principles (see, e.g., Chesters and Welsh 2006: 129; Hardt 2002). It would be interesting to investigate whether or not strategic positions are underpinned by normative commitments. This kind of investigation could further illuminate the relationship between the utopian visions of activists and how they act together to make them a reality.

COLLECTIVE ACTION

When addressing the political practices of the global justice movement, the overwhelming emphasis in the literature is on protest.[17] Particular attention has been paid to "disruptive" modes of protest, from the demonstrations against the WTO and the G8 (Cockburn, St. Clair, and Sekula 2000; Tina 2005) to shoving custard pies or waving golden phalluses in the faces of men in suits at elite conferences (Notes from Nowhere 2003: 246–55, 262–63; Kingsnorth 2003: 146). Our study of feminist antiglobalization activism certainly confirms protest as widespread, in both disruptive and more conventional forms. However, our account in chapter 7 went far beyond this to identify five other types of political practice undertaken by our interviewees that also deserve scrutiny—advocacy, service provision, knowledge production, popular education, and movement building.

To be fair, some commentators on the global justice movement have criticized their colleagues for what they see as a reductive focus on protest and have argued for a broadening of the lens on movement practices to include ongoing activities in communities aimed at transforming everyday life.[18] To this end, accounts have emerged that offer brief glimpses of alternative practices, echoing the range we found in feminist antiglobalization activism. Service provision, for instance, can be seen in efforts to reconnect electricity supplies in the shantytowns of South Africa (Starr 2005: 177; Kingsnorth 2003: 87–123). Popular education is found in a proliferation of initiatives to build critical awareness of global economic and political structures among the wider public (Trapese Collective 2005; see also Coté, Day, and de Peuter 2007: part III). Especially in the more academic-oriented literature, we catch sight of a range of advocacy practices around attempts to pressure various international actors on issues such as debt relief for poor southern countries (Mayo 2005: ch: 9; Reitan 2007: ch. 3; Bandy and Smith 2005: part IV). These glimpses notwithstanding, the full panoply of practices engaged in by global justice movement activists has not yet been systematically studied or adequately conceptualized.

The typology presented in chapter 7 was our attempt at such a study of feminist antiglobalization activist practices. What we would like to do here is draw out some possible areas of research that spring directly from this preliminary effort. On the one hand, there is a question as to whether other movement sectors pursue a similar range of practices and thus whether our typology has wider applicability. On the other hand, there is a need to think more carefully about where movement action takes place. Given the focus on protest in the literature, it is not surprising to find the prevailing site of global justice movement activism presented as "out in the streets." However, it is clear from our research that feminist antiglobalization activist practices are not confined to the streets. This being the case, we suggest the understanding of power elaborated above, and more specifically our argument about the need to disentangle different sites of oppression, provides a useful starting point for thinking about the location of feminist antiglobalization activism. In other words, the body, family, movements, society, economy, state, and environment could be conceptualized also as terrains of political action. The practices discussed in chapter 7, it seems to us, seek to intervene in and transform the relations of oppression reproduced in all of these realms.

A further conceptual line of inquiry concerns Sasha Roseneil's modes of action. In chapter 7, we drew on her distinction, mentioned above, between internal and external modes of action (1995: 71), the latter referring to those activities that confront the outside world and external opponents, and the former to those oriented to building solidarity within the movement. We found this a useful heuristic device for our framing of movement practices insofar as it gave us contrasting end points on a spectrum along which practices could be arrayed. Nonetheless, we also found, as we pointed out in our conclusion of chapter 7, that a strict dichotomy between internal and external modes cannot be sustained. This is because most feminist antiglobalization activist practices are dual-facing, engaging with interlocutors both within and beyond the movement,[19] and because feminist antiglobalization groups typically multitask, pursuing a wide range of practices simultaneously.

Despite the limitations of an internal-external dichotomy, we still find the concept of a mode of action useful, understood in broad terms as a discrete set of political practices underpinned by a coherent rationale. Indeed, we propose that feminist antiglobalization activism embodies a distinctive mode of action that can be characterized as *principled pragmatism*. By principled, we mean that it is driven by a utopian vision that reflects a normative commitment to overturning oppression and to acting in principled ways. By pragmatic, we refer to the imperative to get things done in the here and now.[20] More concretely, pragmatism indicates both a focus on achievable, immediate ends, and a general responsiveness and adaptability to one's environment. In our study, principled pragmatism can be seen, for instance, in popular education efforts to impart practical skills to women. By teaching women to read or to build their own homes, feminist antiglobalization activists are not only helping them to improve their everyday circumstances in very concrete ways, but also seeking to empower them to determine their own lives. It is also evident in practices around service provision. As we showed in chapter 7, our interviewees respond to the needs of women in their communities by offering both physical and psychological aid intended to help heal the ravages of economic deprivation or violence and to rebuild self-esteem. By fusing a principled and pragmatic orientation to action in this way, feminist antiglobalization activists in effect instantiate their ethical vision of a transformed society through concrete actions in women's everyday lives, striving to realize their desired future in the present.

This way of thinking about the practices of feminist antiglobalization activism generates two potential avenues for further work on models of action. To begin with, there is a question as to whether principled pragmatism is unique to feminists within the global justice movement or found more widely. We strongly suspect that the latter may be the case. Hints in this direction are evident in the characterization by some scholars of the utopian dimension of the movement as "an ongoing process of becoming" (Coté, Day, and de Peuter 2007: 13) and as involving an open-ended commitment to multiple alternatives (Santos 2006: 11), in contrast to "totalizing visions of a far-off, perfectly harmonious world" (Juris 2008: 286).

A second possible focus of study concerns the extent to which other modes of action may be at play within the global justice movement. What we described above as "carnivalesque dissent" is a case in point. Based on a "methodology" that refuses dichotomies between "the personal and the political . . . activist and non-activist," and oriented to "transforming and sustaining the inner emotional life of . . . activists" (Klepto and Up Evil 2005: 244–45, 247) this mode of action seems to be bound by a coherent, normative rationale. The "'new' network ontology" (Cumbers, Routledge, and Nativel 2008: 183), invoked in some quarters as typifying the global justice movement, provides a further example. In this regard, analysts have pointed to the deep-rooted normative underpinnings of the network practices that are so widespread in the movement, highlighting democratic and inclusive desires to flatten hierarchies, encourage spontaneity, and incorporate diversity in the struggle for a better world.[21] Again, it might be helpful to understand these normative commitments and their associated practices as constituting a distinct mode of action, this time centering on the creation and sustenance of solidarity in the global justice movement.

FORGING SOLIDARITY

Ever since the phenomenon of "teamsters and turtles" coming together at the Battle of Seattle (Berg 2003), writing on the global justice movement has sought to understand the extent and character of cohesion within it. After all, if this is "a movement of movements," one in which diversity is not only acknowledged but celebrated, on what basis is solidarity possible? We approached this question in chapter 8 through the trope of identity, as do many other writers on the global justice movement (e.g., Chesters and Walsh 2006: 130–34; della Porta 2005; Smith 2002: 209–14).

Among those using this trope, there is a marked tendency to define identities in terms of political ideologies. And despite considerable debate around which ideological identities are present and/or dominant within the movement—ranging from Marxism to social democracy to anarchism[72]— there seems to be consensus that the movement has a "clearly left wing profile" (della Porta 2005: 192). Admittedly, a handful of commentators have drawn attention to the existence of a right-wing, populist antiglobalization position,[73] but by far the majority of them do not. This left-wing characterization is strongly confirmed by our study of feminist antiglobalization activists in chapter 8.

Our work also corroborates a finding made by social movement scholar Donatella della Porta concerning what she calls "tolerant" or "flexible" identities in the global justice movement (2005: 186). Della Porta argues that these identities value "diversity," show a willingness to be "contaminated" by others, and reflect a tendency to "limited identifications" around "concrete objectives" (2005: 186–89; see also Tarrow and della Porta 2005: 237–40). This view resonates with our claims in chapter 8 about the normative value that feminist antiglobalization activists attach to the diversity of identities among women and feminists, and their marked flexibility in the mobilization of ideological categories.

These convergences notwithstanding, chapter 8 brings to light new lines of inquiry on identity. Most obviously, our chapter makes clear that the literature on the global justice movement neglects feminism as an important ideological identity for activists. Yet, as we have demonstrated, a large proportion of our interviewees lay claim to this identity. For this reason, we would be interested to find out whether and to what extent feminist identities are mobilized beyond the specific movement sector that was the focus of our research. In pursuing this question, we need to be open minded as to the meaning and nature of feminist identity. For example, is it being deployed in mixed-gender groups in ways that redefine and transform its meaning?

In addition, chapter 8 foregrounded the role of a whole *type* of identity, namely social identity, which we contrasted to more ideological sources of self-labeling. More specifically, we illustrated that categories such as "woman," "black," "lesbian," and "Muslim," and conjunctural combinations of these, are politicized within feminist antiglobalization activism, serving to precipitate and sustain individual involvement and demarcate collective actors in the form of autonomous organizations. Yet, social identities like these are rarely noted within the global justice movement literature, aside from glimpses in della Porta's discussion of the "heterogeneous bases" of the movement (2005: 180), and in references to nationalist identifications (see, e.g., Juris 2008: 65, 73) and "indigeneity" (e.g., Higgins 2005; MacDonald 2006: ch. 6). Clearly, there is room for further research into the range of social identities mobilized in the global justice movement—what about gay, lesbian, and transsexual identities, for example?—as well as into the detail of how they are constituted and deployed.

Why has social identity as a category been so neglected in global justice movement commentary? We suggest that an underlying anxiety around identity politics may be at work. According to Linda Alcoff (2000), both liberals and leftists have criticized identity politics as separatist in orientation, as reifying identities, and as partisan and solipsistic, incapable of speaking beyond a particular subject position. Alcoff adds that identity politics is seen by leftist critics in particular as operating on the terrain of culture, concerned with a politics of representation and symbols rather than with material interests or social justice. Feminism, or what are seen to be its more identity-oriented components, is often the target of this critique, along with other movements such as those organizing around race and sexuality (see, e.g., Gitlin 1993, 1995; Hobsbawm 1996).[24]

These stereotypical assumptions about identity politics seem to have filtered into the literature on the global justice movement. They are evident in Fred Halliday's dismissal of the movement as lacking political coherence in part because of tendencies within it to suspend "any critical judgement with regard to ethnic, religious, and other 'indigenous' cultures" (Halliday 2000: 127). For others, the strength of the global justice movement lies precisely in the fact that it "has transcended [the] identity politics" of the 1980s "by seeking to forge a new internationalism" (Callinicos 2003: 113) and by moving beyond a narrow focus on cultural "representation" (Klein 2000: 107–8; see also Thomas and Klein 2002).

One problem with these views of the global justice movement is that they rest on a misunderstanding of identity, in general, and social identity, in particular. Although it may well be the case that identities can sometimes be perceived in essentialist ways and used to justify tendencies toward separatist organizing (see batTzedek 1999; Phelan 1989: ch. 3), our research highlights how feminist antiglobalization activists have been able to mobilize identities in open-ended, flexible, other-oriented ways. Assumptions on this score therefore need careful checking against specific empirical instances.

In our view, another problem inherent in the claim that the global justice movement is transcendent of identity politics is that it rests on an assumed antithesis between two models of politics, what feminist scholar Nancy

Fraser describes as the "politics of recognition," in which "[c]ultural domination supplants exploitation as the fundamental injustice," and the "politics of redistribution," concerned with economic injustice (1997: 11–12). Problematizing this dichotomy, Fraser argues that movements hinging on race and gender are "bivalent collectivities" organizing around both these forms of politics simultaneously (1997: 16–17; see critique in Alcoff 2006). Feminist antiglobalization activism, combining as it does, for example, a concern for material inequalities in the labor market and the cultural stigmatization of women's bodies, is certainly bivalent in this sense. Interestingly, Ruth Reitan's recent study of the global justice movement asserts that there is "considerable empirical evidence" that this bivalent orientation can be found more widely (2007: 60–63). For us, this belies any understanding of that movement as solely about a politics of redistribution. It also implies that global justice movement scholars need to be more vigilant about the paradigms of politics on which they rely.

Finally, we want to move to the larger question of how solidarity is forged in the global justice movement. In chapter 8, we focused our efforts on tracing how identities are mobilized, but there are, of course, many other ways of thinking about how activists create and sustain a sense of togetherness and develop a shared commitment to others in political struggle (e.g., Waterman 2000: 140–42). Some of these are touched on in our other chapters. In chapter 4, for instance, our account of what brings our interviewees to feminist antiglobalization activism, and, more specifically, our argument about the role of consciousness of oppression and emotional responses to it, chimes with Reitan's efforts to construct a typology of solidarity based on how individuals become politicized:

> First, among activists at a considerable distance from a threat, *sympathy* with the suffering of others who are deemed worthy of one's support, seems to be the prevailing affective response among those who choose to act, leading to solidarity based on *altruism*. Second, a *perceived connection* between one's own problems or struggle and that of others tends to lead to *empathy* with another's suffering and a sense that its source is at least *remotely threatening* to oneself, which evokes a solidarity based on *reciprocity*. Third, *immediate* proximity to a threat or harm produces *personal suffering*, which can lead activists to seek solidarity relationships with others sharing the same threatened *identity*. (Reitan 2007: 51, emphasis in original)

As is clear from this quote, Reitan's distinction between altruistic, reciprocal, and identity-based solidarity rests on the degree of proximity of individuals to suffering. This framework is useful in highlighting the role of experience and emotional responses, particularly empathy, in the construction of solidarity. Our work, however, raises a question about the stability of Reitan's typology. As we argued in chapter 4, even those who become politicized initially by learning about the suffering of distant others from academic texts may come to perceive themselves as potentially threatened by or as actually suffering oppression. This leaves open the possibility that solidarity based on altruism can shift into a more reciprocal or identity-based sense of solidarity. In addition, our analysis indicates that there are limitations to viewing solidarity entirely as a response to actual or potential suffering. In chapter 4, we pointed to the role of friendship networks as key to bringing individuals into activism and sustaining their commitment, which suggests that solidarity may emerge out of positive social relations with others. Our other chapters hint at yet more possible ingredients for the emergence of solidarity. The development of a common critique of the enemy, the articulation of utopian visions, and engagement in political practices can all, in different ways, function to bind activists together in the pursuit of a shared political project.

FINAL REMARKS

We would like to close by returning to the political significance of our study. We are convinced that feminist antiglobalization activism is not only alive and well in the global justice movement, but shaping this "movement of movements" in profound, albeit often unrecognized, ways. Moreover, bringing "Skeleton woman" out of the shadows will strengthen the movement as a whole. For, as we have argued in this book, feminist critical interrogations of neoliberalism as crosscut by patriarchy and racism can only serve to deepen our understanding of "the enemy" confronting the global justice movement. Feminist utopian thinking, in addition, provides normative inspiration as well as ethical resources for new, more expansive visions of alternative worlds. Guided by both their critical and affirmative analyses, feminist antiglobalization activists have constructed a toolkit of innovative and pragmatic political practices from which others can usefully draw. Finally, our interviewees are bridge builders, mobilizing identities in open-ended and inclusive ways that are of wider significance for a movement composed of such diverse strands. For all these reasons, feminist antiglobalization activism has an important contribution to make to the global justice movement. In their efforts to support that movement and its struggle for other possible worlds, commentators on it must allow Skeleton woman out of the shadows and into the light of day.

NOTES

1. E.g., Broad and Heckscher 2003: 721–24; Starr 2005: 20–21; Katsiaficas 2004; Juris 2008: 39–40.

2. This is on the surface rather puzzling with regard to the more academic commentary on the global justice movement, as the social movement theory on which it often draws has a lot to offer on this score. It seems to us that the question of individual motivation is turned into one of recruitment and studied more at the organizational than the individual level in the social movement theory-influenced scholarship. There is an additional point here to do with levels of analysis, in that social movement scholarship on the global justice movement seems to us to have an overriding concern with "scale shift," or with how and why national movements or organizations are joining up with each other on a transnational scale, or influencing each other across borders (e.g., Reitan 2007; della Porta and Tarrow 2005b; Bandy and Smith 2005). Thus, while national-level studies may include an explanation of why individuals act, this story drops out at the transnational level where work on the spread of ideas and identities, and of organizational form, is more predominant.

3. See IBASE 2005: 17–25; Smith et al. 2008, 50–56; della Porta et al. 2006: 43–49; Reiter et al. 2007: 65–67; Sommier and Combes 2007: 116; Juris 2008: 80; Tarrow 2005: 43–44.

4. See, e.g., Notes from Nowhere 2003: 21; Starr 2005: 9, 16; for a more in-depth analysis, see Sullivan 2005.

5. Recent trends in social movement scholarship and long-standing arguments in feminist theory provide rich theoretical resources for such an endeavor. For the former see Goodwin, Jasper, and Polletta 2001a, 2001b; Jasper 1998; Flam and King 2005; for the latter see Frye 1983: 84–94; Jagger 1989; Taylor 1995; Hercus 1999.

6. There is also a significant strand of analysis that prefers to characterize the real problem as the underlying system of capitalism (e.g., Bircham and Charlton 2001; Callinicos 2003: 26; Carter and Morland 2004; Tormey 2004b).

7. There seems to be no direct equivalent for *pensamiento unico* in English—as there is, for example, in French: *la pensée unique* (Polet 2004a: vii). Perhaps the nearest we have is British Prime Minister Margaret Thatcher's infamous TINA phrase, "There Is No Alternative."

8. See also della Porta 2007b: 16; Moghadam 2009: 13; Coté, Day, and de Peuter 2007: 11; Burbach 2001: 3; Munck 2007: 73; Starr 2000: 151; Smith and Bandy 2005: 12; Waterman 2005: 141.

9. See, e.g., Starr 2000: ch. 1, 150–51; Notes from Nowhere 2003: 109; Sullivan 2005; Birchfield and Freyberg-Inan 2005: 154–61; Callinicos 2003: ch. 1.

10. E.g., Moghadam 2009: 22; International Forum on Globalization 2002: 45; Caffentzis 2005.

11. E.g., Kingsnorth 2003: 320; Klein 2000: 445; Smith 2008: chs. 3, 4; Starr 2005: 47–52.

12. E.g., International Forum on Globalization 2002: 44; Hall 2001; O'Brien 2001; Burbach, Núñez, and Kagarlitsky 1996: 16–19.

13. German 2001; Gruffydd Jones 2005; Sullivan 2005; *On Fire* 2001; Sen and Saini 2005: part 3.

14. See Callinicos 2003: 106–11; Eggert and Guigni 2007: 197–98; Reiter et al. 2007: 67; della Porta et al. 2006: 74–79; Rootes and Saunders 2007: 149; Smith et al. 2008: 14; International Forum on Globalization 2002: 42–46.

15. It is arguably democracy that continues to receive the most attention, with the extensive articulation of aspirations to expand and deepen democracy within society

as well as within the movement (see, e.g., Epstein 2001; Graeber 2002; Polletta 2002: ch. 7; Vysotsky 2003; Starhawk 2002b: 169–78; Toft 2007; Santos 2006: 39–44).

16. We suspect that concerns around bodily integrity (eradicating torture, for example, or protecting sexual choice) may be subsumed in the literature under calls for human rights (e.g., della Porta et al. 2006: 77). However, the analytical and political difficulty here is that rights discourse is transferable; it can be used with regard to a range of harms and social sites, while we want to emphasize the feminist belief that the body as a site of oppression demands a normative focus in its own terms.

17. E.g., Bircham and Charlton 2001; Carter and Morland 2004; Starr 2005; Chesters and Welsh 2006; della Porta and Diani 2006; Bandy and Smith 2005.

18. Crass n.d.; Dixon 2000; Albert 2001; Klein 2002: 23–25, 158.

19. Part of the problem here is that is not always easy to discern who is inside and who is outside the movement with regard to feminist antiglobalization activism. After all, most of the practices of our interviewees seek to engage women in the wider community, who may not themselves be activists but who are treated nonetheless as part of the broader political community.

20. This is not the same as "strategic," which, as we pointed out in chapter 6, can be seen as involving a narrowly instrumental and rational approach to action.

21. See, e.g., Notes from Nowhere 2003: 63–73; Wainwright et al. 2007; Cumbers, Routledge, and Nativel 2008: 185–88; Klein 2002: 16–23; Arquilla and Ronfeldt 2001; Bennett 2005: 213–25. We do not mean by this to suggest that networks and networking within the movement are necessarily horizontal but rather that there is a marked ethical commitment to organize in this way. On this point, we agree with those commentators who warn of the tendency to romanticize networking practices and who argue for the need to subject these relationships to a critical analysis (e.g., Cumbers, Routledge, and Nativel 2008; Routledge, Cumbers, and Nativel 2007; Waterman 2000: 144).

22. See, e.g., Epstein 2001; Kingsnorth 2003: 231–34; Callinicos 2003: ch. 2; Mayo 2005: 24–33.

23. See Starr 2000: 136–44; Rupert 2000; Mayo 2005: 29–31; Munck 2007: ch. 7.

24. A critique of identity politics on this basis has also been articulated within feminism, directed both at women organizing on the basis of specific conjunctural identities (such as lesbians or black women) who are feared to be splintering the movement, and at those seen to be overpreoccupied with articulating and defending women's difference from men (e.g., Mandle n.d.; Benhabib 1994; see also discussion in Ryan 2001).

Appendix

Feminist Antiglobalization Activism

Group Listings

The information that follows is as complete and up-to-date as we could make it as of June 2009. As groups move or disband frequently, and their websites change continually, it should be taken as a guide for research rather than as in any way definitive.

1. Abortion Rights
"Abortion Rights is the national [UK] pro-choice campaign. We are campaigning to defend and extend women's rights and access to safe, legal abortion. We oppose any attack on the 1967 Abortion Act including any attempt to lower the abortion time limit. 40 years after the introduction of safe, legal abortion in Britain women's rights should be advanced not driven back. A consistent three quarters of people support a woman's right to choose in Britain. We believe the law should be brought into line with public opinion—so that women can make their own reproductive decisions without the current unfair legal barriers, obstructions and delays.
"We aim to:

- Oppose any restrictions in women's current rights and access to abortion.
- Improve the current UK abortion law for women, to make abortion available on the request of the woman.
- Improve women's access to, and experience of, abortion—ensure all women in the UK have equal access to safe, legal, and free abortion." (Abortion Rights n.d.)

Contact details:
18 Ashwin Street
London
E8 3DL
Tel: 0207 923 9792
Fax: 0207 923 9792
choice@abortionrights.org.uk
http://www.abortionrights.org.uk

2. AfricaWoman

"Our aim is to encourage African women to develop a new voice in journalism—to develop our personal confidence as opinion formers—to make sure women hit the headlines on issues sidelined by politicians and to learn skills to develop supplements for African newspapers, a wires and news service for African community radio stations, present documentaries for UK TV and radio, and ultimately move as trainers to other parts of the world" (AfricaWoman 2003).
Last available contact details (AfricaWoman 2005):
PO Box
Nairobi 00200
Kenya
Tel: 254-2-2721429
Fax: 254-2-2721439
africawoman@swiftkenya.com
http://www.africawoman.net (not functioning June 2009)

3. Akshara

"Akshara is a women's resource centre, which believes in the power of the word, in the right to information and in its use as a tool for the transformation of individuals and society. Akshara grew out of the contemporary women's movement in India and has gender equality and human rights as its primary concerns in working with young women and men. We have been active in legal campaigns on violence against women, service and support" (Akshara n.d.).
Contact details:
501 Neelambari Road no. 86
Off Gokhale Road
Dadar West
Mumbai 40028
India
Telefax: 91-22-24316082
aksharacentre@vsnl.com
http://www.aksharacentre.org

4. All African Women's Group

"Includes women from Algeria, Bangladesh, Burundi, The Comoros, Ivory Coast, Congo (DRC and Brazzaville), Eritrea, Ethiopia, Kenya, Rwanda, Somalia, Uganda, Zimbabwe. In Africa we organized for survival and for change for ourselves, our families and communities. . . . We came to the UK where we thought our torture would be finished but it has continued. The problem many of us face now is that our asylum claims are denied and we have nowhere to sleep, no money, no food. . . . We are [a] self help group. We have been fighting against detention and deportation, the government's brutal new laws, legal injustices in our cases, racism, destitution, forced dispersal, rape, forced conscription in the countries we fled from, and to get our right to stay in a safe place. We want recognition of our caring work, the same protection and resources that everyone in every country needs like housing, food, healthcare, and schools for our children" (All African Women's Group n.d.).

Contact details:

Crossroads Women's Centre

230a Kentish Town Rd.

London NW5 2AB

UK

Tel: 020 7482 2496

centre@crossroadswomen.net

http://www.allwomencount.net/EWC%20Immigrant/all_african_women.htm

5. All India Democratic Women's Association (AIDWA)

"The All India Democratic Women's Association (AIDWA) is an independent left oriented women's organisation committed to achieving democracy, equality and women's emancipation. One of the largest mass organisations of women in the country, it has an organisational presence in 21 states. The bulk of its 70 lakh membership comprises of rural and urban poor women. It takes up the issues of all women, regardless of caste, class or creed. In policy and practice, it upholds secular values against all forms of fundamentalism, and challenges and resists cultural practices, demeaning to women including those imposed in the name of tradition. AIDWA has led many struggles of women against policies of globalisation, against communalism and sectarian violence, for the eradication of caste discrimination, against all forms of violence against women and oppressed sections. Membership of AIDWA is open to any woman above the age of 16. AIDWA does not accept funds from any foreign funding agency or the government" (AIDWA Maharashtra State Committee n.d.).

Contact details:

121, Vithal Bhai Patel House

Rafi Marg
New Delhi 110001
India
Tel: 00 91 2 3710476/3319566
aidwa@ndb.vsnl.net.in; info@aidwa.org
http://www.aidwaonline.com/index.php

6. Andhra Pradesh Chaitanya Mahila Samakhya (APCMS)

"APCMS is a federation of women['s] organisations. It came into existence on September 24th 1995. Ten women's organisations from different districts in Andhra Pradesh came together to form the federation. Since then, the organisation has been working on several women and people's issues. . . . There is no liberation to the oppressed unless exploiters are brought down. The path to liberation is the new democratic revolution which is against the feudal and imperialist forces. Women's liberation is linked to the liberation of the oppressed people. . . . APCMS [has] organised struggles on issues like dowry, obscenity, social welfare (girls) hostel problems, harassment at workplaces, state repression etc." (APCMS n.d.a).
No up-to-date contact details available.

7. Andhra Pradesh Mahila Samatha Society (APMSS)

"The Andhra Pradesh Mahila Samatha society is a part of the Mahila Samakhya Project which was launched in the state in January 1993. . . . The Mahila Samkhya Project presupposes that education can be a decisive intervention towards women's equality. In this regard, its objectives are:

- To create an environment where women demand knowledge and information.
- Enhance the self-image and self-confidence of women.
- To enable women to determine their own lives and influence their environment, thus empowering them to play a positive role in their own development and the development of society. (APMSS n.d.)

Contact details:
No. 39, Aravind Nagar Colony
Domalguda
Hyderabad—500 029, AP
India
Tel: 00 91 40 27600258
Fax: 00 91 40 27630057
info@apmss.org
http://www.apmss.org

8. Articulação de Mulheres Brasilieras (AMB)

"The Articulação de Mulheres Brasilieras is a nonparty political organization that articulates and empowers feminist struggle and political action of women at the national and international level.

"The AMB agenda is action oriented toward the goal of social transformation and the elimination of inequality, racism, exploitative relation, and for the end of the oppression of all women.

"In order to achieve these objectives, the AMB strengthens the feminist movement, helping to build a political subject and organize actions orientated to the transformation and democratization of the state and society, highlighting different dimensions of politics, culture, and the economy" (AMB n.d., our translation).

Contact details:
AMB Executive Secretary
Rua Real Da Torre
593 Bairro Madalena
CEP 50610-000 Recife
PE, Brasil
Tel: 00 55 (81) 3445 2086
amb@soscorpo.or.br
http://www.articulacaodemulheres.org.br/

9. Articulação de Mulheres Negras Brasilieras (AMNB)

"The AMNB—Network of Black Brazilian Women's Organizations—was founded in September 2000, constituted by twenty-three founding organizations from different regions of Brazil. It was created with the initial objective of bringing black women to the center of the organizing process for the Third World Conference on Racism, Xenophobia and Associated Discrimination (South Africa 2002). In the wake of the conference, the AMNB has dedicated itself to monitoring the recommendations of the Plan of Action and to formulating strategies for inclusive economic development in Brazil, centered on protecting and promoting rights; generating opportunities in the world of work in the city and the countryside; and promoting equality of treatment in all areas of life, based on respect for human diversity and ending racism, sexism, homophobia, and class discrimination in Brazil and throughout Latin America" (AMNB n.d., our translation).

Last known contact details (confirmed in Werneck 2006):
Executive Secretary of AMNB
CRIOLA
Av. Presidente Vargas 482, Sobreloja 203
Centro Rio de Janeiro, CEP 20.071-000
RJ, Brasil

Tel: 00 55 (81) 2158 6194
amnb@uol.com.br
http://www.amnb.org.br

10. Articulacíon Feminista Marcosur (AFM)
"Articulacíon Feminista Marcosur (AFM) is a network of women's groups in Latin America that seeks to amplify the voices of feminists against all forms of social discrimination, oppressions and vulnerabilities. AFM opposes all manifestations of religious, economic and cultural fundamentalisms and propagates for democratic forms of conflict resolution and affirms solidarities and convergences within diversities. It spearheaded the creative and world-renowned campaign 'Your mouth against Fundamentalisms' [and] primarily works on issues of sexual and reproductive rights, democracy and women's political participation" (Feminist Dialogues 2006).
Contact details:
San José 1436
Montevideo 11200
Uruguay
Tel: 598-2 901 8782
Fax: 598-2 902 0393
cotidian@cotidianomujer.org.uy, afm@mujeresdelsur.org.uy
http://www.mujeresdelsur.org.uy

11. Asmita
"Asmita is a resource centre for women that was set up in 1991 to

- create a space for women to come together
- provide a context for critical dialogue and reflection
- facilitate feminist analysis and action on critical issues
- provide resources to women in need.

". . . We work to raise awareness of gender issues at all levels" (Asmita n.d.).
Contact details:
10-3-96, Plot 283, 4th Floor, Street 6, Teacher's Colony
East Marredpalli
Secunderabad 500 026
A.P.
India
Tel: 00 91 40 7733251/7733229
Fax: 00 91 40-7733745
asmitacollective@gmail.com
http://www.asmitacollective.in/index.htm

12. Association for Women's Rights in Development (AWID)
"The Association for Women's Rights in Development (AWID) is an international membership organization connecting, informing and mobilizing people and organizations committed to achieving gender equality, sustainable development and women's human rights. Our goal is to cause policy, institutional and individual change that will improve the lives of women and girls everywhere. We do this by facilitating ongoing debates on fundamental and provocative issues as well as by building the individual and organizational capacities of those working for women's empowerment and social justice.

A dynamic network of women and men around the world, AWID members are researchers, academics, students, educators, activists, business people, policy-makers, development practitioners, funders and more. AWID recognises that our members are our most valuable resource. We have a broad network of expert, committed members interested in sharing their ideas towards viable solutions for gender equality" (AWID 2005).
Contact details:
Toronto Secretariat
215 Spadina Ave., Suite 150
Toronto, Ontario
M5T 2C7
Canada
Tel: (001) 416 594 3773
Fax: (001) 416 594 0330
contact@awid.org
http://www.awid.org/

13. ATTAC—Feminist groups
"The women of feminist ATTAC want:

- Concepts for a humane globalization in which women can live and participate according to their own needs and desires
- A sustainable democratization of economic policy and of the markets
- Financial markets which promote productive activities of men and women and a humane development of our economic system.

"We therefore focus our activities on:

- Making sure that the gender perspective will always be considered and will guide all activities within ATTAC . . .
- Analyzing the effect of economic conditions on women in different social situations . . .
- Pointing out concrete alternatives

- Planning and carrying out 'creative actions'
- Establishing networks with other women/groups that deal with neoliberal globalization and women's issues" (Feminist ATTAC n.d.)

Contact details:
Austria:
FeministATTAC Österreich
Margaretenstr. 166/3/25
A-1050 Wien
Tel: 00 43(1)544 00 10
Fax: 00 43(1)544 00 59
http://www.attac.at/
France:
Commission Genre et Mondialisation
ATTAC France
66-72 rue Marceau, 93100 Montreuil-Sous-Bois
Paris, France
Tel: 01 41 58 17 40
attacfr@attac.org, genre@attac.org, femmes.paris14@attac.org
http://www.france.attac.org/

14. Capetinas
No published information or contact details available.

15. Católicas por les Derechos de Decidir [Catholics for the Right to Decide]
"We are an autonomous movement of Catholic people, engaged in the search for social justice and in changing the prevailing cultural and religious patterns in our societies. We promote women's rights, especially those that refer to sexuality and reproduction. . . . We want women to exercise their sexual rights and reproductive rights in order for them to gain full citizenship both in their society and church. We also want women to hear, respect and recognize their moral capacity for making ethical decisions" (Catholics for the Right to Decide n.d.).
Last known contact details (from Catholics for the Right to Decide n.d.):
Regional Office
C.C.269 Suc. 20(B) 1420 Buenos Aires
Argentina
cddba@wamani.apc.org, catolicasal@wamani.apc.org
http://www.catolicasporelderechoadecidir.org

16. CEMINA—Communicação, Educação e Informação em Gênero
"CEMINA, like many other women's organizations that were created during the 80s, understood that the moment had come for women to use

their voices and assets to occupy a place in society, questioning traditional values, shaking up old structures and streaming new ways forward. We embraced this mission, investing in the idea of 'empowering the voice.' That was it! We opened a channel which enabled not only us, but also our partners, the women from Rio de Janeiro and from Brazil as a whole, to speak candidly about women's issues. The radio program 'Women Speak Up' [Fala Mulher], our first initiative, was created in 1988. The program was initiated by a group of volunteers and soon acquired a more professional profile. It was replicated and continued broadcasting for 10 years. . . . After occupying the radio waves from the North to the South of Brazil, we are working now to apply what we have learned through the radio the new technologies for communication and information (ICTs) in cyber space. . . . The mission of CEMINA is to contribute to the inclusion of issues related to gender and human rights in the realm of communication and information" (CEMINA n.d.a: 1, our translation).
Contact details:
Rua Álvaro Alvim, 21/16°
Centro CEP 20031-010
Rio de Janeiro RJ Brasil
Tel: 00 55-21-2262-1704
Fax: 00 55-21-2262-6454
cemina@cemina.org.br
http://www.cemina.org.br

17. Center for Women's Global Leadership
"The Center for Women's Global Leadership (CWGL) develops and facilitates women's leadership for women's human rights and social justice worldwide. . . . CWGL's programs promote the leadership of women and advance feminist perspectives in policy-making processes in local, national and international arenas. Since 1990, the Center has fostered women's leadership in the area of human rights through women's global leadership institutes, international mobilization campaigns, UN monitoring, global education endeavors, publications and a resource center. The Global Center works from a human rights perspective with an emphasis on violence against women, sexual and reproductive health and socio-economic well-being. The Global Center's programs are in two broad areas of policy and advocacy and leadership development and women's human rights education" (Center for Women's Global Leadership n.d.a).
Contact details:
Douglass College
Rutgers, The State University of New Jersey
160 Ryders Lane
New Brunswick NJ 08901-8555

USA
Tel: 1-732 932 8782
Fax: 1-732 932 1180
cwgl@igc.org
http://www.cwgl.rutgers.edu/

18. Centro Feminista de Estudos e Assessoria (CFEMEA)
"The CFEMEA—Feminist Centre of Study and Assessment is a non-governmental, non-profit making organisation, which works for the citizenship of women and for equality in general. It fights, in an autonomous and non-party political way, for a society and a State that are just and democratic. . . .
"Objectives

- Defend and promote equality of rights and gender equality in legislation, as well as in the planning and implementation of public policy, taking on board the inequalities generated by the intersection of sexist and racist discrimination
- Shine a light on the budgetary process with the view to its democratisation and transparency, as well as incorporating a gender and race perspective into public expenditure" (CFEMEA n.d., our translation)

Contact details:
SCS, Quadra 2, Edifício Goiás, Bloco C, Sala 602
70317-900 Brasília DF
Brazil
Telefax: 00 55 (61) 224 1791
cfemea@cfemea.org.br
http://www.cfemea.org.br/

19. CEPIA—Cidadania, Estudo, Pesquisa, Informação, Ação
"Cepia is a non-governmental, nonprofit organization, dedicated to developing projects that promote human and citizenship rights especially among groups historically excluded from exercising their full citizenship in Brazil. . . . Working from a gender perspective and within a human rights framework, Cepia focuses on issues of health, sexual and reproductive rights, violence and access to justice, poverty and employment. . . . Cepia organizes seminars, meetings and conferences, dialoguing with feminists, social movements, members of the judiciary, lawyers, legislators, medical doctors, health professionals, labor unions, NGOs, opinion makers and civil servants responsible for public policies, so as to broaden the debate on issues related to its agenda" (CEPIA n.d.a).

Contact details:
Rua do Russel 694, apt. 201
22210-010 Rio de Janeiro
RJ, Brazil
Tel: 00 55 21-25586115 or 00 55 21-22052136
cepia@cepia.org.br
http://www.cepia.org.br

20. Codepink

"CODEPINK is a women-initiated grassroots peace and social justice move
ment working to end the wars in Iraq and Afghanistan, stop new wars,
and redirect our resources into healthcare, education, green jobs and other
life-affirming activities. CODEPINK rejects foreign policies based on domination and aggression, and instead calls for policies based on diplomacy,
compassion and a commitment to international law. With an emphasis
on joy and humor, CODEPINK women and men seek to activate, amplify
and inspire a community of peacemakers through creative campaigns and
a commitment to non-violence" (Codepink n.d.).
Contact details:
2010 Linden Avenue, Venice, CA 90291, USA
Tel: (310) 827-4320
info@codepinkalert.org
http://www.codepink4peace.org/

21. Coletivo Feminino Plural

"The group Coletivo Feminino Plural was founded in March 1996, starting
with the initiative of a group of women identified with the feminist struggle
for public policies for women and girls, in defense of human rights and
citizenship. . . . Feminino Plural has the following objectives:

- The defense of the rights of women and girls from the perspective of
  gender and human rights
- The combating of all forms of discrimination and prejudice of gender,
  race, ethnicity, age, or conditions that wear down women and girls,
  whether through norms, laws, positions, behaviors, or actions
- The development of mechanisms, instruments, and public policies to
  fight all forms of discrimination and violence, whether it is physical,
  sexual, psychological, or symbolic
- The compliance with treaties and international conventions on human
  rights and the rights of women
- The guarantee of the exercise of sexual and reproductive rights, free
  from prejudice and with the security of holistic health policies

- For the grassroots and sustainable development of the planet, in ways that ensure work and a quality of life for all women and the end of the exploitation of young children, in particular of girls
- The exercise of substantive citizenship, that is to say that which is effectively lived by women in all areas of their lives, whether in public or private, that will enable them to empower themselves" (Coletivo Feminino Plural 2005, our translation)

Last known contact details (from Coletivo Feminino Plural 2005):
Avenida Salgado Filho, Sen 28
Sl 701, Porto Alegre, RS
90.010-220 Brazil
Tel: 00 51 3221 5298
femininoplural@pop.com.br

22. Collectif National pour les Droits des Femmes (CNDF)
"The National Collective for the Rights of Women is a grouping of feminist associations, of unions and of political parties, constituted on January 24, 1996.

"It has as its ambition to make happen in fact, in practical reality, the formal equality that women have achieved during the twentieth century.

"It fights on all the terrains where women suffer discrimination and unequal treatment, violence, the loss of dignity.

"It intervenes in domains as varied as the reduction of working hours, professional equality, night shifts, community amenities, domestic labor, violence, lesbophobia, the place of women in public life, the struggle against the National Front and its clones, the struggle against sexism, school life, neoliberal globalization, international solidarity. etc. . . ." (CNDF 2007, our translation)
Contact details:
21 ter rue Voltaire
75011 Paris
France
Tel: 01 43 56 36 48
droitsdesfemmes@cndf.ras.eu.org
www.collectifdroitsdesfemmes.org/

23. CRIOLA
"CRIOLA is a Brazilian, non-profit, civil society organization which was founded on September 2, 1992. It is directed by black women of different backgrounds who have returned to work with other Afro-Brazilian women, adolescents and girls primarily in Rio de Janeiro. Since it was established the organization reached around three thousand women, girls, adolescents

and adults. We aim to create and offer programs that confront the racism, sexism and homophobia present in Brazilian society" (CRIOLA n.d.).
Contact details:
Avenida Presidente Vargas 482, Sobreloja 203
Centro, Rio de Janeiro CEP 20071-000
RJ, Brazil
Tel: 21 2518 6194
criola@criola.org.br
http://www.criola.org.br/

24. Dalit Feminist Group
No published information or contact details available.

25. Dalit Women's Federation
No published information or contact details available.

26. Development Alternatives with Women for a New Era (DAWN)
"DAWN began in 1984, on the eve of the international conferences marking the end of the UN Decade for Women, when a group of feminists from the South with similar visions prepared a platform document for that event and held a number of workshops at the NGO Forum in Nairobi. . . . Since then DAWN has continued to influence global debates on development by offering holistic analyses from a South feminist perspective that is both grounded in women's experience and inspired by women's collective strategies and visions. The DAWN network today covers Africa, Asia, Latin America, the Caribbean and the Pacific" (DAWN n.d.a).
Contact details:
Dawn Secretariat
44 Ekpo Abasi Street
Calabar, Cross River State
Nigeria
Tel: 234-87-230929
Fax: 234-87-236298
info@dawnnet.org
http://www.dawnnet.org

27. Fala Preta!
"Fala Preta! Organization of Black Women is a non governmental organization (NGO) founded in April 1997, whose mission is to promote the sustainable human development of the black population through the defense of human rights and citizenship, striving for the elimination of all forms of discrimination and violence, specifically racial and gender discrimination" (Fala Preta! n.d.a).

Contact details:
Rua Vergueiro 434, 2º andar
Aclimação
01504-000 São Paulo, SP
Brazil
Tel: 11 3277 4727
falapret@uol.com.br

28. Feminist Centre, Athens
No English-language published information or contact details.

29. Femmes Solidaires
"Femmes solidaires is a feminist organization for all the women who live in France, whether they are French or immigrants; an organisation for all the women that want to uphold their rights and liberties.

"With a network of over 150 local groups and 25,000 women, Femmes solidaires acts for equality and women's rights in France and all over the world.

"Femmes solidaires acts so that sexism, racialism, violence, poverty and discriminations go back. We also fight to entitle all women to contraception, voluntary abortion and health.

"Femmes solidaires is known as a working class education organization. . . . Femmes solidaires stems from l'Union des Femmes Françaises, born itself of the 'Female Committees of the Résistance' in 1945" (Femmes Solidaires n.d.).
Contact details:
25 Rue du Charolais
75012 Paris
France
Tel: 33 1 40 01 90 90
http://www.femmes-solidaires.org/

30. FEMNET: African Women's Development and Communication Network
"The African Women's Development and Communication Network (FEM-NET) was set up in 1988 to share information, experiences, ideas and strategies among African women's nongovernmental organisations (NGOs) through communications, networking, training and advocacy so as to advance women's development, equality and other women's human rights in Africa.

"FEMNET aims to strengthen the role and contribution of African NGOs focusing [on] women's development, equality and other human rights. It also aims to provide an infrastructure for and a channel through which

these NGOs can reach one another and share information, experiences and strategies [so] as to improve their input into women's development, equality and other women's human rights in Africa. . . . Since its inception in 1988, FEMNET has played a leadership role for African women's NGOs at regional and international decision-making and policy fora" (FEMNET 2009).
Contact details:
KUSCCO Center
Upper Hill-Kilimanjaro Road, off Mara Road
P.O. Box 54562
00200 Nairobi, Kenya
Tel: 254 20 2712971/2
Fax: 254 20 2712974
E-mail: admin@femnet.or.ke
Website: www.femnet.or.ke

31. Flora Tristán: Centro de la Mujer Peruana
"Flora Tristán is a feminist institution which was created in 1979 as a non-profit making, civil association. Its mission is to combat the structural causes which restrict the citizenship of women and/or which affect their ability to exercise citizenship. In consequence, it dedicates itself to pushing for the expansion of citizenship of women and for political and development processes that are responsive to public opinion and which result in equality and gender justice" (Flora Tristán CMP n.d.a, our translation).
Contact details:
Parque Hernán Velarde No 42
Lima 1, Lima
Perú
Tel: (51 1) 433 1457
Fax: (51 1) 433 9500
postmast@flora.org.pe
http://www.flora.org.pe/index.htm

32. Forum Against the Oppression of Women
"FAOW was formed in 1979 as a platform to respond to an extremely unjust judgement on a rape case. Soon from a Forum Against Rape, as it was earlier called, it changed its name to the present one to encompass varied forms of women's oppression. FAOW is part of what in India is recognised as the Autonomous Women's groups which has played a crucial role in this third phase of the women's movement (late 70s onwards). Today it is mainly a campaign group consisting of members from varied background—students, housewives, professional women, lecturers etc. The members meet regularly once in a week and every one puts their voluntary [sic] time in the work that needs to be done. There are no paid staff" (Indianchild n.d.).

Contact details:
29, Bhatia Bhavan, 1st floor
Babrekar Marg
Dadar
Bombay 400028
India
Tel: 91-22-422-2436
inforum@inbb.gn.apc.org

33. Furcaza Feminista
No published information or contact details.
furcaza@riseup.net

34. Global Women's Strike—International Coordination
"The Global Women's Strike was born in 1999, when women in Ireland
decided to welcome the new millennium with a national general strike.
They asked the International Wages for Housework Campaign to support
their call, and we called on women all over the world to make the Strike
global on 8 March 2000. . . . Since 2000 the Strike has been a great success.
It has brought together women in over 60 countries, including grassroots
organisations with impressive track records, who also demand a world that
values all women's work and every life, and who have achieved much. They
are now part of an international network of strike coordinators. . . . With
the theme INVEST IN CARING NOT KILLING, we demand that the $900+
billion now spend on military budgets is used instead for basic survival
needs—clean accessible water, food security, healthcare, housing, education, safety from rape and other violence, protection of our planet—and
therefore for women who are the first carers and the first fighters for the survival of loved ones. We claim for a start the US military budget—over half
the world's military spending—with which 'Corporate America' imposes
its economic and political interests on the whole world. . . . The Global
Women's Strike has extended from taking joint action every 8 March. It is
now a global network that strengthens the ongoing daily struggle of grassroots women (and men)" (James and Lopez 2004).
Contact details:
Crossroads Women's Centre
PO Box 287
London NW6 5QU
UK
Tel: +44 (0)20 7482 2496
Fax: +44 (0)20 7209 4761
womenstrike8m@server101.com
http://globalwomenstrike.net/

35. Grail movement
"Called by spiritual values, The Grail envisions a world of peace, justice and renewal of the earth, brought about by women working together as catalysts for change. Formed in the Netherlands in the 1920s, The Grail is an international women's movement with roots in the spiritual tradition, committed to spiritual search, social transformation, ecological sustainability, and the release of women's creative energy throughout the world. Grail members are bonded in action and faith, working in 20 countries, as individuals and Grail groups, interconnecting regionally, nationally and internationally" (Grailville 2005).
Contact details:
International Coordination:
Nieuwegracht 51
3512LE Utrecht
The Netherlands
Phone: 31-30-234 1894
Fax: 31-30-234 2960
E-mail: iltsecr@planet.nl
http://www.thegrail.org/index.php?lang=en
Brazilian group:
Belo Horizonte (National Headquarters)
Rua Pirapetinga, 390 Bairro Serra
CEP 30220-150 Belo Horizonte/MG
Brazil
Telefax: 31 3225 2224/ 3225 2416
graalbrasilbh@aol.com

36. Indymedia Women
"The imc-women-list exists since summer 2001 and consists of women active in indymedias in Latin America, North America, Europe, the Middle East and Australia. . . . [W]e have discussed in many facets the depressing situation of patriarchal repression in society which unfortunately does not stop at the doorstep of leftist groups" (IMC Women 2005).
Contact details:
http://lists.indymedia.org/mailman/listinfo/imc-women

37. Instituto Eqüit: Gênero, Economia e Cidadania Global
"Our philosophy:
"To contribute to transforming social relations, focusing on gender relations from a feminist view, which seeks to build women's citizenship with regards to democracy and human rights and disregard to market logic.

"Theme Areas:

* Globalization and macroeconomic policy
* Democracy, citizenship and human (economic, social, cultural, environmental and political) rights
* Sustainable development with justice and equity" (Instituto Eqüit n.d.)

Contact details:
Rua da Lapa, 180 salas 908/909 Centro
Rio de Janeiro RJ 20.021-180
Brasil
Tel: 55 (21) 2221 1182/2215-9510
equit@equit.org.br
http://www.equit.org.br

38. International Feminists for a Gift Economy
"International Feminists for a Gift Economy is a group of feminist activists and academics from many countries, who meet irregularly and speak about the gift economy on panels at local and international gatherings" (International Feminists for a Gift Economy).
Contact details:
109 West Johanna St., Austin
TX 78704
USA
Tel: 001 512 444 1672
genvau@aol.com
http://www.gift-economy.com/

39. International Free Women's Foundation/Internationale Vrije Vrouwen Stichting
"The International Free Women`s Foundation has the following aims and principles:

* To encourage and intensify solidarity and communication among women all around the world.
* To promote active participation of women in all fields of social life with their own identity.
* To fight any discrimination against people because of their sex, language, religion, nationality or social situation.
* To promote and extend the engagement of women for social justice, peace and pollution control.
* To create social projects that promote free and democratic relations between members of the society.

- To support women and children who are victims of war and violence.
- To promote education and research work on women's issues.
- Support for social and humanitarian projects for needy women and children in the Middle East and in other parts of the world and international cooperation with women's organisations and individuals are [the] main projects of the IFWF." (International Free Women's Foundation n.d.)

Contact details:
Willebrordusplein 10a, NL-3037 TC Rotterdam
The Netherlands
Tel: +31 (0) 10 465 1800
Fax: +31 (0) 10 265 1460
info@freewomensfoundation.org
http://www.freewomensfoundation.org/

40. International Gender and Trade Network (IGTN)
"IGTN is a network of feminist gender specialists who provide technical information on gender and trade issues to women's groups, NGOs, social movements and governments, and acts as a political catalyst to enlarge the space for a critical feminist perspective and global action on trade and globalization issues.

"IGTN is a Southern-led network that builds South/North cooperation in the work of developing more just and democratic policy from a critical feminist perspective; currently organized in . . . Africa, Asia, Caribbean, Central Asia, Europe, Latin America, Middle East and Gulf, and North America" (IGTN n.d.a).
Contact details:
International Gender and Trade Network Secretariat
Rua da Lapa, 180 / 908 and 909 Lapa
Rio de Janeiro/RJ Brazil 20.021-180
Tel: 55 21 2221-1182
Fax: 55 21 2215-9510
secretariat@igtn.org
http://www.igtn.org/

41. Mahila Jagruthi
"Mahila jagruthi means raising the consciousness of women. Mahila jagruthi is a women's organisation formed in 1994. We seek to analyse women's issues and work towards women's liberation. In this direction, we conduct widespread campaign and consistent struggles against women's oppression and exploitation. We are for joint activities with all democratic women's organizations in their efforts to effect a change in women's lives.

We also actively participate in all democratic women/people's struggles for basic rights, minimum amenities, against caste oppression and class exploitation etc. We are active members of joint action forums against communalism and Globalisation, which pose a great danger to the very survival and dignity of women. Mahila jagruthi functions in Bangalore, shimoga, blegaum and chikmagalur districts" (Mahila Jagruthi n.d.).
Contact details (from Mahila Jagruthi 1998):
No. 29, 2nd Main Road
2nd Cross, Hosahalli
Vijayanagar
Bangalore 560 040
India
mahilajagruthi1994@rediffmail.com

42. Maria Mulher
"Maria Mulher is a feminist organization, coordinated by black women who come from diverse backgrounds, and aiming to carry out interdisciplinary work. It was created in March 1987 and, since then, has struggled for the human rights of women and for the improvement of the living conditions of Afro-descendents. Maria Mulher has the following objectives:

- to combat sexist, ethnic/racial, and social discrimination
- to propose public policies on the possibility of promoting citizenship of women, achieving equality and human rights
- to empower black women to act effectively in society as agents of their own history" (Maria Mulher n.d., our translation)

Contact details:
Travessa Francisco Leonardo Truda, 40 sobreloja
Porto Alegre CEP 90010-050 /RS
Brazil
Tel: 51.3286.8482
Fax: 51.3219.0180
mariamulher@mariamulher.org.br, mariamulher@cpovo.net
http://www.mariamulher.org.br/

43. National Federation of Indian Women (NFIW)
"NFIW was founded in a conference of women held from June 4 to 7, 1954 in the city of Calcutta with participation of 830 women delegates from 18 states of India. . . . The organisation grew its strength among all sections of women belonging to different tribes, castes, religions and other social groupings. It also has membership among women of all economic strata, the agricultural labourers, factory and office workers, those in the field of

academics, and all service sectors, women working in the home-based sector and housewives etc. . . . The NFIW developed good working relation with other women organisations trade unions and NGOs issue to issue. . . . The organisation has been working for legal, social, cultural, political and economic rights of women and has many achievements to its credit" (Communist Party of India n.d.).
Contact details not known.

44. National Network of Autonomous Women's Groups (NNAWG), India
"The National Network of Autonomous Women's Groups (NNAWG) is a coalition of groups and organisations that actively participate within the Women's Movement in India. It was set up in 2004 during the World Social Forum (WSF) in Mumbai, India in response to the need to take feminist political and networking efforts beyond national organising and strongly advocate for visibilising women's issues. NNAWG is closely linked to the National Co-ordination Committee, which initiates and organises the massive 3000 strong national conferences every few years" (Feminist Dialogues 2006).
Contact details:
aksharacentre@vsnl.com

45. NextGENDERation
"The NextGENDERation network is a European network of students and graduates working in various fields of women's, feminist and gender studies (whether these are institutionalised in centers or departments, or not). . . . [It] wants to stand for a type of feminist knowledge politics, deeply concerned with the democratisation of higher education. . . . We work in an autonomous and decentralised way. The idea of NG emerged among a number of young scholars in the context of an ATHENA (a thematic network for women's studies in Europe) meeting. Meanwhile it has travelled in several directions and contexts, through a viral type of feminist politics that we cherish. This means local NG groups look quite different, may or may not be primarily academically-based, and are engaged in different issues, although we share strong feminist, anti-racist, anti-heterosexist and postcolonial standpoints. We have the common space of an e-mail-list to keep in contact, exchange information and ideas about current or possible future projects, and build a stronger European network" (NextGENDERation n.d.).
Contact details:
http://www.nextgenderation.net/

46. Phoenix: Organisation for Woman and Child
"Phoenix is a Women's Organisation, consisting of a group of women from different walks of life. Established in 1991, Phoenix strives for women's and

children's issues based on equal relations. As a concerned organisation of women, it also responds to the other issues of the society such as gender and development, health and reproductive rights, caste-class struggles, minority issues, human rights, socio-economic, cultural and political rights. It emphasizes grassroots activities and believes in community participation at various levels. Phoenix has been a part of the Women's Movement in India and has created a dialogue and network at the district, state and national level on gender and child rights issues. Phoenix adapts an integrated model of development, which establishe[s] linkages between different activities and relating them to a single cause, problem or area of attention. Phoenix would like to form a platform for wider audience for people's participation and representation at the socio-economic and political level, thereby strengthening the process and progressive mechanisms for people's empowerment and sustainable development. Phoenix has developed its ideology from a gender perspective. It started its first step with strengthening grassroots work in rural areas and in urban slums, a task which it still continues to be involved in and is now increasingly concentrating on Research, Network, Policy Advocacy and Publications" (information supplied by e-mail from interviewee Mahe Jabeen, 2004).
Contact details:
10-2-298/72 Shanti Nagar, Masab Tank
Hyderabad
500 028
India
Tel: + 91-40-27151222 or 91 40 22 19240/3303 862
Fax: +91-40-27159040
phoenixwomenorg@yahoo.com

47. REDEH: Rede de Desenvolvimento Humano
"REDEH is a feminist organization that holds as its mission to promote human rights—the basis for equality across sexes, race and ethnicity—and to preserve the environment and to promote environmental sustainable development in public policies through the education of leaders, research and the production of methodological material, the creation of events, seminars and campaigns" (REDEH n.d.a).
Contact details:
Rua Álvaro Alvim 21/16 andar
Rio de Janeiro 20031-010
Brazil
Tel: 55-21-2262-1704
redeh@redeh.org.br
http://www.redeh.org.br/

48. Rede Mulher de Educação
"Created in 1980, Rede Mulher de Educação is a non-governmental organization that promotes and facilitates the inter-connection between women's groups all over Brazil and abroad, constructing a network of services in popular feminist education.

"Rede Mulher de Educação develops actions together with men and women, with mixed institutions . . . to strengthen the capacity to challenge . . . gender unfairness, the sexism in the organizations and [to encourage] valorization of the different feminist contribution to . . . society. . . . [Concretely this means that it] develops formation activities, research, communication and articulation [networking] seeking to strengthen the development of the technical and political competence [of] individual persons, groups and organizations" (Rede Mulher de Educação n.d.).

Contact details:
Rua Coriolano, 28
05047-000 São Paulo
SP Brasil
Tel: 01155 11 3873-2803
Fax: 01155 3862-7050
rdmulher@redemulher.org.br
http://www.redemulher.org.br

49. Sempreviva Organização Feminista (SOF)
"SOF is a feminist nongovernmental organization that has been going since 1963, with its headquarters in the city of São Paulo and its actions having a national scope.

"Our objective is to contribute to the construction of a feminist politics linked to the democratic-popular project, one that will be present in the formulation of proposals and in the organizational processes of social movement struggles. This politics must transform gender relations and favor the self-determination of women.

"Our key public is the women organized in the autonomous women's movement and in the rural and urban popular and workers movements" (SOF n.d., our translation).

Contact details:
R. Ministro Costa e Silva, 36
Pinheiros São Paulo, SP
CEP: 05417-080
Brazil
Tel: (11) 3819-3876
sof@sof.org.br
http://www.sof.org.br/

50. Themis—Assessoria Jurídica e Estudos de Gênero [Legal Counseling and Gender Studies]

"Themis, goddess of Justice, sets each one's rights and duties, both in daily life and under special circumstances, by means of a code inspired by the gods. . . . Transfigured across many centuries . . . , Themis remains the mythical reference of Western civilization, and the inspiration to rethink the current relationship between gender and the Law. . . . Now, in view of the level of social inequalities in Brasil . . . we must reflect about the institution of Law and the process of building identities based on gender, racial and class relations.

"Themis works through three action programmes:

- Popular legal promoters . . .
- Feminist legal advice . . .
- Documentation, Research and Studies Centre
- Mission: Widening the conditions for women to access justice" (Themis n.d.b)

Contact details:
Rua dos Andradas, 1137 Sala 2205
Porto Alegre RS CEP: 90020-007
Brazil
Telefax: 00 55 (51) 3212 0104
themis@themis.org.br
http://www.themis.org.br/

51. Umas e Outras

"The group aims at discussion and organising of homosexual women on the national scene, creating events and other alternatives to meetings to exchange experiences amongst lesbians. The presentation of videos, writing workshops, dance classes, football and the creation of a library with resources for women, that develop debates—they also participate in the organisation of the lesbian parade in the GLBT Pride March in São Paulo" (Diálogo Joven 2005, our translation).
Contact details no longer available online.

52. Women in Black

"Women in Black is a world-wide network of women committed to peace with justice and actively opposed to injustice, war, militarism and other forms of violence. As women experiencing these things in different ways in different regions of the world, we support each other's movements. An important focus is challenging the militarist policies of our own governments. We are not an organisation, but a means of communicating and a formula for action. . . . Any group of women anywhere in the world at any time may organize a Women in Black vigil against any manifestation of violence, militarism or war. Women in Black (WiB) actions are generally women only. Our actions often take the form of women wearing black, standing in a public place in silent, non-violent vigils at regular times and intervals, carrying placards and handing out leaflets. . . . [In addition to vigils] we use many other forms of non-violent direct action such as sitting down to block a road, entering military bases and other forbidden zones, refusing to comply with orders, and "bearing witness." Wearing black in some cultures signifies mourning, and feminist actions dressed in black convert women's traditional passive mourning for the dead in war into a powerful refusal of the logic of war" (Women in Black n.d.a).

Contact details:
International:
vigils@womeninblack.org
http://www.womeninblack.org/
In the UK:
c/o Maypole Fund
PO Box 14072
London N16 5WB
WiBinfo@gn.apc.org
http://www.womeninblack.org.uk/

53. Women Living Under Muslim Laws (WLUML)
"Women Living Under Muslim Laws is an international solidarity network that provides information, support and a collective space for women whose lives are shaped, conditioned or governed by laws and customs said to derive from Islam. For more than two decades WLUML has linked individual women and organisations. It now extends to more than 70 countries ranging from South Africa to Uzbekistan, Senegal to Indonesia and Brazil to France. . . . Our name challenges the myth of one, homogenous Muslim world. . . . The network aims to strengthen women's individual and collective struggles for equality and their rights, especially in Muslim contexts" (WLUML 2005).

Contact details:
International Coordination Office
PO Box 28445
London, N19 5NZ
UK
Tel: +44 207 263 0285
Fax: +44 207 561 9882
wluml@wluml.org
http://www.wluml.org/english/index.shtml

54. Women Speak Out
"Women Speak Out is an open collective of DIY, anarcho feminists who sporadically create spaces for constructive larking and opinionated exchange" (Women Speak Out 2001b).
Contact details:
wso-london-subscribe@yahoogroups.com
womenspeakout-subscribe@yahoogroups.com
http://www.geocities.com/womenspeakout/

55. Women's Environment and Development Organization (WEDO)
"WEDO is an international organization that advocates for women's equality in global policy. It seeks to empower women as decision makers to achieve economic, social and gender justice, a healthy, peaceful planet and human rights for all.

"Through the organization's program areas—Gender and Governance, Sustainable Development, Economic and Social Justice, and U.S. Global Engagement—WEDO emphasizes women's critical role in the social, economic and political spheres. . . . WEDO does advocacy in key global forums such as the UN, supports the efforts of women's organizations worldwide, and engages U.S. women on foreign policy" (WEDO n.d.a).
Contact details:
355 Lexington Ave., 3rd Floor
New York, NY 10017
USA
Tel: (212) 973-0325
Fax: (212) 973-0335
wedo@wedo.org
http://www.wedo.org/

56. Women's Environmental Network (WEN)
"Women's Environmental Network is the only organisation in the UK working consistently for women and the environment. Our vision is of

- A world where women are aware of their ability to change the environment for the better and actively come together to do so.

"Our strategic aims are:

1. Empowering women to make positive environmental change.
2. Increasing awareness of women's perspectives on environmental issues.
3. Influencing decision-making to achieve environmental justice for women.

"Formed in 1988, it is a registered charity funded by members, donations and grant support. Central to WEN's approach is the belief that women have the right to information to enable them to make fair choices. We also believe a precautionary approach is healthiest for people and the planet" (WEN n.d.a).
Contact details:
4 Pinchin Street
PO Box 30626
London E1 1TZ
UK
Tel: 00 44 (0)20 7481 9004
info@wen.org.uk
http://www.wen.org.uk/

57. Women's Global Network for Reproductive Rights (WGNRR)
"The Women's Global Network for Reproductive Rights (WGNRR) is an autonomous, feminist and grassroots network of groups and individuals from every continent who aim to achieve and support reproductive and sexual health rights (RSHR) for women everywhere. WGNRR has dedicated itself to the grassroots and to bringing their voices to policy and lobbying levels. We define RSHR as interrelated, basic human rights which enable women to have safe, responsible and fulfilling sex lives and the self determination to freely decide if, when and how often to have children, free from coercion, discrimination and violence. This includes the right of access to safe, legal abortion" (WGNRR n.d.a).
Contact details:
Vrolikstraat 453-D
1092TJ Amsterdam
The Netherlands
Tel: +31 20 620 9672
Fax: +31 20 622 2450
office@wgnrr.nl
http://www.wgnrr.org/

58. Women's International Coalition for Economic Justice (WICEJ)
"The Women's International Coalition for Economic Justice (WICEJ) is a space that links women's organizations and builds relationships between the issues of women's rights, women's economic justice, women's multiple discrimination and peace and security. Founded to address macroeconomic policy-making in the UN system, WICEJ is addressing new strategic venues for action and ways for women to collaborate across venues to advance economic justice and all women's human rights. We are working to build bridges among feminists and women's groups who organize around

health, violence and reproductive rights, and those who organize around development, macro-economic policy and economic justice; bridges across regions of the world; bridges among women in trade unions and women's NGOs; and bridges across lines of race, ethnicity, caste, class and sexual orientation" (WICEJ n.d.b).
Contact details:
12 Dongan Place #206
New York, NY 10040
USA
info@wicej.org
http://www.wicej.addr.com/

59. Women's International League for Peace and Freedom (WILPF)
"The Women's International League for Peace and Freedom (WILPF) is an international Non Governmental Organization (NGO) with national sections, covering all continents with an international secretariat based in Geneva, and a New York office focused on the work of the United Nations.
"Since its establishment in 1915, WILPF has brought together women from around the world who are united in working for peace by non-violent means, promoting political, economic and social justice for all.
"What WILPF does

- Lobbies governments on international, national and local levels
- Connects communities with the international scene, through national sections
- Participates in, collaborates and networks with international institutions and global movements
- Develops reference, education and action tools through websites, conferences, seminars and publications
- Monitors and contributes to the work of the UN
- Ensures a gender perspective" (WILPF n.d.c)

Contact details:
International Office
1, rue de Varembé
Case Postale 28
1211 Geneva 20
Switzerland
Tel: (+41 22) 919 70 80
Fax: (+41 22) 919 70 81
info@wilpf.ch, inforequest@wilpf.ch
http://www.wilpf.int.ch/

60. World March of Women
"The World March of Women is an international feminist action movement connecting grass-roots groups and organizations working to eliminate the causes at the root of poverty and violence against women. We struggle against all forms of inequality and discrimination directed at women. Our values and actions are directed at making political, economic and social change. They center on the globalization of solidarity; equality between women and men, among women themselves and between peoples; the respect and recognition of diversity among women; the multiplicity of our strategies; the appreciation of women's leadership; and the strength of alliances among women and with other progressive social movements" (World March of Women n.d.d).
Contact details:
International Secretariat
R. Ministro Costa e Silva 36
Pinheiros
São Paulo, SP
CEP: 05417-080
Brazil
Tel: 55 11 3032-3243
info@marchemondiale.org
http://www.marchemondiale.org/

References

Aboim, Maria Luiza. No date. "Brazil—Domestic Violence and the Women's Movement." http://endabuse.forumone.com/programs/printable/display.php3?DocID =96 (June 8, 2009).

Abortion Rights. 2004. "Voicing Women's Right to Choose." Leaflet obtained at the European Social Forum, London, November 2004.

———. No date. "Who We Are." http://www.abortionrights.org.uk/content/ view/39/57/ (June 17, 2009).

Ackerly, Brooke, and Jacqui True. 2006. "Studying the Struggles and Wishes of the Age: Feminist Theoretical Methodology and Feminist Theoretical Methods." Pp. 241–69 in *Methodologies for International Relations*, ed. Brooke Ackerly, Maria Stern, and Jacqui True. Cambridge: Cambridge University Press.

AfricaWoman. 2003. "About AfricaWoman." http://www.africawoman.net/about .php (June 27, 2005, no longer available).

———. 2005. *AfricaWoman*. Special G8 Gleneagles Edition. http://www.william bowles.info/africa/afr_woman.pdf (June 14, 2009).

Akshara. No date. "Akshara." Flyer obtained at Feminist Dialogues, Porto Alegre, January 2005.

Albert, Michael. 2001. "The Movements against Neoliberal Globalization from Seattle to Porto Alegre." http://www.zmag.org/albertgreecetalk.htm (April 19, 2001, no longer available).

Albrecht, Lisa, and Brewer, Rose M. 1990. *Bridges of Power: Women's Multicultural Alliances*. Philadelphia: New Society Publishers.

Alcoff, Linda Martín. 2000. "Who's Afraid of Identity Politics?" In *Reclaiming Identity: Realist Theory and the Predicament of Postmodernism*, ed. Paula M. L. Moya and Michael Hames-Garcia. Berkeley: University of California Press. http://www .alcoff.com/content/afraidid.html (June 17, 2009).

——. 2006. "The Political Critique of Identity," chapter 2 of Alcoff's *Visible Identities: Race, Gender and the Self*. http://www.alcoff.com/content/chap2polcri.html (June 17, 2009).

All African Women's Group. No date. "The All African Women's Group." http://www.allwomencount.net/EWC%20Immigrant/all_african_women.htm (June 13, 2009).

Allen, Amy. 1998. "Rethinking Power." *Hypatia* 13, no. 1: 21–40.

——. 2008. "Power and the Politics of Difference: Oppression, Empowerment and Transnational Justice." *Hypatia* 23, no. 3: 156–72.

All India Democratic Women's Association (AIDWA). 2002. *AIDWA: Perspectives, Interventions and Struggles (1998–2001)*. New Delhi: AIDWA.

——. No date a. *Women in Struggle: The Andhra Pradesh Experience*. Brinda Karat on behalf of AIDWA.

——. No date b. "Introducing AIDWA." Leaflet picked up at AIDWA workshop, World Social Forum, Mumbai, January 2004.

All India Democratic Women's Association (AIDWA) Maharashtra State Committee. No date. "Globalise the Struggle against Globalisation!" Flyer obtained at AIDWA workshop, World Social Forum, Mumbai, January 2004.

Allwood, Gill, and Khursheed Wadia. 2002. "French Feminism: National and International perspectives." *Modern and Contemporary France* 10, no. 2: 211–23.

Alvarez, Sonia E. 1990. *Engendering Democracy in Brazil: Women's Movements in Transition Politics*. Princeton, NJ: Princeton University Press.

——. 1998. "Latin American Feminisms 'Go Global': Trends of the 1990's and Challenges for the New Millennium." Pp. 294–324 in *Cultures of Politics, Politics of Cultures: Re-Visioning Latin American Social Movements*, ed. Sonia Alvarez, Evelina Dagnino, and Arturo Escobar. Boulder, CO: Westview Press.

——. 2004 [1999]. "Advocating Feminism: The Latin American Feminist NGO 'Boom'." Pp. 122–48 in *Feminist Politics, Activism and Vision: Local and Global Challenges*, ed. Luciani Ricciutelli, Angela Miles, and Margaret H. McFadden. London: Zed Books.

——. No date. "Translating the Global: Effects of Transnational Organizing on Local Feminist Discourses and Practices in Latin America." Global Solidarity Dialogue. http://www.antenna.nl/~waterman/alvarez.html (June 8, 2009).

Alvarez, Sonia E., with Nalu Faria and Miriam Nobre. 2004. "Another (Also Feminist) World Is Possible: Constructing Transnational Spaces and Global Alternatives from the Movements." Pp. 199–206 in *World Social Forum: Challenging Empires*, ed. Jai Sen, Anita Anand, Arturo Escobar, and Peter Waterman. New Delhi: Viveka Foundation.

Amoore, Louise, ed. 2005. *The Global Resistance Reader*. London: Routledge.

Andhra Pradesh Chaitanya Mahila Samakhya (APCMS). No date a. "APCMS." Flyer obtained at Mumbai Resistance, January 2004.

——. No date b. *Manifesto and Constitution*. Hyderabad: APCMS, obtained at Mumbai Resistance, January 2004.

Andhra Pradesh Mahila Samatha Society (APMSS). No date. "Together We Make a Path." Leaflet obtained at APMSS office. Hyderabad, India, January 2005.

Andrijasevic, Rutvica, and Sarah Bracke. 2003. "Coming to Knowledge, Coming to Politics: A Reflection on Feminist Practices from the NextGENDERation Network." Script for *Multitudes,* March 2003. http://www.nextgenderation.net/texts/ multitudes.pdf (June 17, 2009).

Andrijasevic, Rutvica, Sarah Bracke, and Christina Gamberi. 2002. "Nextgenderation Network at the European Social Forum: A Feminist Intervention." http:// nextgenderation.let.uu.nl/esf2002/article.html (June 17, 2009).

Antrobus, Peggy. 2004. *The Global Women's Movement: Origins, Issues and Strategies.* London: Zed Books.

Anzaldúa, Gloria. 1987. *Borderlands/La Frontera: The New Mestiza.* San Francisco, CA: Aunt Lute Books.

Arksey, Hilary, and Peter Knight. 1999. *Interviewing for Social Scientists: An Introductory Resource with Examples.* London: SAGE.

Arquilla, John, and David F. Ronfeldt. 2001. *Networks and Netwars.* RAND Corporation.

Articulação de Mulheres Brasileiras (AMB). No date. "Sobre a AMB." http://www .articulacaodemulheres.org.br/publique/cgi/cgilua.exe/sys/start.htm?infoid=244 &sid=20 (June 15, 2005, no longer available).

Articulação de Mulheres Negras Brasileiras (AMNB). No date. AMNB Homepage. http://www.amnb.org.br/ (June 15, 2009).

Articulación Feminista Marcosur (AFM). 2002. "The Navigator's Notebook." http:// www.mujeresdelsur.org.uy/campana/libro_ing1.htm (June 17, 2009).

——. 2003a. "III World Social Forum, Porto Alegre, 23rd to 28th January 2003, Electronic Newsletter no. 1." http://www.dawn.org.fj/global/worldsocialforum/ socialforum.html (October 12, 2005, no longer available).

——. 2003b. "World Social Forum 2003: Report on the Activities of the ARTICULACIÓN FEMINISTA MARCOSUR." http://www.mujeresdelsur.org.uy/fsm/2003/ report03.htm (June 7, 2009).

——, No date. "Campaign against Fundamentalism, People Are Fundamental." http:// www.mujeresdelsur.org.uy/index_i.htm [click on campaigns] (June 7, 2009).

Asmita. No date. "Asmita: Resource Centre for Women." Leaflet obtained at Asmita office, Secunderabad, January 2004.

Association for Women and Human Rights in Development (AWID). 2005. "About AWID." http://www.awid.org/go.php?pg=about (June 11, 2005; document no longer available online; new formulation of AWID's values available http://www .awid.org/eng/About-AWID/What-is-AWID, June 7, 2009).

——. 2008. "Young Feminist Activism Program." http://www.awid.org/eng/About -AWID/AWID-Initiatives/Young-Feminist-Activism-Program (June 17, 2009).

Banaszak, Lee Ann, Karen Beckwith, and Dieter Rucht, eds. 2003. *Women's Movements Facing the Reconfigured State.* Cambridge: Cambridge University Press.

Bandy, Joe, and Jackie Smith, eds. 2005. *Coalitions across Borders: Transnational Protest and the Neoliberal Order.* Lanham, MD: Rowman and Littlefield.

Banks, Olive. 1986. *Becoming a Feminist: The Social Origins of 'First Wave' Feminism.* Brighton: Wheatsheaf Books.

Bartky, Sandra Lee. 1990. *Femininity and Domination: Studies in the Phenomenology of Oppression.* New York: Routledge.

——. 1995. "Agency: What's the Problem?" Pp. 178–93 in *Provoking Agents: Gender and Agency in Theory and Practice,* ed. Judith Kegan Gardiner. Urbana: University of Illinois Press.

batTzedek, Elliot. 1999. "Identity Politics and Racism: Some Thoughts and Questions." *Rain and Thunder,* no. 5. http://www.feminist-reprise.org/docs/iprace.htm (June 8, 2009)

Beaulieu, Elsa, and Julia di Giovanni. 2003. "The March at the 3rd Intercontinental Youth Camp," *Newsletter* 6, no. 1. http://www.worldmarchofwomen.org/bulletin_liaison/2003/2003_02/en#d (June 17, 2009).

Beckwith, Karen. 2000. "Beyond Compare? Women's Movements in Comparative Perspective." *European Journal of Political Research* 37, no. 4: 431–68.

——. 2003. "The Gendering Ways of States: Women's Representation and State Reconfiguration in France, Great Britain and the United States." Pp. 169–202 in *Women's Movements Facing the Reconfigured State,* ed. Lee Ann Banaszak, Karen Beckwith, and Dieter Rucht. Cambridge: Cambridge University Press.

Beleoken, Elvire. 2002. "Report: The African Social Forum, Bamako, Mali, 5–9 January 2002." http://www.africansocialforum.org/doc/fsa/bmk/Report%20on%20Bamako.pdf (June 8, 2009).

Bell, Daniel. 1960. *The End of Ideology: On the Exhaustion of Political Ideas in the Fifties.* Glencoe, IL: Free Press.

Benhabib, Seyla. 1992. *Situating the Self: Gender, Community and Postmodernism in Contemporary Ethics.* New York: Routledge.

——. 1994. "From Identity Politics to Social Feminism: A Plea for the Nineties." *Philosophy of Education.* http://www.ed.uiuc.edu/eps/PES-Yearbook/94_docs/BENHABIB.HTM (June 8, 2009).

Bennett, W. Lance. 2005. "Social Movements beyond Borders: Understanding Two Eras of Transnational Activism." Pp. 203–26 in *Transnational Protest and Global Activism,* ed. Donatella della Porta and Sidney Tarrow. Lanham, MD: Rowman and Littlefield.

Berg, Bruce. 2004. *Qualitative Research Methods,* 5th ed. Boston: Pearson.

Berg, John C. 2003. *Teamsters and Turtles: US Progressive Political Movements in the 21st Century.* Lanham, MD: Rowman and Littlefield.

Beuchler, Steven M. 2000. *Social Movements in Advanced Capitalism: The Political Economy and Cultural Construction of Social Activism.* New York: Oxford University Press.

——. 2004. "The Strange Career of Strain and Breakdown Theories of Collective Action." Pp. 47–66 in *The Blackwell Companion to Social Movements,* ed. David A. Snow, Sara Soule, and Hanspeter Kriesi. Oxford: Blackwell.

Bhaiya, Abha, and Kalyani Menon-Sen. 1996. *Feminist Training: Precepts and Practice—Experiences in the Mahila Samakhya Programme.* No publication details, book obtained at World Social Forum, Mumbai, India, January 2005.

Bircham, Emma, and John Charlton, eds. 2001. *Anti-capitalism: A Guide to the Movement,* 2nd ed. London: Bookmark.

Birchfield, Vicki, and Annette Freyberg-Inan. 2005. "Organic Intellectuals and Counter-Hegemonic Politics in the Age of Globalisation: The Case of ATTAC." Pp. 154–73 in *Critical Theories, International Relations and "the Anti-Globalisation Movement,"* ed. Catherine Eschle and Bice Maiguashca. London: Routledge.

Blee, Kathleen, and Verta Taylor. 2002. "Semi-structured Interviewing in Social Movement Research." Pp. 92–117 in *Methods of Social Movement Research,* ed. Bert Klandermans and Suzanne Staggenborg. Minneapolis: University of Minnesota Press.

Boserup, Ester. 1970. *Woman's Role in Economic Development*. London: Allen & Unwin.

Bouchier, David. 1979. "The Deradicalisation of Feminism: Ideology and Utopia in Action." *Sociology* 13, no. 3: 387–402.

Braidotti, Rosi, Ewa Charkiewicz, Sabina Hausler, and Saskia Wieringa. 1997. "Women, the Environment and Sustainable Development." Pp. 54–61 in *The Women, Gender and Development Reader Nalini*, ed. Nalini Visvanathan, Lynne Duggan, Laurie Nisonoff, and Nan Wiegersma. London: Zed Press.

Brecher, Jeremy, Tim Costello, and Brendan Smith. 2000. *Globalization from Below: The Power of Solidarity*. Cambridge, MA: Southend Press.

Brenner, Johanna. 2004. "Transnational Feminism and the Struggle for Global Justice." Pp. 25–34 in *World Social Forum: Challenging Empires*, ed. Jai Sen, Anita Anand, Arturo Escobar and Peter Waterman. New Delhi: Viveka Press.

Broad, Robin, ed. 2002. *Global Backlash: Citizen Initiatives for a Just World Economy*. Lanham, MD: Rowman and Littlefield.

Broad, Robin, and Heckscher, Zahara. 2003. "Before Seattle: The Historical Roots of the Current Movement against Corporate-Led Globalisation." *Third World Quarterly* 24, no. 4: 713–28.

Brown, Wendy. 1993. "Wounded Attachments." *Political Theory* 21, no. 3: 390–410.

Bryson, Valerie. 1999. "Patriarchy: A Concept Too Useful to Lose?" http://www.psa. ac.uk/journals/pdf/5/1999/bryson.pdf (June 7, 2009).

Burbach, Roger. 2001. *Globalization and Postmodern Politics: From Zapatistas to High-Tech Robber Barons*. London: Zed Books.

Burbach, Roger, Orlando Núñez, and Boris Kagarlitsky. 1996. *Globalization and Its Discontents: The Rise of Postmodern Socialisms*. London: Pluto Press.

Burdick, John. 1992. "Rethinking the Study of Social Movements: The Case of Christian Base Communities in Urban Brazil." Pp. 171–84 in *The Making of Social Movements in Latin America*, ed. Arturo Escobar and Sonia Alvarez. Boulder, CO: Westview Press.

Burrows, Nancy. 2002. "The World March of Women at the World Social Forum in Porto Alegre, Brazil, from January 31–February 5, 2002." http://www.ffq.qc.ca/marche2000/en/fsm2002b.html (June 17, 2009).

Buttel, Frederick H., and Kenneth A. Gould. 2004. "Global Social Movement(s) at the Crossroads: Some Observations on the Trajectory of the Anti-Corporate Globalization Movement." *Journal of World-Systems Research* 10, no. 1: 37–66.

Bystydzienski, Jill M., and Steven P. Schacht, eds. 2001. *Forging Radical Alliances across Difference: Coalition Politics for the New Millennium*. Lanham, MD: Rowman and Littlefield.

Caine, Barbara. 1997. *English Feminism, 1780–1980*. Oxford: Oxford University Press.

Caffentzis, George. 2005. "Dr. Sachs, Live8 and Neoliberalism's Plan B." Pp. 51–60 in *Shut Them Down: The G8, Gleneagles 2005 and the Movement of Movements*, ed. David Harvie, Keir Milburn, Ben Trott, and David Watts. Leeds: Dissent! and Autonomedia.

Caldwell, Kia Lilly. 2004. "Racialized Boundaries: Women's Studies and the Question of 'Difference' in Brazil." *Hemispheric Dialogues* 2. http://lals.ucse.edu/hemispheric_dialogues/dialogues/caldwell.html (November 28, 2004, no longer available).

Callinicos, Alex. 2003. *An Anti-capitalist Manifesto.* Cambridge: Polity Press.
———. 2004. "Building on the Success of the London ESF." http://www.resist.org .uk/?q=node/749 (June 19, 2009).
Calman, Leslie J. 1992. *Toward Empowerment: Women and Movement Politics in India.* Boulder, CO: Westview Press.
Canel, Eduardo. 2004. "New Social Movement Theory and Resource Mobilization Theory: The Need for Integration." http://www.idrc.ca/en/ev-54446-201-1-DO_TOPIC.html (June 17, 2009).
Caney, Simon. 2008. "Global Justice: From Theory to Practice." Pp. 27–43 in *Globalization and the Politics of Justice,* ed. Barry K. Gills. London: Routledge.
Carter, John, and David Morland. 2004. "Anti-capitalism: Are We All Anarchists Now?" Pp. 8–28 in *Anti-capitalist Britain,* ed. John Carter and David Morland. Cheltenham: New Clarion Press.
Catholics for the Right to Decide. No date. "Catholics for the Right to Decide (CDD) Came into Being in Latin America in 1987." English-language flyer, obtained at the World Social Forum, Mumbai, January 2004.
Catholics for the Right to Decide in Mexico. No date. "We Are Women, We Are Catholic and We Are in the Struggle." English language document. http://www .catholicsforchoice.org/lowbandwidth.engmexico.html (April 11, 2006, no longer available).
CEMINA, (Communicação, Educação e Informação em Gênero). No date a. "Communicação, Educação e Informação em Genero" [Communication, Education and Information on Gender], bilingual Portuguese-English document obtained at REDEH office, Rio de Janeiro, January 2005.
———. No date b. Cemina Home Page. http://www.cemina.org.br/a_index.asp (June 17, 2009).
Centro de Midia Independente (CMI) Brasil. 2005. "Manifestação Denuncia a Violência contra Mulher no Acampamento da Juventude [Demonstration Denouncing Violence against Women in the Youth Camp]." http://www.midia independente.org/pt/blue//2005/01/305254.shtml (June 17, 2009).
Centro Feminista de Estudos e Assessoria (CFEMEA). No date. "Apresentação [Introduction]." http://www.cfemea.org.br/quemsomos/apresentacao.asp (June 17, 2009).
Center for Women's Global Leadership (CWGL). No date a. "About CWGL." http:// www.cwgl.rutgers.edu/globalcenter/about.html (June 17, 2009).
———. No date b. "Leadership Development and Women's Human Rights Education." http://www.cwgl.rutgers.edu/globalcenter/leadership/leadership.html (June 17, 2009).
CEPIA—Cidadania, Estudo, Pesquisa, Informação, Ação. No date a. "Our Mission." http://www.cepia.org.br/en/default.asp (June 17, 2009).
———. No date b. "Programs." http://www.cepia.org.br/en/programas.asp (June 17, 2009).
Chang, K., and L. Ling. 2000. "Globalization and Its Intimate Other: Filipina Domestic Workers in Hong Kong." Pp. 27–43 in *Gender and Global Restructuring: Sighting, Sites and Resistances,* ed. Marianne H. Marchand and A. S. Runyan. London: Routledge.

Charles, Nickie. 2000. *Feminism, the State and Social Policy.* Basingstoke: Palgrave.

Charlton, Sue Ellen. 1997. "Development as History and Process." Pp. 7–13 in *The Women, Gender and Development Reader,* ed. Nalini Visvanathan, Lynne Duggan, Laurie Nisonoff, and Nan Wiegersma. London: Zed Press.

Chesters, Graeme, and Ian Welsh. 2006. *Complexity and Social Movements: Multitudes at the Edge of Chaos.* London: Routledge.

Cochrane, Regina. 2004. "Another World Via 'Diversity'?: Ecofeminism at the 2004 World Social Forum." *Women and Environments* Fall/Winter, 15–18.

Cockburn, Alexander, Jeffrey St. Clair, and Allan Sekula. 2000. *Five Days That Shook the World: Seattle and Beyond.* London: Verso.

Cockcroft, James. 2003. "Report on Porto Alegre 2003." http://www.forum socialmundial.org.br/noticias_textos.php?cd_news=249 (June 8, 2009).

Codepink. No date. "About Us." http://www.codepink4peace.org/article. php?list=type&type=3 (June 17, 2009).

Coletivo Feminino Plural. 2005. "Feminino Plural: Cidadania e direitos humanos das mulheres e das meninas" [Feminino Plural: Citizenship and Human Rights of Women and Girls]. Leaflet obtained at interview with Telia Negrão, Porto Alegre, January 22, 2005.

Collectif National pour les Droits des Femmes (CNDF). 2002. "Accueil de la petite enfance–emploi–partage des tâches" [Childcare–Work–Job Sharing]. http://www .collectifdroitsdesfemmes.org/spip.php?article7 (June 8, 2009).

———. 2007. "Qui Sommes Nous" [Who We Are]. http://collectifdroitsdesfemmes .org/spip.php?article4 (June 17, 2009).

———. No date a. "Homepage." http://www.collectifdroitsdesfemmes.org/ (June 17, 2009).

———. No date b. No title. First line reads "Le Collectif national pour les Droits des Femmes mène une campagne 'Accueil de la petite enfance–employ–partage des tâches'" [The National Collective for the Rights of Women leads a campaign 'Childcare–Work–Job-Sharing']. http://www.collectifdroitsdesfemmes.org/camp. html (June 11, 2005, no longer available).

Collins, Patricia Hill. 1998. "It's All in the Family: Intersections of Gender, Race and Nation." *Hypatia* 13, no. 3: 62–82.

———. 2000. *Black Feminist Thought: Knowledge, Consciousness, and the Politics of Empowerment,* 2nd ed. London: Routledge.

Collins, Pauline. 2002. "Another Europe Is Possible: The European Social Forum Held at Palfarri via Cenni, Florence, 5th–10th November 2002." http://ukwilpf .org.uk/NewsArticles/europeansocialforumreport.html (June 15, 2005, no longer available).

Combahee River Collective. 1977. "The Combahee River Collective Statement." http://circuitous.org/scraps/combahee.html (June 17, 2009).

Communist Party of India. No date. No title: Communist Party of India—Mass Organizations. http://www.cpi.org.in/CPI-MassOrgBody.htm (June 17, 2009).

Conway, Janet. 2007a. "Transnational Feminisms and the World Social Forum: Encounters and Transformations in Anti-globalization Spaces." *Journal of International Women's Studies* 8, no. 3: 49–70. http://www.bridgew.edu/SOAS/jiws/ April07/Conway.pdf (June 13, 2009).

———. 2007b. "Reflections on the 3rd International Feminist Dialogues: Notes from a Newcomer." *Journal of International Women's Studies* 8, no. 3: 211–13. http://www.bridgew.edu/SOAS/jiws/April07/Conway1.pdf (June 17, 2009).

Corcoran-Nantes, Yvonne. 2000. "Female Consciousness or Feminist Consciousness? Women's Consciousness Raising in Community-Based Struggles in Brazil." Pp. 81–100 in *Global Feminisms since 1945*, ed. Bonnie Smith. London: Routledge.

Cornwall Grail Group. No date. "Why Is It Called the Grail?" http://thomas.home.igc.org/cornwall/historyname.htm (June 15, 2005, no longer available).

Corrêa, Sonia. 2003. "Abortion Is a Global Political Issue." *DAWN Supplement for the World Social Forum, Porto Alegre, 23–28 January 2003.* http://www.dawn.org.fj/global/worldsocialforum/socialforum.html (June 30, 2003, no longer available).

Corrêa, Sonia, and Rosalind Petchesky. 1994. "Reproductive and Sexual Rights: A Feminist Perspective." Pp. 107–23 in *Population Policies Reconsidered: Health, Empowerment and Rights*, ed. G. Sen, A. Germain, and L. Chen. Boston: Harvard School of Public Health.

Costain, Anne N. 1994. *Inviting Women's Rebellion: A Political Process Interpretation of the Women's Movement.* Baltimore: Johns Hopkins University Press. (Originally published 1992)

Coté, Mark, Richard J. F. Day, and Greig de Peuter. 2007. *Utopian Pedagogy: Radical Experiments against Neoliberal Globalization.* Toronto: University of Toronto Press.

Crass, Chris. No date. "Beyond the Whiteness—Global Capitalism and White Supremacy: Thoughts on Movement Building and Anti-racist Organising." http://colours.mahost.org/articles/crass4.html (June 14, 2009).

Crenshaw, Kimberle. 1998. "Demarginalizing the Intersection of Race and Sex: A Black Feminist Critique of Antidiscrimination Doctrine, Feminist Theory, and Antiracist Politics." Pp. 314–43 in *Feminism and Politics*, ed. Anne Phillips. Oxford: Polity Press.

CRIOLA. No date. "CRIOLA: Organização de Mulheres Negras. Somos Parte de um movimento internacional que luta para reinventar o mundo" [CRIOLA: Organization of Black Women. We Are Part of an International Movement to Reinvent the World]. Leaflet, bilingual Portuguese/English, obtained at CRIOLA office, January 2005.

Crossette, Barbara. 2003. "The Role of Women." Pp. 137–56 in *Understanding Contemporary India*, ed. Sumit Ganguly and Neil DeVotta. London: Lynne Reinner.

Crossley, Neil. 2002. *Making Sense of Social Movements.* Buckingham: Open University Press.

Cruells, Eva. 2004. "The Exclusivity of the London ESF." *Digital Futures* Winter, 2–3.

Cumbers, Andy, Paul Routledge, and Corrine Nativel. 2008. "The Entangled Geographies of Global Justice Networks." *Progress in Human Geography* 32, no. 2: 183–201.

Curtin, Jennifer. 2006. "Gendering Political Representation in the Old and New Worlds of Westminster." Pp. 236–51 in *Representing Women in Parliament: A Comparative Study*, ed. Marian Sawer, Manon Tremblay, and Linda Trimble. London: Routledge.

Dalton, Russell. 2005. "Social Modernization and the End of Ideology Debate: Patterns of Ideological Polarisation." http://www.socsci.uci.edu/~rdalton/archive/jjps06.pdf (June 17, 2009).

Danaher, Kevin, and Roger Burbach, eds. 2000. *Globalize This! The Battle against the World Trade Organization and Corporate Rule*. Monroe, ME: Common Courage Press.

DAWN. 2000. "World Social Forum: Changes to the Agenda." *Dawn Informs*, November, 9.

——. 2001. No title, text begins "DAWN'S gender-focussed perspective on development was firmly present in; the planning and implementation of the First World Social Forum." *Dawn Informs*, February, 3.

——. 2002. "Globalization and Fundamentalism: A Genderscape." In *Addressing the World Social Forum: A DAWN Supplement*. http://www.dawn.org.fj/global/worldsocialforum/socialforum.html (Jun 30, 2003, no longer available).

——. No date a. "About Dawn." http://www.dawnnet.org/about.html (June 17, 2009).

——. No date b. "Regional Training Institute." http://www.dawnnet.org/regions/rti.html (June 11, 2009).

Day, Richard J. F. 2005. *Gramsci Is Dead: Anarchist Currents in the Newest Social Movements*. London: Pluto Press.

De Angelis, Massimo. 2004. "Evaluating the London ESF." *Eurotopia—European Social Forum: Debating the Challenges for Its Future*. http://www.euromovements.info/newsletter/masimo.htm (June 7, 2009).

De Goede, Marieke. 2005. "Carnival of Money: Politics of Dissent in an Era of Globalizing Finance." Pp. 379–91 in *The Global Resistance Reader*, ed. Louise Amoore. London: Routledge.

della Porta, Donatella. 2005. "Multiple Belongings, Tolerant Identities and the Construction of 'Another Politics': Between the European Social Forum and the Local Social Fora." Pp. 175–202 in *Transnational Protest and Global Activism*, ed. Donatella della Porta and Sidney Tarrow. Lanham, MD: Rowman and Littlefield.

——, ed. 2007a. *The Global Justice Movement: Cross National and Transnational Perspective*. Boulder, CO: Paradigm

——. 2007b. "The Global Justice Movement: An Introduction." Pp. 1–28 in *The Global Justice Movement: Cross National and Transnational Perspectives*, ed. Donatella della Porta. Boulder, CO: Paradigm.

della Porta, Donatella, Massimiliano Andretta, Lorenzo Mosca, and Herbert Reiter. 2006. *Globalization from Below: Transnational Activists and Protest Networks*. Minneapolis: University of Minnesota Press.

della Porta, Donatella, and Mario Diani. 2006. *Social Movements: An Introduction*, 2nd ed. Oxford: Blackwell.

della Porta, Donatella, and Sidney Tarrow. 2005a. "Transnational Processes and Social Activism: An Introduction." Pp. 1–17 in *Transnational Protest and Global Activism*, ed. Donatella della Porta and Sidney Tarrow. Lanham, MD: Rowman and Littlefield.

——, eds. 2005b. *Transnational Protest and Global Activism*. Lanham, MD: Rowman and Littlefield.

De Mond, Nadia. 2003. "ESF: Feminism and the Movement." *International ViewPoint Online Magazine* 4, no. 354, November. http://www.internationalviewpoint.org/spip.php?article125 (June 17, 2009).

Desai, Manisha. 2002. "Transnational Solidarity: Women's Agency, Structural Adjustment and Globalisation." Pp. 15–33 in *Women's Activism and Globalization: Linking Local Struggles and Transnational Politics,* ed. Nancy A. Naples and Manisha Desai. London: Routledge.

Diálogo Joven. 2005. "Especial: Foro Social Mundial 2005—Jóvenes: También Luchamos para Cambiar el Mundo" [Special Issue for the World Social Forum 2005—Youth: Part of the Struggle for a Better World] 1, 3: p. 4. Newspaper obtained at Feminist Dialogues, Porto Alegre, World Social Forum.

Diani, Mario. 2002. "Network Analysis." Pp. 173–200 in *Methods of Social Movement Research,* ed. Bert Klandermans and Suzanne Staggenborg. Minneapolis, MN: University of Minnesota Press.

———. 2003a. "Introduction: Social Movements, Contentious Actions and Social Networks: 'From Metaphor to Substance?'" Pp. 1–18 in *Social Movements and Networks: Relational Approaches to Collective Action,* ed. Mario Diani and Doug McAdam. Oxford: Oxford University Press.

———. 2003b. "Networks and Social Movements: A Research Programme." Pp. 299–319 in *Social Movements and Networks: Relational Approaches to Collective Action,* ed. Mario Diani and Doug McAdam. Oxford: Oxford University Press.

Di Giovanni, Julia. 2004. "After Mumbai: World Social Forum Report." *Newsletter* 7, no. 1 (March). http://www.worldmarchofwomen.org/bulletin_liaison/2004/2004_03/en#art3 (June 17, 2009).

Diniz, Simone Grilo, Cecilia de Mello e Souza, and Ana Paula Portella. 2001. "Not Like Our Mothers." Pp. 31–68 in *Negotiating Reproductive Rights: Women's Perspectives across Countries and Cultures,* ed. Rosalind Petchesky and Karen Judd. London: Zed Press.

Dixon, Chris. 2000. "Finding Hope after Seattle: Rethinking Radical Activism and Building a Movement." http://users.resist.ca/~chrisd/reflecting/afterseattle.htm (June 14, 2009).

Drainville, Andre. 2004. *Contesting Globalization: Space and Place in the World Economy.* London: Routledge.

Duchen, Claire. 1986. *Feminism in France: From May 1968 to Mitterrand.* London: Routledge & Kegan Paul.

Duddy, Janice. 2004a. "4th World Social Forum: Interview with Carol Barton." http://www.mujeresdelsur.org.uy/fsm/2004/i_dialogues35.htm (June 17, 2008).

———. 2004b. "What Were the Experiences of AWID Staff at the WSF?" *Resource Net Friday File,* 165. http://www.awid.org/eng/Issues-and-Analysis/Library/What-were-the-experiences-of-AWID-staff-at-the-WSF (June 11, 2009).

Duke, Dawn. 2003. "Alzira Rufino's A Casa de Cultura de Mulher Negra as a Form of Female Empowerment: A Look at the Dynamics of a Black Women's Organisation in Brazil Today." *Women's Studies International Forum* 26, no. 4: 357–68.

Dybeck, Amanda. 2003. "ESF 2: Another Step Forward." http://www.resist.org.uk/reports/archive/paris_esf/index.html (August 29, 2008, no longer available).

Earth, Barbara. 1996. "Structural Adjustment and Its Effects on Health and Education in Tanzania." *Canadian Women's Studies* 16, no. 3: 123–28.

Egan, Carolyn, and Michelle Robidoux. 2001. "Women." Pp. 81–91 in *Anti-capitalism: A Guide to the Movement*, ed. Emma Bircham and John Charlton. London: Bookmark Publications.

Eggert, Nina, and Marco Guigni. 2007. "The Global Justice Movement in Switzerland." Pp. 184–209 in *The Global Justice Movement: Cross-national and Transnational Perspectives*, ed. Donatella della Porta. Boulder, CO: Paradigm.

Epstein, Barbara. 2001. "Anarchism and the Anti-globalization Movement." *Monthly Review* 53, no. 4. http://www.monthlyreview.org/0901epstein.htm (June 17, 2009).

Eschle, Catherine. 2001. *Global Democracy, Social Movements and Feminism*. Boulder, CO: Westview Press.

———. 2004a. "Feminist Studies of Globalisation: Beyond Gender, Beyond Economism?" *Global Society* 18, no. 2: 97–125.

———. 2004b. "Constructing 'the Anti-globalisation Movement.'" *International Journal of Peace Studies* 9, no. 1: 61–84.

———. 2005. "Skeleton Women: Feminism and the Antiglobalization Movement." *Signs: Journal of Women in Politics and Culture* 30, no. 3: 1741–70.

Eschle, Catherine, and Bice Maiguashca, eds. 2005. *Critical Theories, International Relations and 'the Anti-Globalisation Movement'*. London: Routledge

———. 2006. "Bridging the Academic/Activist Divide: Feminist Activism and the Teaching of Global Politics." *Millennium: Journal of International Studies* 35, no. 1: 119–37.

Estima, Fernanda. 2003. "The World March of Women at the World Social Forum 2003." *Newsletter* 6, no. 1(February). http://www.worldmarchofwomen.org/bulletin liaison/2003/2003_02/en#c (June 17, 2009).

Ette, Mercy. 2007. "Empowerment." Pp. 146–60 in *The Impact of Feminism on Political Concepts and Debates*, ed. Georgina Blakely and Valerie Bryson. Manchester: Manchester University Press.

Eurotopia. No date. *European Social Forum: Debating the Challenges for Its Future*. http://www.euromovements.info/newsletter/ (June 17, 2009).

Fala Preta! No date a. "Fala Preta! A Black Organization for the Third Millennium." Leaflet obtained at Fala Preta! offices, January 2005.

———. No date b. "Objetivos." http://www.falapreta.org.br/objetivos.htm (June 11, 2005, no longer available).

Feminist ATTAC. No date. "Feminist Attac" [English Translation Part 1]. http://www.attac.at/907.html (June 11, 2005, no longer available).

Feminist Dialogues. 2006. "Coordinating Group 2007." http://feministdialogues.isiswomen.org/index.php?option=com_content&view=article&id=25&Itemid=122 (June 11, 2009).

———. 2009. "Feminist Dialogues Home Page." http://feministdialogues.isiswomen.org/ (June 17, 2009).

Femmes Solidaires. No date. "Femmes Solidaires: A Feminist Organisation for All Women." Leaflet obtained at feminist café in St. Denis, Paris, ESF, November 2003.

FEMNET. 2009. "About FEMNET: Background and History." http://www.femnet.or.ke/subsection.asp?ID=1 (June 13, 2009).

Fisher, William F., and Thomas Ponniah, eds. 2003. *Another World Is Possible: Popular Alternatives to Globalization at the World Social Forum*. London: Zed Books.

Flam, Helena, and Debra King. 2005. *Emotions and Social Movements*. London: Routledge.

Flora Tristán CMP. No date a. "Centro de la Mujer Peruana Flora Tristán" [Center for Peruvian Women Flora Tristán]. http://www.flora.org.pe/mision.htm (June 17, 2009).

———. No date b. "Red Nacional Mujer Rural" [National Network of Rural Women]. http://www.flora.org.pe/red_mujer_rural.htm (June 17, 2009).

———. No date c. "Biblioteca Flora Tristán" [Flora Tristán library]. http://www.flora.org.pe/biblioteca.htm (June 17, 2009).

———. No date d. "Campaña 28 de Setiembre" [September 28 Campaign]. http://www.flora.org.pe/setiembre28.htm (June 17, 2009).

Foerster, Amy. 2009. "Contested Bodies: Sex Trafficking and Transnational Politics." *International Feminist Journal of Politics* 11, no. 2: 151–73.

Fowlkes, Diane. 1997. "Moving from Feminist Identity Politics to Coalition Politics through a Feminist Materialist Standpoint of Intersubjectivity in Gloria Anzaldua's Borderlands/La Fronter: The New Mestiza." *Hypatia* 12, no. 2: 105–24.

Francisco, Gigi. 2001. "Women Make Their Mark at the World Social Forum." *Dawn Informs*, February, 1–3.

Frankenberg, Ruth. 1993. "Growing up White: Feminism, Racism and the Social Geography of Childhood." *Feminist Review* 45: 51–84.

Fraser, Nancy. 1997. *Justice Interruptus: Critical Reflections on the "Postsocialist" Condition*. New York: Routledge.

Freeman, Jo. 2003. "The Women's Movement." Pp. 22–31 in *The Social Movements Reader: Cases and Concepts*, ed. Jeff Goodwin and James M. Jasper. Oxford: Blackwell.

Friedan, Betty. 1963. *The Feminine Mystique*. New York: Norton.

Frye, Marilyn. 1983. *The Politics of Reality: Essays on Feminist Theory*. Trumansburg, NY: Crossing Press.

Fukuyama, Francis. 1989. "The End of History?" *National Interest* 16, Summer: 3–18.

Gandhi, Nandita, and Shah, Nandita. 1991. *The Issues at Stake: Theory and Practice in the Contemporary Women's Movement in India*. New Dehli: Kali for Women.

Gardiner, Judith Kegan. 1995. "Introduction." Pp. 1–20 in *Provoking Agents: Gender and Agency in Theory and Practice*, ed. Judith Kegan Gardiner. Urbana: University of Illinois Press.

Gelb, Joyce. 1986. "Feminism in Britain: Politics without Power?" Pp. 103–21 in *The New Women's Movement*, ed. Drude Dahlerup. London: Sage.

———. 1990. "Feminism and Political Action." Pp. 137–55 in *Challenging the Political Order: New Social and Political Movements in Western Democracies*, ed. R. Dalton and M. Kuelchler. Cambridge: Polity Press.

German, Lindsey. 2001. "War." Pp. 123–34 in *Anti-capitalism: A Guide to the Movement*, 2d ed., ed. Emma Bircham and John Charlton. London: Bookmark.

Gerring, John. 1997. "Ideology: A Definitional Analysis." *Political Research Quarterly* 50 (4): 957–94.

Gills, Barry K. 2008. "The Global Politics of Justice." Pp. 1–4 in *Globalization and the Global Politics of Justice*, ed. Barry K. Gills. London: Routledge.

Gitlin, Todd. 1993. "The Rise of 'Identity Politics': An Examination and Critique." *Dissent* (Spring): 172–77.

———. 1995. *Twilight of Common Dreams: Why America Is Wracked with Culture Wars.* New York: Henry Holt.

Gleason, Philip. 1983. "Identifying Identity: A Semantic History." *Journal of American History* 69, no. 4: 910–31.

Global Women's Strike. 2003. *Global Women's Strike* [newspaper], no. 2, November.

———. 2004a. "Call for a Women's Day at the European Social Forum." http://www.globalwomenstrike.net/English2004/WomensDayLetter.htm (June 17, 2009).

———. 2004b. "Response to the Opposition to a Women's Day at the European Social Forum in London." Letter dated June 15, 2004, obtained at Crossroads centre, November 2004.

———. 2004c. "Women's Open Day: Invisible Workers Centre Stage." Flyer. http://www.globalwomenstrike.net/ESFWomensDay.htm (June 17, 2009).

———. No date. "The Demands of the Strike." http://www.globalwomenstrike.net/NewStrike/NewDemands.htm (June 17, 2009).

Goodwin, Jeff, and James M. Jasper, eds. 2003. *The Social Movement Reader: Cases and Concepts.* Oxford: Blackwell.

Goodwin, Jeff, James M. Jasper, and Francesca Polletta. 2001a. "Introduction: Why Emotions Matter." Pp. 1–24 in *Passionate Politics: Emotions and Social Movements,* ed. Jeff Goodwin, James M. Jasper, and Francesca Polletta. Chicago: University of Chicago Press.

———, eds. 2001b. *Passionate Politics: Emotions and Social Movements.* Chicago: University of Chicago Press.

Gouws, Amanda. 2007. "Ways of Being: Feminist Activism and Theorizing at the Global Feminist Dialogues in Porte Alegre, Brazil, 2005." *Journal of International Women's Studies,* 8, no. 3: 28–36. http://www.bridgew.edu/soas/jiws/April07/Gouws.pdf (June 17, 2009).

Graeber, David. 2002. "The New Anarchists." *New Left Review* no. 13(January–February): 61–73.

———. 2007. "The Shock of Victory." http://news.infoshop.org/article.php?story=2007graeber-victory (June 17, 2009).

Grail. No date. "About Us." http://www.thegrail.org/index.php?menu=2&lang=en (June 8, 2009).

Grailville. 2005. "About the Grail and Building Community." http://grailville.org/home.php?ID=2 (June 17, 2009).

Grey, Mary. 2005. "Dalit Women and the Struggle for Justice in a World of Global Capitalism." *Feminist Theology* 14, no. 1: 127–49.

Gruffydd Jones, Branwen. 2005. "Globalisations, Violences and Resistances in Mozambique: The Struggles Continue." Pp. 53–73 in *Critical Theories, International Relations and "the Anti-Globalisation Movement,"* ed. Catherine Eschle and Bice Maiguashca. London: Routledge.

Grzybowski, Cândido. 2002. "Is a More Feminine World Possible?" *Dawn Informs,* May, 19.

Hadden, Jennifer, and Sidney Tarrow. 2007. "Spillover or Spillout? The Global Justice Movement in the United States after 9/11." *Mobilization* 12, no. 4: 359–76.

Hagemann-White, Carol. 2002. "Violence against Women in the European Contexts, Histories, Prevalences, Theories." Pp. 31–48 in *Thinking Differently: A Reader in European Women's Studies,* ed. Gabriele Griffin and Rosi Braidotti. London: Zed.

Hall, Ronnie. 2001. "Environment." Pp. 57–68 in *Anti-capitalism: A Guide to the Movement,* 2nd ed., ed. Emma Bircham and John Charlton. London: Bookmark.

Halliday, Fred. 2000. "Getting Real about Seattle." *Millennium: Journal of International Studies* 29, no. 1: 123–29.

Hanmer, Jalina. 2002. "Violence Militarism and War." Pp. 267–81 in *Thinking Differently: A Reader in European Women's Studies,* ed. Gabriele Griffin and Rosi Braidotti. London: Zed.

Haralanova, Christina. 2005. "Is There an Equal Space for Women's Rights Discussions at the Forum?" *Les Penelopes.* http://www.penelopes.org/Anglais/article.php3?id_article=1213 (June 17, 2009).

Haraway, Donna. 1988. "Situated Knowledges: The Science Question in Feminism and the Privilege of Partial Perspective." *Feminist Studies* 14, no. 3: 575–99.

Harding, Sandra. 1987. "Introduction: Is There a Feminist Method?" Pp. 1–14 in *Feminism and Methodology,* ed. Sandra Harding. Bloomington: Indiana University Press.

———. 1991. *Whose Science? Whose Knowledge? Thinking from Women's Lives.* Ithaca, NY: Cornell University Press.

———. 1992. "Subjectivity, Experience and Knowledge: An Epistemology from/for Rainbow Coalition Politics." *Development and Change* 23, no. 3: 175–93.

Hardt, Michael. 2002. "Porto Alegre: Today's Bandung?" http://www.forumsocial-mundial.org.br/dinamic/eng_b_Michael_Hardt.php (June 17, 2009).

Hardt, Michael, and Antonio Negri. 2000. *Empire.* Cambridge, MA: Harvard University Press.

———. 2003. "Foreword." Pp. xvi–xix in *Another World Is Possible: Popular Alternatives to Globalization at the World Social Forum,* ed. William F. Fisher and Thomas Ponniah. Novia Scotia: Fernwood.

Hardtman, Eva-Maria. 2003. *'Our Fury Is Burning': Local Practice and Global Connections in the Dalit Movement.* Stockholm: Stockholm University.

Hartmann, Betsy. 1994. "Consensus and Contradiction on the Road to Cairo." *WGNRR Newsletter* 47, no. 3: 10–11.

Harvie, David, Keir Milburn, Ben Trott, and David Watts. 2005. *Shut Them Down! The G8, Gleneagles 2005 and the Movement of Movements.* Leeds: Dissent!

Hawken, Paul. 2000. "Skeleton Woman Visits Seattle." Pp. 14–34 in *Globalize This!,* ed. Kevin Danaher and Roger Burbach. Monroe, ME: Common Courage Press.

Hawkesworth, Mary. 2006. *Globalization and Feminist Activism.* Lanham, MD: Rowman and Littlefield.

Held, David. 1995. *Democracy and the Global Order: From the Global State to Cosmopolitan Governance.* Cambridge: Polity Press.

Hennessy, Rosalind. 1995. "Women's Lives/Feminist Knowledge: Feminist Standpoint as Ideology Critique." http://english.illinoisstate.edu/Strickland/495/henness1.html (August 19, 2009).

Hennig, Brett. 2004. "Hypocrisy in the UK European Social Forum Process." http://www.indymedia.org.uk/en/2004/01/284424.html (June 17, 2009).

Hercus, Cheryl. 1999. "Identity, Emotion, and Feminist Collective Action." *Gender and Society* 13, no. 1: 34–55.

———. 2005. *Stepping Out of Line: Becoming and Being a Feminist.* New York: Routledge.

Hierro, Graciela. 1994. "Gender and Power." *Hypatia* (1): 173–83.

Higgins, Nick. 2005. "Lessons from the Indigenous: Zapatista Poetics and a Cultural Humanism for the Twenty First Century." Pp. 87–102 in *Critical Theories, International Relations and "the Anti-Globalisation Movement,"* ed. Catherine Eschle and Bice Maiguashca. London: Routledge.

Hobsbawm, Eric. 1996. "Identity Politics and the Left." *New Left Review,* 217: 38–47.

Hodkinson, Stuart. 2002. "Another European Social Forum Is Necessary: Reflections on Florence, Italy, 6–10 November 2002." *Red Pepper.* http://www.redpepper.org.uk/intarch/x-anotheresf.htm (December 16, 2005, no longer available).

hooks, bell. 1981. *Ain't I a Woman: Black Women and Feminism.* Boston, MA: South End Press.

Hubbard, Gill. 2003. "European Social Forum: Paris on My Mind." *Socialist Review.* http://www.socialistreview.org.uk/article.php?articlenumber=8692 (June 11, 2009).

Huijg, Dieuwertje. 2003a. "Porto Alegre 26th of January 2003." *Daily Impressions from Porto Alegre.* http://www.nextgenderation.net/projects/alterglobalisation/wsf2003/report3.html (June 17, 2009).

———. 2003b. "Porto Alegre 27th of January 2003." *Daily Impressions from Porto Alegre.* http://www.nextgenderation.net/projects/alterglobalisation/wsf2003/report4.html (June 17, 2009).

Iannello, Kathleen P. 1992. *Decisions without Hierarchy: Feminist Interventions in Organization Theory and Practice.* New York: Routledge.

IBASE (Brazilian Institute of Social and Economic Analyses). 2005. "An X-ray of Participation in the 2005 Forum: Elements for Debate." Rio de Janeiro: IBASE. http://www.ibase.br/userimages/relatorio_fsm2005_INGLES2.pdf (June 17, 2009).

IMC Women. 2003. "IMC Womyn Proposal." http://www.docs.indymedia.org/view/Global/ImcWomynProposal (June 15, 2005, no longer available).

Indianchild.com. No date. "NGOs in India (Women)." http://www.indianchild.com/women_ngos_in_india.htm (June 17, 2009).

Instituto Eqüit. No date. "Eqüit Institute." Leaflet (English), obtained at Instituto Eqüit office, Rio de Janeiro, January 2005.

International Feminists for a Gift Economy. No date. No title. http://www.gift-economy.com/international.html (June 17, 2009).

International Forum on Globalization. 2002. "Alternatives to Economic Globalisation." Pp. 42–46 in *Global Backlash: Citizen Initiatives for a Just World Economy,* ed. Robin Broad. Lanham, MD: Rowman and Littlefield.

International Free Women's Foundation. No date. "Aims and Principles of the International Free Women's Foundation." http://www.freewomensfoundation.org/english/aims/aimsindex.htm (June 17, 2009).

International Gender and Trade Network (IGTN). 2005. "Trade Agreements." http://www.igtn.org/page/trade/ (June 15, 2005, no longer available).

———. No date a. "IGTN Homepage." http://www.igtn.org/ (June 17, 2009).

———. No date b. "IGTN." Leaflet obtained at Equit office, January 2005.

International League of Peoples' Struggles (ILPS). 2004a. "Mumbai Resistance 2004." http://www.ilps-news.com/central-info-bureau/events/mumbai-resistance -2004/ (June 17, 2009).

———. 2004b. "Why Mumbai Resistance." http://www.ilps-news.com/central-info -bureau/events/mumbai-resistance-2004/why-mumbai-resistance-2004/ (June 17, 2009).

International Prostitutes Collective. No date. "International Prostitutes Collective Home page." http://www.prostitutescollective.net/ (June 17, 2009).

International Women's Health Coalition. 2008. "CFEMEA: Keeping Feminists Tapped into National Politics." http://www.iwhc.org/index.php?option=com _content&task=view&id=183&Itemid=95 (June 7, 2009).

Jacoby, Tami. 2006. "From the Trenches: Dilemmas of Feminist IR Fieldwork." Pp. 153–73 in *Feminist Methodologies for International Relations*, ed. Brooke Ackerly, Maria Stern, and Jacqui True. Cambridge: Cambridge University Press.

Jaggar, Alison. 1989. "Love and Knowledge: Emotion in Feminist Epistemology." Pp. 145–71 in *Gender/Body/Knowledge: Feminist Reconstructions of Being and Knowing*, ed. Alison Jaggar and Susan R. Bordo. New Brunswick, NJ: Rutgers University Press.

Jagori. No date. "Looking Back at the Contemporary Indian Women's Movement." http://www.jagori.org/wom_movement.htm (March 1, 2004, no longer available).

James, Selma, and Nina Lopez. 2004. "8th March 2004: Calling All Women, 5th Global Women's Strike . . . " http://www.globalwomenstrike.net/English2004/8_ march_2004.htm (June 17, 2009).

Jasper, James M. 1998. "The Emotions of Protest: Effective and Reactive Emotions in and around Social Movements." *Sociological Forum* 13, no. 3: 397–424.

———. 2003. "The Emotions of Protest." Pp. 153–62 in *The Social Movements Reader: Cases and Concepts*, ed. Jeff Goodwin and James M. Jasper. Oxford: Blackwell.

Jayawardena, Kumari. 1986. *Feminism and Nationalism in the Third World*. London: Zed Books.

Jeffers, Esther, and Christiane Marty (coordinators), and Catherine Bloch London, Helena Hirata, Esther Jeffers, Francois Lille, Martine Lurol, Christiane Marty, Jacqueline Penit, Claude Piganiol-Jacquet, Evelyne Rochedereux, Josette Trat, Stephanie Treillet, and Sophie Zafari (authors). 2003. *Quand les Femmes se Heurent à La Mondialisation* [When Women Are Confronted by Globalisation]. Paris: ATTAC and Mille et Une Nuits.

Jenkins, J. Craig. 1983. "Resource Mobilization Theory and the Study of Social Movements." *Annual Review of Sociology* 9: 527–53.

Jenson, Jane. 1996. "Representations of Difference: The Varieties of French Feminism." Pp. 73–114 in *Mapping the Women's Movement*, ed. Monica Threlfall. London: Verso.

John, Mary. 1998. "Feminisms and Internationalisms: A Response from India." *Gender and History* 10, no. 3: 539–48.

Johnson, Greg. 2002. "The Situated Self and Utopian Thinking." *Hypatia* 17, no. 3: 20–44.

Juris, Jeffrey S. 2005. "Youth and the World Social Forum." http://ya.ssrc.org/ transnational/Juris/ (June 17, 2009).

———. 2008. *Networking Futures: The Movements against Corporate Globalization.* London: Duke University Press.

Kahn, Nighat Said. 2004. "Up against the State: The Women's Movement in Pakistan." In *Feminist Politics, Activism and Vision*, ed. Luciana Ricciutelli, Angela Miles, and Margaret. London: Zed. http://www.oise.utoronto.ca/cwse/Nighat%20 Lecture%203.pdf (June 7, 2009).

Kantola, Johanna. 2006. *Feminists Theorize the State.* London: Palgrave Macmillan.

Kaplan, Caren. 1994. "The Politics of Location as Transnational Feminist Critical Practice." Pp. 137–52 in *Scattered Hegemonies: Postmodernity and Transnational Feminist Practices*, ed. Caren Kaplan and Inderpal Grewal. Minneapolis: University of Minnesota Press.

Karadenizli, Maria, Bénédicte Allaert, and Carmen de la Cruz. 2003. "'Another World Is Possible . . . It's on HER Way!' A WIDE Report on the World Social Forum." https://www.igloo.org/libraryservices/download-nocache/Library/vz/womenind/wideposi/anotherw (June 11, 2009).

Karat, Brinda. 1997. "The Multiple Struggles of Women." *Frontline: India's National Magazine* 14, no. 9. http://www.flonnet.com/fl1419/14190890.htm (June 7, 2009).

———. 2002. "Introduction." In *AIDWA: Perspectives, Interventions and Struggles (1998–2001).* New Delhi: AIDWA.

———. 2005. *Survival and Emancipation: Notes from Indian Women's Struggles.* Gurgaon, India: Three Essays Collective.

Karat, Brinda, and Jagmati Sangwan. No date. "Concepts/Frameworks of Family Violence—Community Codes and 'Honour' Killings: The Haryana Experience." Unpublished paper, obtained at AIDWA workshop, World Social Forum, January 2004.

Katsiaficas, George. 2004. "Seattle Was Not the Beginning." Pp. 3–10 in *Confronting Capitalism: Dispatches from a Global Movement*, ed. Eddie Yuen, Daniel Burton-Rose, and George Katsiaficas. Brooklyn, NY: Soft Skull Press.

Katzenstein, Mary Fainsod. 1990. "Feminism within American Institutions: Unobtrusive Mobilization in the 1980's." *Signs: Journal of Women in Culture and Society* 16, no. 1: 27–54.

———. 2003. "Discursive Activism by Catholic Feminists." Pp. 249–53 in *The Social Movements Reader: Cases and Concepts*, ed. Jeff Goodwin and James M. Jasper. Oxford: Blackwell.

Keck, Margaret E., and Kathryn Sikkink. 1998. *Activists beyond Borders: Advocacy Networks in International Politics.* Ithaca, NY: Cornell University Press.

Kerr, Joanna. 2002. "From 'WID' to 'GAD' to Women's Rights: The First Twenty Years of AWID." http://awid-org.sitepreview.ca/eng/Issues-and-Analysis/Library/From-WID-to-GAD-to-Women-s-Rights-The-First-Twenty-Years-of-AWID (June 7, 2009).

Khullar, Mala. 1997. "Emergence of the Women's Movement in India." *Asian Journal of Women's Studies* 3, no. 2: 94–129.

Kingsnorth, Paul. 2003. *One No, Many Yeses: A Journey to the Heart of the Global Resistance Movement.* London: Free Press.

Klein, Naomi. 2000. *No Logo.* London: Flamingo.

———. 2001. "World Social Forum: A Fete for the End of History." *The Nation*, March 19, 2001. http://www.nadir.org/nadir/initiativ/agp/free/wsf/fete.htm (June 17, 2009).

———. 2002. *Fences and Windows: Dispatches from the Front Lines of the Globalization Debate*. London: Flamingo.

———. 2003. "More Democracy—Not More Political Strongmen." *The Guardian*, February 3. http://www.forumsocialmundial.org.br/dinamic.php?pagina=balanco_klein_2003in (June 17, 2009).

———. 2004. "Reclaiming the Commons." Pp. 219–29 in *A Movement of Movements: Is Another World Really Possible?*, ed. Tom Mertes. London: Verso.

Klepto, Kolonel, and Major Up Evil. 2005. "The Clandestine Insurgent Rebel Clown Army Goes to Scotland via a Few Other Places." Pp. 243–54 in *Shut Them Down! The G8, Gleneagles 2005, and the Movement of Movements*, ed. David Harvie, Keir Milburn, Ben Trott, and David Watts. London: Dissent and Autonomedia.

Klugman, Barbara. 2007. "Parallel or Integrated 'Other Worlds': Possibilities for Alliance-Building for Sexual and Reproductive Rights." *Journal of International Women's Studies* 8, no. 3, 88–112. http://www.bridgew.edu/soas/jiws/April07/Klugman.pdf (June 17, 2009).

Knight, Danielle. No date. "Seeing beyond the Numbers: The Human Costs of Population Control in Brazil." *Z Magazine*. http://zena.secureforum.com/Znet/zmag/articles/sept96knight.htm (November 28, 2004, no longer available).

Koopman, Sara. 2007. "A Liberatory Space? Rumors of Rapes at the 5th World Social Forum, Porto Alegre, 2005." *Journal of International Women's Studies* 8, no. 3, 149–63. http://www.bridgew.edu/SOAS/jiws/April07/Koopman.pdf (June 17, 2009).

Kricorian, Nancy. No date. "Direct Action and Street Theater." http://www.codepink4peace.org/article.php?id=330 (June 7, 2009).

Kriesi, Hanspeter. 1996. "The Organizational Structure of New Social Movements in a Political Context." Pp. 152–48 in *Comparative Perspectives on Social Movements*, ed. Doug McAdam, John D. McCarthy, and Mayer N. Zald. Cambridge: Cambridge University Press.

Kubrin, David. 2004. "Scaling the Heights to Seattle." Pp. 21–28 in *Confronting Capitalism: Dispatches from a Global Movement*, ed. Eddie Yuen, Daniel Burton-Rose, and George Katsiaficas. Brooklyn, NY: Soft Skull Press.

Kumar, Radha. 1993. *The History of Doing: An Illustrated Account of Movements for Women's Rights and Feminism in India, 1800–1990*. New Delhi: Kali for Women.

Kumar, Sandhya. 2004. "Women and the WSF." http://www.india-seminar.com/2004/535/535%20comment.htm (June 7, 2009).

Latoures, Aurelie. 2007. "Gender in the Bamako Polycentric World Social Forum (2006): Is Another World Possible." *Journal of International Women's Studies* 8, no. 3: 164–83. http://www.bridgew.edu/SoAS/JIWS/April07/Latoures.pdf (June 17, 2009).

Leclerc, Anne. 2003. "Success of Assembly for Women's Rights." *International Viewpoint Online Magazine* 4, no. 355 (December). http://www.internationalviewpoint.org/spip.php?article111 (June 17, 2009).

Leite, José. 2005. *The World Social Forum: Strategies of Resistance*, trans. Traci Romine. Chicago: Haymarket Books.

Lofland, John, and Lyn H. Lofland. 1995. *Analyzing Social Settings: A Guide to Qualitative Observation and Analysis*, 3rd ed. Belmont, NY: Wadsworth.

Loveli, Peggy A. 2006. "Race, Gender and Work in Sao Paulo Brazil, 1960–2000." *Latin American Research Review* 41, no. 3: 63–86.

Lovenduski, Joni, and Vicky Randall. 1993. *Contemporary Feminist Politics: Women and Power in Britain*. Oxford: Oxford University Press.

Lugones, María. 1990. "Playfulness, 'World'-Traveling, and Loving Perception." Pp. 390–402 in *Making Face, Making Soul/Haciendo Caras: Creative and Critical Perspectives by Feminists of Color*, ed. Gloria Anazaldúa. San Francisco: Aunt Lute Books.

Lyshaug, Brenda. 2006. "Solidarity without 'Sisterhood'? Feminism and the Ethics of Coalition Building." *Politics and Gender* 2, no. 1: 77–100.

MacDonald, Kevin. 2006. *Global Movements: Action and Culture*. Oxford: Basil Blackwell.

Mackinnon, Catharine. 1987. "Feminism, Marxism, Method and the State." Pp. 135–56 in *Feminism and Methodology*, ed. Sandra. Milton Keynes: Open University Press.

Madhok, Sujata. 2004. "Women: Background and Perspective." Infochange. http://infochangeindia.org/20021004593 1/Women/Backgrounder/Women -Background-Perspective.html (June 17, 2009).

———. No date. "Background and Perspective." http://www.infochangeindia.org/ WomenIbp.jsp (June 7, 2009).

Mahila Jagruthi. 1998. *Women and Communalism*. Bangalore: Mahila Jagruthi.

———. 2001. *Women's Liberation: A Mahila Jagruthi Perspective*. Bangalore: Mahila Jagruthi.

———. 2004. "Commodification of Women Due to Imperialist Globalisation." Paper presented at "The Impact of Imperialist Globalization on Women," workshop at Mumbai Resistance, January 2004.

———. No date. "Mahila Jagruthi." Leaflet obtained at Mumbai Resistance, Mumbai, January 2004.

Mahila Samakhya Uttar Pradesh. No date. "Mahila Samakhya Uttar Pradesh." Leaflet obtained at World Social Forum, Mumbai, India, January 2005.

Maiguashca, Bice. 2006a. "Rethinking Power from the Point of View of Resistance: The Politics of Gender." In *International Political Economy and Poststructural Politics*, ed. Marieka de Goede. Basingstoke: Palgrave Macmillan.

———. 2006b. "Making Feminist Sense of the Anti-globalization Movement: Some Reflections on Methodology and Method." *Global Society* 20, no. 2.

Mandle, Joan D. No date. "How Political Is the Personal? Identity Politics, Feminism and Social Change." http://userpages.umbc.edu/~korenman/wmst/ identity_pol.html (June 17, 2009).

Marchand, Marianne, and Anne Sisson Runyan. 2000a. "Feminist Sightings of Global Restructuring: Conceptualizations and Reconceptualizations." Pp. 1–22 in *Gender and Global Restructuring: Sighting, Sites and Resistances*, ed. Marianne H. Marchand and A. S. Runyan. London: Routledge.

———, eds. 2000b. *Gender and Global Restructuring: Sightings, Sites and Resistances*. London: Routledge.

Maria Mulher. No date. "Maria Mulher." Leaflet obtained at interview with Noelci Homero, Porto Alegre, January 2005.

Marin, Gustavo. 2002. "Beyond Porto Alegre." http://www.forumsocialmundial. org.br/dinamic/eng_b_GustavoMarin.php (June 17, 2009).

Marshall, Barbara. 2000. *Configuring Gender*. Ontario: Broadview.

Mayo, Marjorie. 2005. *Global Citizens: Social Movements and the Challenge of Globalization*. Toronto: Canadian Scholars' Press.

McCarthy, John D., and Mayer N. Zald. 1973. *The Trend of Social Movements in America: Professionalization and Resource Mobilization*. Morristown, NJ: General Learning Press.

McKay, George, ed. 1998. *DiY Culture: Party and Protest in Nineties Britain*. London: Verso.

McKenna, Erin. 2001. *The Task of Utopia: A Pragmatist and Feminist Perspective*. New York: Rowman and Littlefield.

Melucci, Alberto. 1989. *Nomads of the Present: Social Movements and Individual Needs in Contemporary Society*. London: Radius.

Mertes, Tom, ed. 2004. *A Movement of Movements: Is Another World Really Possible?* London: Verso

Messer-Davidow, Ellen. 1995. "Acting Otherwise." Pp. 23–51 in *Provoking Agents: Gender and Agency in Theory and Practice*, ed. Judith Kegan. Urbana: University of Illinois Press.

Mies, M. 1982. *The Lacemakers of Narsapur: Indian Housewives Produce for the World Market*. London: Zed Press.

Miles, Angela. 1996. *Integrative Feminisms: Building Global Visions, 1960s–1990s*. London: Routledge.

Ming, Wu. 2004. "Why Not Show Off about the Best Things: A Few Quick Notes on Social Conflict in Italy and the Metaphors Used to Describe It." Pp. 235–42 in *Confronting Capitalism: Dispatches from a Global Movement*, ed. Eddie Yuen, Daniel Burton-Rose, and George Katsiaficas. Brooklyn, NY: Soft Skull Press.

Moghadam, Valentine M. 1995. "Market Reforms and Women's Economic Status: Eastern Europe, Russia, Vietnam and China." *Development* [Special Issue], no. 1: 61–66.

———. 2000. "Economic Restructuring and the Gender Contract: A Case Study of Jordan." Pp. 99–115 in *Gender and Global Restructuring: Sightings, Sites and Resistances*, ed. Marianne Marchand and Anne Sisson Runyan. London: Routledge.

———. 2001. "Transnational Feminist Networks: Collective Action in an Era of Globalization." Pp. 111–39 in *Globalization and Social Movements*, ed. Pierre Hamel, Henri Lustiger-Thaler, Jan Nederveen Pieterse, and Sasha Roseneil. Basingstoke: Palgrave.

———. 2005. *Globalizing Women: Transnational Feminist Networks*. Baltimore: Johns Hopkins University Press.

———. 2009. *Globalization and Social Movements: Islamism, Feminism and the Global Justice Movement*. Lanham, MD: Rowman and Littlefield.

Mohanty, Chandra. 1998. "Feminist Encounters: Locating the Politics of Experience." Pp. 254–72 in *Feminism and Politics*, ed. Ann Philipps. Oxford: Oxford University Press.

———. 2003. *Feminism without Borders: Decolonizing Theory, Practicing Solidarity*. Durham: Duke University Press.

Mollo, Maria de Lourdes Rollemberg, and Alfredo Saad-Filho. No date. "The Neoliberal Decade: Reviewing the Brazilian Economic Transition." http://netx.u-paris10.fr/actuelmarx/m4mollo.htm (April 21, 2009).

Moraga, Cherríe, and Gloria Anzaldúa. 1983. *This Bridge Called My Back: Writings by Radical Women of Color.* New York: Kitchen Table Press.

Morton, Adam David. 2002. "'La Resurecion del Maiz': Globalisation, Resistance and the Zapatistas." *Millennium* 31, no. 1: 27–54.

Moya, Paula. 1997. "Postmodernism, 'Realism' and the Politics of Identity: Cherríe Moraga and Chicana Feminism." Pp. 125–50 in *Feminist Genealogies, Colonial Legacies, Democratic Futures,* ed. M. Jacqui Alexander and Chandra Talpade Mohanty. New York: Routledge.

———. 2001. "Introduction: Reclaiming Identity." In *Reclaiming Identity: Realist Theory and the Predicament of Postmodernism,* ed. Paula Moya and Michael Hames-Garcia. Berkeley: University of California Press. Reprinted in *Cultural Logic* 3, no. 2. http://clogic.eserver.org/3-1&2/moya.html (June 8, 2009).

"Mumbai Resistance." 2004. *The Spark,* February 19. http://home.clear.net.nz/pages/wpnz/feb19-04mumbairesistance.htm (January 11, 2006, no longer available).

Munck, Ronaldo. 2007. *Globalization and Contestation: The New, Great Counter-Movement.* London: Routledge.

NAARI Today. 2001. "Akshara: An NGO's Profile." http://www.naaritoday.com/womensnetwork/ngos/akshara.html (June 17, 2009).

Naples, Nancy A. 2002. "Changing the Terms of Community Activism, Globalization and the Dilemmas of the Transnational Feminist Praxis." Pp. 3–14 in *Women's Activism and Globalization: Linking Local Struggles and Transnational Politics,* ed. Nancy A. Naples and Manisha Desai. New York: Routledge.

Naples, Nancy A., and Manisha Desai, eds. 2002. *Women's Activism and Globalization: Linking Local Struggles and Global Politics.* London: Routledge.

Nash, Jennifer. 2008. "Re-thinking Intersectionality." *Feminist Review* 89: 1–15.

National Women's History Project. No date. "Why Women's History?" http://www.nwhp.org/aboutnwhp/index.php (June 11, 2009).

Newland, Kathleen. 1988. "From Transnational Relationships to International Relations: Women in Development and the International Decade for Women." *Millennium: Journal of International Studies* 17, no. 3: 507–16.

New Vistas Publications. 2003. *WSF: Dissent or Diversion?* Delhi: New Vistas Publications.

NextGENDERation. No date. "Involve Yourself!" http://www.nextgenderation.net/mission.html (June 17, 2009).

Notes from Nowhere, eds. 2003. *We Are Everywhere: The Irresistible Rise of Global Anti-capitalism.* London: Verso.

Oakley, Anne. 1981. "Interviewing Women: A Contradiction in Terms." Pp. 30–61 in *Doing Feminist Research,* ed. Helen Roberts. London: Routledge & Kegan Paul.

Obando, Ana Elena. 2005. "Sexism in the World Social Forum: Is Another World Possible?" *WHRNet,* February. http://www.awid.org/eng/Issues-and-Analysis/Library/Sexism-in-the-World-Social-Forum-Is-Another-World-Possible (June 11, 2009).

O'Brien, Mark. 2001. "Labour." Pp. 69–80 in *Anti-capitalism: A Guide to the Movement,* 2nd ed., ed. Emma Bircham and John Charlton. London: Bookmark.

Office for National Statistics. 2005. "Annual Survey of Hours and Earnings—2005 Results." http://www.statistics.gov.uk/StatBase/Product.asp?vlnk=14203 (August 27, 2009).

———. 2009. "Labor Force Survey." http://www.statistics.gov.uk/StatBase/Source .asp?vlnk=358&More=Y (August 17, 2009).

Oliveira, Guacira C. No date. "Against Fundamentalisms." http://www.mujeresdelsur .org.uy/campana/libro_ing7.htm (June 7, 2009).

Oliver, Pamela, and Hank Johnston. 2000. "What a Good Idea! Frames and Ideologies in Social Movement Research." http://www.ssc.wisc.edu/~oliver/PROTESTS/ ArticleCopies/Frames.2.29.00.pdf (June 17, 2009).

Oloo, Onyango. 2006. "Gendering WSF Nairobi 2007." http://globalpolicy.org/ ngos/advocacy/conf/2006/0720gendering.htm (June 17, 2009).

On Fire: The Battle of Genoa and the Anti-capitalist Movement. 2001. United Kingdom: One-Off Press.

Ong, A. 1987. *Spirits of Resistance and Capitalist Discipline: Factory Women in Malaysia.* Albany: State University of New York Press.

Parmar, Pratibha. 1989. "Other Kinds of Dreams." *Feminist Review* no. 31: 55–65.

Patel, Pragna. 2001. "Creating Alternative Spaces: Black Women in Resistance," interview by Paminder Parbha. Pp. 153–68 in *Women Resist Globalization: Mobilizing for Livelihood and Rights,* ed. Sheila Rowbotham and Stephanie Linkogle. London: Zed.

Pateman, Carole. 1998. "The Patriarchal Welfare State." Pp. 241–68 in *Feminism, The Public and the Private,* ed. Joan Landes. Oxford: Oxford University Press.

Patomäki, Heikki. 2008. "Global Justice: A Democratic Perspective." Pp. 5–26 in *Globalization and the Global Politics of Justice,* ed. Barry K. Gills. London: Routledge.

Patomäki, Heikki, and Teivo Teivainen. 2005. "The Post-Porto Alegre World Social Forum: An Open Space or a Movement of Movements?" http://www.forum socialmundial.org.br/dinamic.php?pagina=bal_teivo_fsm2005_in (June 17, 2009).

Petchesky, Rosalind Pollack. 1994. "A Feminist Perspective on Reproductive and Sexual Rights." *Political Environments* (1): 22–25.

———. 2003. *Global Prescriptions: Gendering Health and Human Rights.* London: Zed Press.

Peters, Cynthia. 2002. "Another World Is Possible." *Zmagazine.* http://www.zmag .org/zmag/viewArticle/13248 (June 17, 2009).

Phelan, Shane. 1989. *Identity Politics: Lesbian Feminism and the Limits of Community.* Philadelphia: Temple University Press.

Phoenix, Anne. 2001. "Practising Feminist Research: The Intersection of Gender and 'Race' in the Research Process." Pp. 203–19 in *Feminism and Race,* ed. Kum-Kum Bhavnani. Oxford: Oxford University Press.

Pianta, Mario, and Raffaele Marchetti. 2007. "The Global Justice Movements: The Transnational Dimension." Pp. 29–51 in *The Global Justice Movement: Cross-National and Transnational Perspectives,* ed. Donatella della Porta. Boulder, CO: Paradigm.

Platt, Gerald M., and Rhys H. Williams. 2002. "Ideological Language and Social Movement Mobilization: A Sociolinguistic Analysis of Segregationists' Ideologies." *Sociological Theory* 20, no. 3: 328–59.

Plows, Alexandra. 2004. "Activist Networks in the UK: Mapping the Build-Up to the Anti-globalization Movement." Pp. 95–113 in *Anti-capitalist Britain*, ed. John Carter and Dave Morland. London: New Clarion Press.

Polet, François. 2004a. "Introduction." Pp. vii–xi in *Globalizing Resistance: The State of Struggle*, ed. Francois Polet and CETRI, with translations by Victoria Bawtree. London: Pluto Press, in association with Louvain-La-Neuve, Belgium: Tricontinental Centre (CETRI).

———, ed. 2004b. *Globalizing Resistance: The State of Struggle*, with translations by Victoria Bawtree. London: Pluto Press.

———, ed. 2007. *The State of Resistance: Popular Struggles in the Global South*. London: Zed Press.

Polletta, Francesca. 2002. *Freedom Is an Endless Meeting: Democracy in American Social Movements*. Chicago: University of Chicago Press.

Ponniah, Thomas, and William F. Fisher. 2003. "Introduction: The World Social Forum and the Reinvention of Democracy." Pp. 1–20 in *Another World Is Possible: Popular Alternatives to Globalization at the World Social Forum*, ed. William F. Fisher and Thomas Ponniah. London: Zed Books.

Pratt, Minnie Bruce. 1988. "Identity: Skin, Blood, Heart." Pp. 11–63 in *Yours in Struggle: Three Feminist Perspectives on Anti-semitism and Racism*, ed. Elly Bulkin, Minnie Bruce Pratt, and Barbara Smith. Ithaca, NY: Firebrand Books.

Pringle, Rosemary, and Sophie Watson. 1998. "Women's Interests and the Post-structuralist State." Pp. 203–23 in *Feminism and Politics*, ed. Anne Phillips. Oxford: Oxford University Press.

Rajan, Rajeswari Sunder. 2003. *The Scandal of the State: Women, Law and Citizenship in Postcolonial India*. Durham: Duke University Press.

Ramazanoğlu, Caroline. 1989. *Feminism and the Contradictions of Oppression*. London: Routledge.

Ramazanoğlu, Caroline, with Janet Holland. 2002. *Feminist Methodology: Challenges and Choices*. London: Sage.

Randall, Vicky. 1992. "Great Britain and the Dilemmas for Feminist Strategy in the 1980s: The Case of Abortion and Reproductive Rights." Pp. 80–94 in *Women's Movements Facing the Reconfigured State*, ed. Lee Ann Banaszak, Karen Beckwith, and Dieter Rucht. Cambridge: Cambridge University Press.

Ray, Raka. 1999. *Fields of Protest: Women's Movements in India*. Minneapolis: University of Minnesota Press.

Reagon, Bernice Johnson. 1998. "Coalition Politics: Turning the Century." Pp. 242–53 in *Feminism and Politics*, ed. Anne Phillips. Oxford: Oxford University Press.

Rebick, Judy. 2002. "Catching up with the Call." *Dawn Informs*, May: 17–18.

REDEH. No date a. "REDEH Homepage." http://www.redeh.org.br/ing/index.htm [English version] (June 15, 2005, no longer available).

———. No date b. "Background." http://www.redeh.org.br/ing/index.htm (June 15, 2005, no longer available).

———. No date c. "Education." http://www.redeh.org.br/ing/index.htm (June 15, 2005, no longer available).

———. No date d. "Research and Documentation." http://www.redeh.org.br/ing/index.htm (June 15, 2005, no longer available).

Rede Mulher de Educação. No date. "Rede Mulher de Educação (Women's Network)." English language leaflet obtained at office, Sao Paulo, January 2005.

Reinharz, Shulamit. 1992. *Feminist Methods in Social Research*. Oxford: Oxford University Press.

Reitan, Ruth. 2007. *Global Activism*. London: Routledge.

Reiter, Herbert, with Massimiliano Andretta, Donatello della Porta, and Lorenzo Mosca. 2007. "The Global Justice Movement in Italy." Pp. 2–78 in *The Global Justice Movement: Cross-National and Transnational Perspectives*, ed. Donatella della Porta. Boulder, CO: Paradigm Press.

"A Report from Mumbai Resistance 2004 and the World Social Forum, Mumbai." 2004. http://revcom.us/a/1232/awtwns-mumbai.htm (June 8, 2009).

Research Unit on Political Economy. 2003. *The Economics and Politics of the World Social Forum: Lessons for the Struggle against 'Globalisation.'* Mumbai: Sai Shakti Press.

Reyes, Oscar, and Stuart Hodgkinson. 2004. "A Democratic Forum Is Possible." *Red Pepper*, January. http://www.redpepper.org.uk/A-democratic-forum-is-possible (June 17, 2009).

Rich, Adrienne. 1986. *Blood, Bread and Poetry: Selected Prose 1979–1985*. New York: W.W. Books.

Richter, Judith, and Loes Keysers. 1994. "Toward a Common Agenda? Feminists and Population Agencies on the Road to Cairo." *Development* 1: 50–55.

Rootes, Christopher, and Claire Saunders. 2007. "The Global Justice Movement in Great Britain." Pp. 128–56 in *The Global Justice Movement: Cross-National and Transnational Perspectives*, ed. Donatella della Porta. Boulder, CO: Paradigm.

Rosenberg, Martha. 2002. "Which Other World Is Possible." *WGNRR Newsletter*, no. 75 (March). http://www.wgnrr.nl//newsletter/NL75eng.pdf (February 13, 2008, no longer available).

Roseneil, Sasha. 1995. *Disarming Patriarchy: Feminism and Political Action at Greenham*. Buckingham: Open University Press.

———. 2000. *Common Women, Uncommon Practices: The Queer Feminisms of Greenham*. London: Cassell.

Routledge, Paul, Andrew Cumbers, and Corinne Nativel. 2007. "Grassrooting Network Imaginaries: Relationality, Power and Mutual Solidarity in Global Justice Networks." *Environment and Planning A* 39: 2575–92.

Rowbotham, Sheila. 1977. *Hidden from History: 300 Years of Women's Oppression and the Fight against It*. London: Pluto.

Rowbotham, Sheila, and Stephanie Linkogle, eds. 2001. *Women Resist Globalization: Mobilizing for Livelihood and Rights*. London: Zed.

Roy, Arundhati. 2004. "Confronting Empire." Speech at World Social Forum, Porto Alegre, Brazil, January 27, 2003. Pp. 243–46 in *Confronting Capitalism: Dispatches from a Global Movement*, ed. Eddie Yuen, Daniel Burton Rose, and George Katsiaficas. Brooklyn, NY: Soft Skull Press.

Rucht, Dieter. 1990. "The Strategies and Action Repertoires of New Movements." Pp. 157–75 in *Challenging the Political Order: New Social and Political Movements in Western Democracies*, ed. Russell Dalton and Manfred Keuchler. Oxford: Oxford University Press.

Runyan, Anne Sisson, and Marianne H. Marchand. 2000. "Conclusion: Feminist Approaches to Global Restructuring." Pp. 225–30 in *Gender and Global Restructuring: Sightings, Sites and Resistance*, ed. Marianne H. Marchand and Anne Sisson Runyan. London: Routledge.

Rupert, Mark. 2000. *Ideologies of Globalization: Contending Visions of a New World Order*. London: Routledge.

Rupp, Leila J., and Verta Taylor. 1999. "Forging Feminist Identity in an International Movement: A Collective Identity Approach to Twentieth Century Feminism." *Signs: Journal of Women in Culture and Society* 24, no. 2: 263–86.

Ryan, Barbara. 2001. "Introduction—Identity Politics: The Past, the Present and the Future." Pp. 1–18 in *Identity Politics in the Women's Movement*, ed. Barbara Ryan. New York: New York University Press.

Salazar, Martha. 2004. "Fourth World Social Forum." Mumbai, India, January 16–21, 2004. *WIDE Briefing Paper*. Brussels: WIDE.

Sandoval, Chela. 1995. "Feminist Forms of Agency and Oppositional Consciousness: US Third World Feminist Criticism." Pp. 208–28 in *Provoking Agents: Gender and Agency in Theory and Practice*, ed. Judith Kegan Gardiner. Chicago: University of Illinois Press.

Santiago, Maria M. 2005. "Building Global Solidarity through Feminist Dialogues." http://www.isiswomen.org/wia/wia2-04/mari.htm (June 9, 2008, no longer available).

Santos, Boaventura de Sousa. 2006. *The Rise of the Global Left: The World Social Forum and Beyond*. London: Zed Books.

Sargent, Lydia, and Michael Albert. 2004. "Another World Is Possible but Apparently Unimaginable." Commentary. *Z Magazine* (March): 6–8.

Sarkar, Tanika, and Urvashi Butalia. 1995. "Introductory Remarks." Pp. 1–9 in *Women and the Hindu Right*, ed. Tanika Sarkar and Urvashi Butalia. New Delhi: Kali for Women.

Schnews. 2002. "Women Speak Out: Radical Dairy London, 8–10 March 2002." http://www.schnews.org.uk/sotw/women-speak-out.htm (June 17, 2009).

Schweikert, Patrocinio P. 1995. "What Are We Doing? What Do We Want? Who Are We? Comprehending the Subject of Feminism." Pp. 229–48 in *Provoking Agents: Gender and Agency in Theory and Practice*, ed. Judith Kegan Gardiner. Urbana: University of Illinois Press.

Seel, Benjamin, Matthew Paterson, and Brian Docherty, eds. 2000. *Direct Action in British Environmentalism*. London: Routledge.

Sempreviva Organização Feminista (SOF). No date. "Feminismo, Movimento Social e Transformação são as razões de ser da SOF—Sempreviva Organização Feminista" [Feminism, Social Movement and Transformation as the Reason for the Existence of SOF]. http://www.sof.org.br/ (June 17, 2009).

Sen, Gita, and Caren Grown. 1987. Development, Crises and Alternative Visions: Third World Women's Perspectives. New York: Monthy Review Press.

Sen, Jai. 2004. "A Tale of Two Charters." Pp. 72–75 in *World Social Forum: Challenging Empires*, ed. Jai Sen, Anita Anand, Arturo Escobar, and Peter Waterman. New Delhi: Viveka Press.

Sen, Jai, and Mayuri Saini. 2005. *Talking New Politics: Are Other Worlds Possible?* New Delhi: Zubaan.

Shah, Nandita. 2004. "Building Politics of Solidarity: Women's Movement and Other Social Movements." Speech at Asia Pacific NGO forum for Beijing Plus 10, Bangkok, July 2. http://ap-ngo-forum.isiswomen.org/downloads/forumpapers/nandita_shah_speech.pdf (June 7, 2009).

Shepard, Benjamin, and Roland Hayduk, eds. 2002. *From Act UP to the WTO: Urban Protest and Community Building in the Era of Globalization.* London: Verso.

Slatter, Claire. 2002. "Beyond the Theory-Practice-Activism Divide." http://www.wicej.addr.com/readings/slatter.pdf (May 21, 2009).

Smith, Jackie. 2002. "Globalizing Resistance: The Battle of Seattle and the Future of Social Movements." Pp. 207–27 in *Globalization and Resistance: Transnational Dimensions of Social Movements,* ed. Jackie Smith and Hank Johnston. Lanham, MD: Rowman and Littlefield.

———. 2008. *Social Movements for Global Democracy.* Baltimore: Johns Hopkins University Press.

Smith, Jackie, and Joe Bandy. 2005. "Introduction: Cooperation and Conflict in Transnational Protest." Pp. 1–17 in *Coalitions across Borders: Transnational Protest and the Neoliberal Order,* ed. Joe Bandy and Jackie Smith. Lanham, MD: Rowman and Littlefield.

Smith, Jackie, and Hank Johnston. 2002. "Globalization and Resistance: An Introduction." Pp. 1–10 in *Globalization and Resistance: Transnational Dimensions of Social Movements,* ed. Jackie Smith and Hank Johnston. Lanham, MD: Rowman and Littlefield.

Smith, Jackie, Marina Karides, Marc Becker, Dorval Brunelle, Christopher Chase-Dunn, Donatella della Porta, Rosalba Icaza Garza, Jeffrey S. Juris, Lorenza Mosca, Ellen Reese, Peter (Jay) Smith, and Rolando Vázquez. 2008. *Global Democracy and the World Social Forum.* Boulder, CO: Paradigm Press.

Smyth, Ines. 1998. "Gender Analysis of Family Planning: Beyond the 'Feminist vs. Population Control' Debate." Pp. 217–38 in *Feminist Visions of Development: Gender Analysis and Policy,* ed. Cecile Jackson and Ruth Pearson. London: Routledge.

Snow, David. 2001. "Collective Identity and Expressive Forms." Center for the Study of Democracy Paper 01/07. http://repositories.cdlib.org/cgi/viewcontent.cgi?article=1016&context=csd (June 17, 2009).

Social Movements International Network. No date. "Social Movement International Network Homepage." http://www.movsoc.m2014.net/?lang=en (June 7, 2009).

Sommier, Isabelle, and Helène Combes. 2007. "The Global Justice Movement in France." Pp. 103–27 in *The Global Justice Movement: Cross-National and Transnational Perspectives,* ed. Donatella della Porta. Boulder, CO: Paradigm.

Squires, Judith. 1999. *Gender in Political Theory.* Cambridge: Polity Press.

Stanley, Liz, and Sue Wise. 1993. *Breaking Out Again: Feminist Ontology and Epistemology,* 2nd ed. London: Routledge.

Starhawk. 2002a. "CODEPINK—Women's Pre-Emptive Strike for Peace: Call to Action." http://www.starhawk.org/activism/activism-writings/codepink.html (June 8, 2009).

———. 2002b. *Webs of Power: Notes from the Global Uprising.* Gabriola Island, BC: New Society.

Starr, Amory. 2000. *Naming the Enemy: Anti-corporate Movements Confront Globalization.* London: Zed.

———. 2005. *Global Revolt: A Guide to the Movements against Globalisation*. London: Zed.

Stienstra, D. 2000. "Dancing Resistance from Rio to Beijing: Transnational Women's Organizing and the United Nations Conferences, 1992–6." Pp. 209–24 in *Gender and Global Restructuring: Sighting, Sites and Resistances*, ed. Marianne Marchand and Anne Sisson Runyan. London: Routledge.

Stoltz Chinchilla, Norma. 1992. "Marxism, Feminism and the Struggle for Democracy in Latin America." Pp. 37–51 in *The Making of Social Movements in Latin America*, ed. Arturo Escobar and Sonia Alvarez. Boulder, CO: Westview Press.

Studlar, Donley T. 2006. "Women and Westminster: Descriptive Representation in the United Kingdom." Pp. 83–101 in *Representing Women in Parliament: A Comparative Study*, ed. Marian Sawer, Manon Tremblay, and Linda Trimble. London: Routledge.

Sudbury, Julia. 1998. *'Other Kinds of Dreams': Black Women's Organisations and the Politics of Transformation*. London: Routledge.

Sullivan, Sian. 2005. "'We Are Heartbroken and Furious!': Violence and the (Anti-) Globalisation Movement(s)." Pp. 174–94 in *Critical Theories, International Relations and "the Anti-globalisation Movement,"* ed. Catherine Eschle and Bice Maiguashca. London: Routledge.

Sutton, Liz. 2002. "Speak Out for Trade Justice." Speech given at debate "Is Fair Trade Possible in a Consumer Society," part of the Trade Justice Movement's lobby of parliament, June 19. http://www.wen.org.uk/general_pages/Newsitems/ni_tradejustice.htm (June 7, 2009).

Tarrow, Sidney. 1998. *Power in Movement: Social Movements and Contentious Politics*, 2nd ed. Cambridge: Cambridge University Press.

———. 2005. *The New Transnational Activism*. Cambridge: Cambridge University Press.

Tarrow, Sidney, and Donatella della Porta. 2005. "Conclusion: 'Globalization,' Complex Internationalism, and Transnational Contention." Pp. 227–46 in *Transnational Protest and Global Activism*, ed. Donatella della Porta and Sidney Tarrow. Lanham, MD: Rowman and Littlefield.

Taylor, Verta. 1995. "Watching for Vibes: Bringing Emotions into the Study of Feminist Organizations." Pp. 223–33 in *Feminist Organizations: Harvest of the New Women's Movement*, ed. Myra Marx Ferree and Patricia Yancey Martin. Philadelphia: Temple University Press.

———. 1998. "Feminist Methodology in Social Movements Research." *Qualitative Sociology* 21, no. 4: 357–79.

Taylor, Verta, and Nancy E. Whittier. 1992. "Collective Identity in Social Movement Communities: Lesbian Feminist Mobilization." Pp. 104–29 in *Frontiers in Social Movement Theory*, ed. Aldon D. Morris and Carol McClurg Mueller. New Haven: Yale University Press.

Themis. No date a. "Campanhas—Violência sexual é crime" [Campaigns—Sexual Violence and Crime]. http://www.themis.org.br/themis/modules.php?name=Content&pa=showpage&pid=28 (June 15, 2005, no longer available).

———. No date b. "Themis: Legal Counselling and Gender Studies." English language leaflet obtained at Themis office, January 2005.

Thomas, Lyn, and Naomi Klein. 2002. "Interview with Naomi Klein." *Feminist Review* 70: 46–56.

Tina, Kara N. 2005. "This Is How We Do It." Pp. 27–37 in *Shut Them Down! The G8, Gleneagles 2005 and the Movement of Movements,* ed. David Harvie et al. London: Dissent and Autonomedia.

Toft, Amoshaun. 2007. "Prefigurative Politics in the Pro-Democracy Movement." *Harbinger: A Journal of Social Ecology* 2, no. 1. http://www.social-ecology.org/2001/10/prefigurative-politics-in-the-pro-democracy-movement/ (June 14, 2009).

Tormey, Simon. 2004a. "The 2003 European Social Forum: Where Next for the Anti-Capitalist Movement?" *Capital and Class.* http://findarticles.com/p/articles/mi_qa3780/is_200401/ai_n9366221/ (June 11, 2009).

———. 2004b. *Anti-capitalism: A Beginners Guide.* Oxford: One World.

Trapese Collective. 2005. "Getting Off the Activist Beaten Track." Pp. 119–25 in *Shut Them Down! The G8, Gleneagles 2005 and the Movement of Movements,* ed. David Harvie et al. London: Dissent and Autonomedia.

Triggs, Sheila. 2004. "Forced Marriages and Love Matches: UK WILPF at the London ESF, a Political Education." Unpublished paper, November 2004.

Umas e Outras. 2003. "A Experiência do Grupo Umas & Outras está Transformando a Vida de Muitas Mulheres" [The Experience of the Group Umas & Outras in Transforming the Lives of Many Women]. http://www.grupoumaseoutras.com.br/arquivos/frame_grupo.htm (June 15, 2005, no longer available).

———. No date. "Atividades Exclusivas para Mulheres Seja Bem-Vinda" [Women-Only Activities, All Women Welcome]. Flyer obtained at Umas e Outras offices, São Paulo, January 2005.

UNIFEM Gender Responsive Budgeting. 2005. "Brazil." http://www.gender-budgets.org/content/view/38/126/ (June 7, 2009).

Valentine, Gill. 2007. "Theorizing and Researching Intersectionality: A Challenge for Feminist Geography." *Professional Geographer* 59, no. 1: 10–21.

Vargas, Virgina. 2001. "Is Another World Possible?" http://www.socialwatch.org/en/informesTematicos/38.html (June 17, 2009).

———. 2002. "A Space of Our Own." *Dawn Informs* (May): 20–21.

———. 2003. "Feminism, Globalization and the Global Justice and Solidarity Movement." *Cultural Studies* 17, no. 6: 905–20.

———. 2004. "The World Social Forum 3 and Tensions in the Construction of Alternative Thinking." Pp. 228–32 in *World Social Forum: Challenging Empires,* ed. Jai Sen, Anita Anand, Arturo Escobar, and Peter Waterman. New Delhi: Viveka Press.

Vysotsky, Stanislav. 2003. "Women's Movements, Anti-globalization and Prefigurative Politics." http://home.comcast.net/~vysotsky.s/women_and_globalization.pdf (June 14, 2009).

Wainwright, Hilary. 2002. "Porto Alegre by the Arno." http://www.tni.org/detail_page.phtml?page=archives_wainwright_esf (June 7, 2009).

———. 2005. "World Social Forum on Trial." *Red Pepper.* http://www.redpepper.org.uk/article391.html (June 17, 2009).

Wainwright, Hilary, Oscar Reyes, Marco Berlinguer, Fiona Dove, Mayo Fuster i Morrell, and Joan Subirats, eds. 2007. *Networked Politics: Rethinking Political Organisation in an Age of Movements and Networks—Work in Progress.* Amsterdam: Transnational Institute.

Walby, Sylvia. 1990. *Theorising Patriarchy.* Oxford: Basil Blackwell.

———. 2002. "Feminism in a Global Era." *Economy and Society* 31: 533–57.

Waller, Marguerite, and Sylvia Marcos. 2005. *Dialogue and Difference: Feminisms Challenge Globalization.* Basingstoke: Palgrave Macmillan.

Waterman, Peter. 2000. "Social Movements, Local Places, Globalized Spaces: Implications for 'Globalization from Below.'" Pp. 135–49 in *Globalization and the Politics of Resistance*, ed. Barry K. Gills. Basingstoke: Palgrave.

———. 2002. "The Still Unconsummated Marriage of International Unionism and the Global Justice Movement." http://www.commoner.org.uk/01-5groundzero. htm (June 17, 2009).

———. 2003. "From Agreements of Comrades to the Reinvention of Emancipation: The 3rd World Social Forum, Porto Alegre, Brazil, January 23–8, 2003," draft March 15, 2003.

———. 2005. "Talking across Difference in an Interconnected World of Labor." Pp. 141–61 in *Coalitions across Borders: Transnational Protest and the Neoliberal Order*, ed. Jackie Smith and Joe Bundy. Lanham, MD: Rowman and Littlefield.

Waters, Sarah. 2004. "Mobilising against Globalisation: ATTAC and the French Intellectuals." *West European Politics* 27, no. 5: 854–74.

Weber, Cynthia. 2005. *International Relations Theory: A Critical Introduction.* London: Routledge.

Weir, Alison. 2008a. "Home and Identity: In Memory of Iris Marion Young." *Hypatia* 23, no. 3: 4–21.

———. 2008b. "Global Feminism and Transformative Identity Politics." *Hypatia* 23, no. 4: 110–33.

Wennerhag, Magnus. 2008. "The Politics of the Global Movement." *Eurozine.* http://www.eurozine.com/articles/2008-05-02-wennerhag-en.html (June 14, 2009).

Werneck, Jurema. 2006. "Incorporação das Dimensões de Gênero e de Igualdade racial e étnica nas Ações de Combate à Pobreza e à Desigualdade: A visão da Articulação de Organizações de Mulheres Negras Brasileiras/AMNB" [Incorporating the Aspects of Gender and Racial and Ethnic Inequalities in Action to Combat Poverty and Inequality: The Vision of the Network of Organizations of Black Women/AMNB]. http://www.amnb.org.br/incorporacao%20racial%20e%20 etnica%20.pdf (June 17, 2009).

Whitaker, Francisco. No date. "World Social Forum: Origins and Aims." http://www.fsmt.org.co/eng-origen.htm (June 17, 2009).

Whittier, Nancy. 2003. "Sustaining Commitment among Radical Feminists." Pp. 103–15 in *The Social Movements Reader: Cases and Concepts*, ed. Jeff Goodwin and James M. Jasper. London: Blackwell.

WHRnet. 2005. "An Interview with Ticiana Studart." http://www.awid.org/eng/issues-and-Analysis/Library/An-Interview-with-Ticiana-Studart (August 12, 2009).

Wichterich, Christa. 2000. *The Globalized Woman: Reports from a Future of Inequality.* London: Zed.

Willis, Patricia. 2007. "A Conversation with Onyango Oloo at the WSF Nairobi 2007." *Journal of International Women's Studies* 8, no. 3: 199–210. http://www.bridgew.edu/soas/jiws/april07/Willis.pdf (June 11, 2009).

Wilson, Ara. 2007. "Feminism in the Space of the World Social Forum." *Journal of International Women's Studies* 8, no. 3: 10–27. http://www.bridgew.edu/soas/jiws/April07/Wilson.pdf (June 17, 2009).

Women against Rape. No date. "Black Women's Rape Action Project/Women against Rape." http://www.womenagainstrape.net/WhoWeAreContactUs/WhoWeAre .htm (June 17, 2009).

Women in Black. No date a. "About Women in Black." http://www.womeninblack .org/en/about (August 19, 2009).

———. No date b. "Start a Vigil." http://www.womeninblack.org/en/startavigil (August 19, 2009).

Women in Black UK. No date a. "Women in Black Actions." http://www.womenin black.org.uk/Actions.htm (June 17, 2009).

———. No date b. "Latest." http://www.womeninblack.org.uk/Latest.htm (June 7, 2009).

Women Living Under Muslim Laws (WLUML). 2005. "About WLUML." http:// www.wluml.org/english/about.shtml (June 15, 2005, no longer available).

Women's Environmental Network (WEN). 2002. "Visions for a Healthier Planet." http://www.wen.org.uk/general_pages/visions_web.pdf (June 17, 2009).

———. 2003a. *Briefing: Getting Lippy.* December. London: WEN.

———. 2003b. "Prevention Call at Cancer Conference." *WEN News,* Winter: 12.

———. 2004. "Concerned about the Future? Take Action for a Healthier Planet." Leaflet obtained at WEN office, November 2004.

———. No date a. "About WEN." http://www.wen.org.uk/general_pages/about.htm (June 17, 2009).

———. No date b. "Women Taking Action for a Healthier Planet." Leaflet obtained at WEN office, London, October 2004.

Women's Environment and Development Organization (WEDO). 2002. "Planet Earth, Meet Planeta Femea." *WEDO News and Views* 15, no. 1: 5.

———. No date a. "About Wedo: Mission and Goals." http://www.wedo.org/ aboutus.aspx?mode=mission (June 15, 2005, no longer available).

———. No date b. "Our Story." http://www.wedo.org/about/our-story (June 7, 2009).

———. No date c. "About Wedo." http://www.wedo.org/about (June 11, 2009).

Women's Environment and Development Organization (WEDO), REDEH, and the Heinrich Boll Foundation. 2002. "Women's Action Agenda for a Healthy and Peaceful Planet: A Decade of Women's Advocacy for Sustainable Development." http://www.minuhemmati.net/publi/WAA2015_Brochure_2002.pdf (June 17, 2009).

Women's Global Network for Reproductive Rights (WGNRR). 2007. "Call for Action 2007: Safe Abortion to Save Women's Lives!" http://www.wgnrr.nl/pdf/ cfa2007eng.pdf (September 1, 2008, no longer available).

———. No date a. "About WGNRR: Who Are We?" http://www.wgnrr.org/index .php?option=com_frontpage&Itemid=1 (June 11, 2009).

———. No date b. "About WGNRR: Who Are We?" http://www.wgnrr.nl/home .php?page=1&sub=1&type=menu (July 13, 2005; specific text quoted no longer available).

———. No date c. "The WGNRR Newsletter." http://www.wgnrr.org/index.php ?option=com_content&task=view&id=30&Itemid=8 (June 7, 2009).

Women's International Coalition for Economic Justice (WICEJ). 2003. "Women's Voices from Porto Alegre." http://www.wicej.addr.com/wsf03/note1.html (May 25, 2009).

———. No date a. "About WICEJ." http://www.wicej.addr.com/about.html (June 17, 2009).

———. No date b. "Women's International Coalition for Economic Justice: Mobilizing Women for Economic Justice." Leaflet obtained at World Social Forum, women's orientation session, January 27, 2004, Porto Alegre, Brazil.

Women's International League of Peace and Freedom (WILPF). 2007. "Constitution and Bylaws." http://www.wilpf.int.ch/history/constitution.htm (June 17, 2009).

———. No date a. "History of WILPF." http://www.wilpf.int.ch/history/hindex.htm (June 17, 2009).

———. No date b. "Racial Justice." http://www.wilpf.int.ch/racialjustice/index.htm (June 17, 2009).

———. No date c. "About Us." http://www.wilpf.int.ch/AboutUs/index.htm (June 17, 2009).

Women Speak Out. 2001a. "Women Speak Out." http://www.fempages.org/EFAU.htm (June 17, 2009).

———. 2001b. "Women Speak Out." Flyer for November 2001, London meeting. http//www.geocities.com/womenspeakout.history.htm (July 15, 2005, no longer available).

———. 2002. "Holloway Prison Demonstration—March 2002." http://www.geocities.com/womenspeakout/hollowaydem.htm (June 17, 2009).

———. No date. "Women Speak Out! [History]." http://www.geocities.com/women speakout.history.htm (July 15, 2005, no longer available).

World March of Women. 1999a. "Advocacy Guide to Women's World Demands: A World in Need of Change." http://www.marchemondiale.org/publications/cahier/c_02/en/base_view (June 17, 2009).

———. 1999b. "Eliminating Poverty." http://www.marchemondiale.org/publications/cahier/c_03/en/base_view (June 12, 2009).

———. 2003a. "2003 World Social Forum: Perspective of Women of the World March of Women." http://www.forumsocialmundial.org.br/dinamic.php?pagina=bal_march_mulher_ing (June 17, 2009).

———. 2003b. "The World Social Forum: A Process for Us to Appropriate." *World March of Women Newsletter* 6, no. 4. http://www.marchemondiale.org/bulletin_liaison/2003/2003_12/en (June 11, 2009).

———. 2004a. "Vision Leading to Action." http://www.marchemondiale.org/en/actions.html (July 13, 2005, no longer available).

———. 2004b. "Women's Global Charter for Humanity." http://www.marchemondiale.org/qui_nous_sommes/charte/en (June 12, 2009).

———. 2004c. "Women's Global Charter for Humanity—Supporting Document 1: The Charter—Another Way to 'March.'" http://www.marchemondiale.org/en/charter_accomp1.html (July 13, 2005, no longer available).

———. 2004d. "2003 WSF: Perspective of Women." Pp. 233–34 in *World Social Forum: Challenging Empires*, ed. Jai Sen, Anita Anand, Arturo Escobar, and Peter Waterman. New Delhi: Viveka Foundation.

———. No date a. "Goals of the World March of Women." http://www.marchemondiale.org/qui_nous_sommes/objectifs/en/base_view (June 17, 2009).

———. No date b. "World March of Women." Introduction pamphlet. http://www.marchemondiale.org/qui_nous_sommes/en/ (June 11, 2009).

————. No date c. "Adhesion to the World March." http://www.marchemondiale .org/membres/devenez_membre/cmicarticle.2005-12-16.5999069685/en (June 12, 2009).

————. No date d. "Who We Are." http://www.marchemondiale.org/qui_nous_ sommes/en/ (June 17, 2009).

World Social Forum. 2002. "World Social Forum Charter of Principles." http:// www.forumsocialmundial.org.br/main.php?id_menu=4&cd_language=2 (June 17, 2009).

————. 2003. "Panels." http://www.forumsocialmundial.org.br/main.php?id_ menu=7_2_1&cd_language=2 (August 12, 2009).

————. 2004a. "Structure of Indian Process." http://www.wsfindia.org/?q=node/5 (June 17, 2009).

————. 2004b. "India Working Organisations." http://www.wsfindia.net/IWClist .php (February 22, 2008, no longer available).

————. 2004c. "WSF 2005 Will Be Held in Porto Alegre." http://www.forum socialmundial.org.br/noticias_01.php?cd_news=954 (June 17, 2009).

————. 2004d. "Methodology of WSF 2005." http://www2.forumsocialmundial.org .br/main.php?id_menu=5_4&cd_language=2 (June 17, 2009).

————. 2005a. "Closing Ceremony." http://www.forumsocialmundial.org.br/ dinamic.php?pagina=encerra2005_ing (June 17, 2009).

————. 2005b. "World Social Forum 2005 Memorial." http://www.forumsocial mundial.org.br/main.php?id_menu=14_5&cd_language=2 (June 7, 2009).

————. 2006. "Background of the WSF Process." http://www.forumsocialmundial .org.br/main.php?id_menu=2&cd_language=2 (June 13, 2009).

Young, Iris Marion. 1990. *Justice and the Politics of Difference*. Princeton, NJ: Princeton University Press.

————. 1994. "Gender as Seriality: Thinking about Women as a Social Collective." *Signs: Journal of Women in Culture and Society* 19, no. 3: 713–38.

Yuen, Eddie. 2004. "Introduction." Pp. vii–xxix in *Confronting Capitalism: Dispatches from a Global Movement*, ed. Eddie Yuen, Daniel Burton-Rose, and George Katsiaficas. Brooklyn, NY: Soft Skull Press.

Yuen, Eddie, Daniel Burton-Rose, and George Katsiaficas, eds. 2004. *Confronting Capitalism: Dispatches from a Global Movement*. Brooklyn, NY: Soft Skull Press.

Zehetbauer, Linda. 2003. "Report about WILPF Participation at the European Social Forum." http://www.wilpf.int.ch/events/ESF-03.htm (October 22, 2005, no longer available).

Index

About the Authors

Bice Maiguashca is a Senior Lecturer in the Department of Politics at the University of Exeter, UK. Her current research and teaching interests include feminism and "the politics of resistance," more generally, as well as social and political theory. She is author or coauthor of, among others, "Rethinking Globalised Resistance: Feminist Activism and Critical Theorising in IR" (with Catherine Eschle), in the *British Journal of Politics and International Relations* (May 2007); "Making Feminist Sense of the Anti-Globalization Movement: Some Reflections on Methodology and Method," in *Global Society* (Spring 2006); and "Theorising Knowledge from Women's Political Practices: The Case of the Women's Reproductive Rights Movement," in the *International Feminist Journal of Politics* (June 2005). She is also coeditor, with Catherine Eschle, of *Critical Theories, International Relations and "the Anti-Globalisation Movement"* (2005).

Catherine Eschle is a Senior Lecturer in the Department of Government at the University of Strathclyde, Glasgow, UK. Her research and teaching interests lie at the intersections of feminism, international relations, globalization, social movements, and social change. Related publications include "Skeleton Women: Feminism and the Anti-Globalisation Movement," in *Signs: Journal of Women in Culture and Society* (2005). She is coeditor, with Bice Maiguashca, of *Critical Theories, International Relations and "the Anti-Globalisation Movement"* (2005), and author of the monograph *Global Democracy, Social Movements, and Feminism* (2001). She has recently developed a focus on feminism, nuclear weapons discourses, and peace activism, working with Claire Duncanson of Edinburgh University.

Together, they have published "Gender and the Nuclear Weapons State: A Feminist Critique of the UK Government's White Paper on Trident," in *New Political Science* (2008). She is coeditor of the *International Feminist Journal of Politics*.